Equity Warriors

*To equity warriors—past, present, and future—dedicated to
fulfilling the promise of public education for each and every student*

Equity Warriors

Creating Schools That Students Deserve

George S. Perry, Jr.
with Joan Richardson

Foreword by Larry Leverett

A Joint Publication

FOR INFORMATION:

Corwin
A SAGE Company
2455 Teller Road
Thousand Oaks, California 91320
(800) 233-9936
www.corwin.com

SAGE Publications Ltd.
1 Oliver's Yard
55 City Road
London EC1Y 1SP
United Kingdom

SAGE Publications India Pvt. Ltd.
B 1/I 1 Mohan Cooperative Industrial Area
Mathura Road, New Delhi 110 044
India

SAGE Publications Asia-Pacific Pte. Ltd.
18 Cross Street #10-10/11/12
China Square Central
Singapore 048423

President: Mike Soules
Associate Vice President and Editorial Director: Monica Eckman
Program Director and Publisher: Dan Alpert
Senior Content Development Editor: Lucas Schleicher
Content Development Editor: Mia Rodriguez
Editorial Assistant: Natalie Delpino
Production Editor: Tori Mirsadjadi
Copy Editor: Amy Marks
Typesetter: C&M Digitals (P) Ltd.
Cover Designer: Scott Van Atta
Marketing Manager: Sharon Pendergast

Library of Congress Cataloging-in-Publication Data

Names: Perry, George S., Jr., 1954- author.

Title: Equity warriors : creating schools that students deserve / George S. Perry, Jr. with Joan Richardson ; foreword by Larry Leverett.

Description: Thousand Oaks, California : Corwin, 2022. | Includes bibliographical references and index.

Identifiers: LCCN 2021045718 | ISBN 9781071851371 (paperback) | ISBN 9781071851388 (epub) | ISBN 9781071851401 (epub) | ISBN 9781071851418 (pdf)

Subjects: LCSH: Educational equalization—United States. | Educational leadership—United States.

Classification: LCC LC213.2 .P466 2022 | DDC 379.2/6—dc23/eng/20211012
LC record available at https://lccn.loc.gov/2021045718

This book is printed on acid-free paper.

22 23 24 25 26 10 9 8 7 6 5 4 3 2 1

Contents

Foreword

By Larry Leverett

An organization cannot flourish—at least, not for long—on the actions of the top leader alone. Schools and districts need many leaders at many levels.

Michael Fullan, 2002

The pandemic and the national reckoning on racism have taken the bandage off the deep racial disparities in health, education, wealth, and numerous other systems that perpetuate systemic failures for Black and Latinx children in America. As painful as this period has been, it also has awakened many white Americans to the need to do more to resolve the disparities in all facets of American life.

That means this is a very hopeful moment.

It means we may be at a place where most Americans can agree that inequities exist in our schools and that it's time to address them because they diminish all of us. Hopefully, that means we may finally be able to make the changes that we need. But we cannot make those changes by using the thinking we relied on in the past.

Believing that only the leader at the top can effect change is thinking we should have left behind in the last century. It didn't work well then, and it definitely won't deliver what we need for our future. The work of equity requires all of us to bring our best selves to the front. Regardless of our role, we have work to do, and that is work that we must do together.

Advancing equity has been George Perry's life work. I've known and worked with George since I was a rookie superintendent in Englewood, New Jersey, and George was my go-to partner. I continue to draw on his knowledge to inform the work of the New Jersey Network of Superintendents, a 12-year-old professional community of practice that focuses on capacity building of equity-focused superintendents.

In 2006, we framed the work of the Panasonic Foundation to focus on equity-driven systemic change by supporting superintendents and school boards in large urban districts that were struggling with organizational cultures experiencing various forms of resistance to advancing equity. Then we went to work! George led several partnership teams that engaged superintendents, school boards, and central office leadership teams in developing systemic approaches to creating and sustaining equitable practices, policies, plans, and support systems. The foundation partnered with Perry and Associates, Inc., to advance equity from the classroom to the boardroom, relying on their experience in coaching teacher and school leaders at all levels, as well as the district leaders who support them. Our courageous partner districts made and sustained gains on our shared mission to "break the links" between race, poverty, and educational outcomes by improving the academic and social success of ALL students: ALL MEANS ALL.

For this book, George draws on his experience working with schools and districts across the country. He does not offer a prescription for how to achieve equity in schools. Instead, he suggests new and proven ways of thinking about how such a goal can be accomplished. He rightly understands that urgency means educators must redirect the system we have and that leaders at all levels of the enterprise have work that only they can do. As George demonstrates with story after story, educators have been successful at working within the existing system and producing change. If others can do it, you can do it too!

We experienced this kind of change in the cause of equity when I was superintendent in Plainfield, New Jersey. When I arrived, the district was 90 percent Black and Latinx students, with 75 percent of the students qualifying for free or reduced-price meals. Fewer than 25 percent of the students met minimum performance levels on state tests. The community was disengaged and apathetic. Low expectations prevailed. Collective bargaining units were constantly in conflict with the school board and district leadership. The school board was focused on patronage, jobs, and contracts with preferred vendors. Students and staff had a low sense of efficacy, and most residents and staff had little faith that improvement was possible. Parents suspected that the school system that had failed them would also fail their children. Naming and blaming was a too-frequent activity in the organization.

But, during my eight-year tenure in Plainfield, we were able to rock and roll on tackling system issues and made significant progress on a number of student performance outcomes. We moved toward an equity-focused culture. We became a mission-centered school district that engaged students; parents; staff at all levels; unions; clergy; and community, business, and nonprofit leaders in planning the transformation of the

Plainfield Public Schools. We faithfully marched toward reinvigorating the spirit and culture of the school and community and set this as our mission statement: "Whatever it takes to build an educational system for all students to achieve academic and social success. No alibis. No excuses. No exceptions."

My work as superintendent changed to include much more time in classrooms. I broadened my knowledge of best instructional practices to create access and success for all learners so that I could become a more effective observer in classrooms. Because I had experienced the value of personal reflection, I encouraged staff at all levels of the organization to engage in the rituals and routines of reflective practice. I studied superintendents who had embraced their responsibility to address racial disparities. I actively sought out proof points of districts and schools that were thinking differently about how to break the links between academic and social success and the race, ethnicity, and socioeconomic status of students.

Because I changed how I worked, the district could change how it worked. We provided opportunities for teachers, parents, and community members to share responsibility for moving equity work forward—ensuring that we included critics as well as supporters. We collected data and shared it to support transparency regarding our progress and failures. We distributed leadership to provide a clear decision-making process. We shifted staff development from sit-and-get sessions facilitated by outside experts to offerings led by our own teachers, principals, or central office staff. Self-organized parent groups explored solutions to real-life challenges and barriers that adversely affected student success. The board worked closely with me to develop equity-focused policies and monitored the implementation of adopted policies and processes that encouraged equity and accountability. We included the community in dozens of community-centered conversations that were held in living rooms, community spaces, and churches and helped refine the changes we needed. Plainfield became the pearl of my career as a superintendent.

In Plainfield, we coined the term "equity warriors" to name those who embraced this cause. People were proud to be known as equity warriors and celebrate the contributions of everyone who was invested in making change happen.

- Equity warriors passionately lead and embrace the mission of high levels of achievement for all students, regardless of race, social class, ethnicity, culture, disability, or language proficiency. Regardless of their role in a school, district, or community, equity warriors see themselves as having the power to influence the teaching and learning agenda in meaningful ways.

- Equity warriors often act outside their formally assigned roles. Their influence is not based on hierarchical roles. They communicate effectively and persistently with diverse publics to influence the core business of schools and districts. They participate successfully in cross-functional teams. They work to improve their knowledge, skills, and dispositions. They engage in risk-taking. They model the values, beliefs, and behaviors for others to emulate in the quest for higher levels of learning for all groups of children and youth.

- Equity warriors are driven by personal values and beliefs, and have an area of knowledge or expertise that they are passionate about. They contribute freely to equity work beyond their assigned role and are willing to grow and learn to become more effective in advancing the equity agenda in their school, district, or community. They are committed to social justice and recognize that any effort to achieve equitable outcomes for *all* learners requires their participation and presence in the generation of solutions.

Today's leaders must create conditions that will grow cohorts of equity warriors who are willing to engage in the sustained work necessary to achieve equity. These warriors must operate at all levels of the organization. As George rightly points out in this book, leaders at the district level have different work to do from leaders at the school level. All of that work is significant, and all of it must occur simultaneously and in concert. Achieving equity in school systems demands no less.

The time is right for us to move forward. Seize the opportunities presented by this moment to move your schools and districts toward equitable learning for all children. Become an equity warrior!

Acknowledgments

First and foremost, I thank Laurie Perry, my wife and life partner, our sons George III and Jeffrey, daughter-in-law Kristen, and my parents, George and Della Perry, for their love, support, and inspiration. They stood by me even though I was less of a presence in their daily lives than was right or than they deserved. They permitted me to be an equity warrior.

Equity warriors are part of a critical mass. In politics, diplomacy, and warfare, there is no "I," only we. Most often, the "we" in this book refers to the Perry and Associates consultant team, an extraordinary group of equity warriors who are committed to social justice and are gifted leaders and teachers of adults and students. Their deep instructional knowledge and their passion for equity and learning continue to inspire admiration. They are dedicated district and school practitioners who gave of themselves to coach others and deserve much of the credit for supporting our partner districts. They are Ivan Alba, Allan Alson, Holly Culbertson, Laurie Hinzman, Connie Jensen, Lamont Jackson, Staci Monreal, Irella Perez, Sandy Rogers, Tiffiny Shockley Jackson, Cynthia Terry, and Jennifer White. I am indebted to Cynthia, Holly, Lamont, and Tiffiny for their critical read and feedback on earlier drafts, and their contributions to this book.

Another extraordinary group of equity warriors is the Perry and Associates team of researchers and writers responsible for our efforts to advance special education reform in New York City. The "we" in this case is a team of research and policy advocates that included Carol Wright, Nancy Baez, and Elizabeth Rockett Sullivan; research associates Kaili Baucum Sanderson, Joyvin Benton, Tonya Leslie, Joseph Nelson, Liza Pappas, and Elizabeth Rivera Rodas; and assistants Hanna Baker, Adam Briones, Melissa Brown, and Brad Reina.

I was fortunate to have M. Hayes Mizell, a champion of civil rights and middle school reform, as a mentor, critical friend, and supporter. Hayes asked the tough questions about any school reform effort, including professional learning, that did not lead to student achievement. He held a high standard for advancing equity; provided districts, schools, and support organizations with enormous resources as director of Edna McConnell Clark

Foundation's Program for Student Achievement; and held us all accountable for delivering on the vision.

In 1995, with a newly minted doctorate, I joined the Panasonic Foundation as a senior consultant. The foundation's mission was to partner with school districts willing to break the links among race, poverty, and social outcomes for all students: All Means All. I am indebted to its first executive director, Sophie Sa, for the opportunity to learn and explore ways to advance equity alongside school board members, superintendents, and union leaders across the country. The learning opportunities allowed me to collaborate with some of the leading education researchers, reformers, and practitioners as we applied cutting-edge thinking to the real-world complexity of school districts.

I used to think that I knew what it meant to advance equity. It wasn't until Larry Leverett became the foundation's executive director that I understood that advancing equity requires each of us to look inward and challenge ourselves. He was my mentor and guide, and we pushed each other through hard conversations informed by the reality of public education. Larry and our colleagues, particularly Barbara Anderson, Kaili Baucum Sanderson, and Alan Alson, helped me wrestle with questions about race and privilege. We shared values and a commitment to advancing equity, which allowed us to challenge and question each other and self-reflect without blame and divisiveness. Together, we created a safe space to experience the struggle and grow in our understanding of what it takes to effect meaningful change.

Advancing equity is a journey. Our three decades of advancing equity with districts and schools across the United States allows us to draw on many examples of equity work, some successful, some not. We are able to draw on specific schools and districts to show the reality of how equity efforts play out in practice. Some of the many equity warriors it has been my privilege to know are named in the examples taken from our first-hand experiences working with the following districts and schools: Atlanta, Boston, Baltimore County (Maryland), Chicago, Corpus Christi (Texas), East Baton Rouge (Louisiana), Elgin (Illinois), Flint (Michigan), Hartford (Connecticut), Jefferson County (Louisville, Kentucky), Los Angeles, Long Beach (California), Marin City (California), Metropolitan Nashville, Milwaukee, Montgomery County (Maryland), Newark (New Jersey), New Jersey districts, New York City, Norfolk (Virginia), Oakland (California), Portland (Oregon), Roanoke (Virginia), Santa Fe and rural northern New Mexico districts, and Stamford (Connecticut).

I did not know Dan Alpert before we submitted our proposal to Corwin, or so I thought. Many of the books on my bookshelf that have contributed to my learning and influenced my thinking were published by Dan and Corwin. His contributions to advancing equity and broadening our knowledge are immense. On the first read, Dan understood the possibility of having leaders from the classroom to the boardroom engage together in a multidimensional approach to advance equity. His excitement, support, and encouragement pushed us to get this done. I am grateful to Dan and the Corwin team of Lucas Schleicher, Mia Rodriguez, Natalie Delpino, Tori Mirsadjadi, Amy Marks, and Scott Van Atta.

Finally, Joan Richardson deserves much of the credit for *Equity Warriors* becoming a reality. I met Joan when she was communications director for the National Staff Development Council, which is now Learning Forward. I would read her editor's columns and marvel at her skills and insights when she served as editor in chief of *Phi Delta Kappan* magazine for 10 years. I jumped at the opportunity to collaborate with her, and the result is this book. I could not have anticipated the effort needed for this project. Joan has been there, patiently, every step of the way. She is an honest thought partner and colleague who guides, clarifies, and pushes. I deeply appreciate her contributions to the content; her nudging and redirection; as well as the time, effort, and expertise she gave to create this book. It is not an oversimplification to say that *Equity Warriors* would not have happened without her.

PUBLISHER'S ACKNOWLEDGMENTS

Corwin gratefully acknowledges the contributions of the following reviewers:

Sean Beggin
Associate Principal
Anoka-Hennepin Schools—Secondary Technical Education Program
Anoka, MN

Ray Boyd
Principal
West Beechboro Primary School, Department of Education
Perth, Western Australia

Janet Crews
Coordinator of Professional Learning
Clayton School District
Clayton, MO

Ken Darvall
Principal
Tema International School
Tema, Ghana

Freda Hicks
School Partnerships
North Carolina Central University
Durham, NC

Rachael Lehr
Associate Principal
West Beechboro Primary School
Perth, Western Australia

Marianne L. Lescher
School Principal, PreK–8th Grade
Kyrene Traditional Academy
Chandler, AZ

Roseanne Lopez
Associate Superintendent
Amphitheater Public Schools
Tucson, AZ

Neil MacNeill
Principal
Ellenbrook Primary School
Ellenbrook, Western Australia

Jacie Maslyk
Assistant Superintendent
Hopewell Area School District
Aliquippa, PA

Courtney Miller
Assistant Principal and Co-Founder of Inclusive
   Teacher Academy
Upland High School
Upland, CA

Cathy Patterson
Retired Elementary Assistant Principal and Teacher
Walnut Valley Unified School District
Walnut, CA

About the Authors

From October 2018 to December 2021, George S. Perry, Jr., Ph.D., served in the New York City Department of Education and the Chancellor's Office as the director of school leadership and organizational alignment. In this role, George supported the assessment, alignment, and implementation of citywide equity and values-centered leadership development for teacher, school, and district leaders.

Before joining the New York City Department of Education, George was executive director of Perry and Associates, Inc., a national consulting firm, founded in 2001, that acts on its commitment to social justice and equity by assisting district and school leaders to improve the academic achievement of *all* students.

George has 40 years of experience in education at the national, state, and local levels. George directed experienced, highly successful consultant teams in building instructional leadership capacity at the district and school levels. He and his colleagues assisted school boards, superintendents, and district and school leaders to transform central offices to support schools; strengthen instructional leadership capacity by fostering vertical coherence from the classroom to the boardroom; redesign systemwide systems of support for students with disabilities and family engagement; strengthen principal instructional leadership; accelerate middle and high school level academic achievement; and develop prototype curricula.

George and his colleagues guided over 100 underperforming schools in Corpus Christi, Flint, Long Beach, Los Angeles, and San Diego to raise and sustain student achievement by improving instruction, building on strengths, and using data and research-based strategies.

The district and school partnerships have been successful in raising student achievement, closing achievement gaps, and preparing students for college and careers. Three partner districts have won the prestigious Broad Prize for Urban Education, awarded annually for raising student achievement and closing achievement gaps.

In addition, George served as the senior education advisor during the 2013 campaigns and on the transition teams of Mayor Marty Walsh of Boston and Mayor Bill de Blasio of New York City.

Beginning in 1994, George was a senior consultant with the Panasonic Foundation, working on district-level, systemic improvement and assisting school boards, superintendents, and district and association/union leaders to "break the links" between race, poverty, and achievement for all students: All Means All. In this role, George assisted district leaders on their journey toward advancing equity as a "critical friend" and coach. With his support, leaders built their capacity to think and plan strategically and systemically, identify barriers to improvement, and address significant challenges through creating conditions for systemwide change and enhancing leadership skills and actions.

George holds a doctorate in public policy analysis from the University of Illinois at Chicago, a master of education degree from Harvard University, a master of business administration degree from Babson College, and a bachelor of science with honors in secondary education from Northeastern University.

For more information or to share your experiences as an equity warrior, join us at www.equity-warriors.com.

Joan Richardson is known as an excellent editor, writer, and researcher with deep expertise about education and for being a creative and strategic thinker who excels at transforming publications and rethinking organizational efforts to deepen impact in schools and influence quality of learning. In addition to spending hundreds of hours visiting U.S. schools, she has extensive experience visiting and writing about schools abroad—Canada, China, Denmark, England, Finland, France, Germany, Haiti, and the Netherlands.

She was editor in chief of *Phi Delta Kappan* magazine, the flagship publication of PDK International (pdkintl.org), for 10 years and also director of the PDK Poll of the Public's Attitudes Toward the Public Schools, the nation's longest-running public opinion survey about K–12 education.

Before joining PDK in 2008, Joan served as communications director for the National Staff Development Council (now Learning Forward) for 12 years. In that position, she was executive editor of *JSD* and also the creator, editor, and writer for the NSDC newsletters—*The Learning Principal, The Learning System, Tools for Schools,* and *Teachers Teaching Teachers (T3)*—and manager of the organization's extensive website. She also directed NSDC's book publishing operations and website, and its media outreach efforts.

Prior to her work in the nonprofit sector, Joan worked for 22 years as a newspaper reporter and editor. In her last newspaper job, with the *Detroit Free Press*, she focused on issues and trends in education, including coverage of the early days of charter schools in Michigan. Her previous newspaper jobs included stints at the *Indianapolis Star* and the *Peoria Journal Star*.

She designed and launched *All Things PLC*, a magazine published by Solution Tree Press. She is the author of *From the Inside Out: Learning From the Positive Deviance in Your Organization* (NSDC, 2004). She served on the Grosse Pointe (Michigan) Board of Education for six years, including one term as president.

Joan was a Michigan Journalism Fellow (1988–1989), studying the economics of globalization on American business and American life. She received her bachelor's degree in journalism and history from Indiana University.

INTRODUCTION

THE FIERCE URGENCY OF NOW

We are now faced with the fact that tomorrow is today. We are confronted with the fierce urgency of now. . . . We may cry out desperately for time to pause in her passage, but time is deaf to every plea and rushes on. . . . We must move past indecision to action.

Martin Luther King Jr., 1967

What if we acted . . . now . . . using what we know rather than just continuing to talk about advancing equity and raising the achievement of all children?

Advancing equity and challenging implicit bias and systemic racism requires a systemic response by district and school leaders and by their community partners. It requires district- and school-level leadership working in concert at a scale comparable to the challenges. It is possible. My colleagues and I have been there and seen the challenges met.

WHERE DO WE START?

With the fierce urgency of now! We can't squander precious time hoping to reinvent or revolutionize public education to address the vestiges of systemic bias, advance equity, and raise the achievement of all students. Our best path to advance equity is to acknowledge and understand the complexity of existing structures and systems and make them work for each and every student.

Somehow, many well-intentioned attempts have failed because they have not recognized existing structures and systems as tools that we can leverage to achieve our goals. Instead, they fight them. They waste resources in repeating cycles of reinventing and designing duplicative alternatives that contain the same flaws. They lose public confidence by doing so.

We are not going to eliminate the structures and systems that we have. Accept that. Wringing our hands and commiserating about how they work against the best interest of students and education professionals will not advance equity. In fact, it will slow our progress.

Instead, let's devote our time and energy to eliminate bias and oppression by activating systems and structures to work for all students, which is exactly what privileged families have been doing for decades upon decades. We should hold up as our standard the one set by John Dewey more than 100 years ago: What the best and wisest parent wants for their own child, that must be what the community wants for all of its children (Dewey, 1902, p. 3).

THE ROOTS OF INEQUITY GO DEEP

Advancing equity does not mean being blind to the past. In fact, we will be stronger moving forward if we fully understand that the roots of public education are planted in the soil of racism and sexism. Creating structures and systems that serve all children means that we are battling centuries of a mindset that ensures children would be treated differently according to the color of their skin, their gender, their abilities, or their economic status.

The early public schools were designed with white boys in mind (Carpenter, 2013). In many locations, not even white girls were allowed to attend public schools when boys were present (Kaestle, 1983, p. 28). Girls were relegated to attending schools early in the day before boys arrived or during the summer when families needed boys at home for agricultural chores. When white girls were admitted to school, their coursework focused on skills that would make them good wives and mothers (Kaestle, 1983, p. 54). Not until the 1970s did the laws and social norms begin to change toward believing that girls could and should learn as much at school as boys.

The road forward was far more challenging for children of color. Here are a few examples.

Public schools in the 1700s and 1800s were never intended to be used by Black children. By the 1830s, most Southern states forbid teaching enslaved people to read and write (Black, 2020, p. 89). After emancipation, states in the South rewrote their constitutions to guarantee a free public education for all children, but that change actually benefited poor white children more than Black children (Black, 2020, pp. 110–111). By the turn of the century, the concept of "separate but equal" meant Black and white children attended different schools supported by vastly different resources. The U.S. Supreme Court even agreed that Georgia could tax Black and white citizens equally even though a community provided a high school only for white children (Butchart, 2020; *Cumming v. Richmond County Board of Education*, 1899).

States weren't alone in ensuring that white children got more than Black children. Federal housing policies and lending practices ensured that neighborhoods would be segregated which meant the neighborhood schools they attended also would be segregated (Rothstein, 2017, pp. 132–137). Properties in Black areas of towns were valued less and, since school funding was largely tied to property taxes, schools in less affluent areas received less money for books and building maintenance, further exacerbating the inequities.

The 1954 U.S. Supreme Court case *Brown v. Board of Education* may have decreed that segregated schools are "inherently unequal," but massive protests followed efforts to actually have Black and white children sit in the same classrooms. The passage of the Civil Rights Act in 1964 outlawed discrimination in programs receiving federal money and authorized the federal government to require school districts to desegregate. By the 1970s, the U.S. Supreme Court had ruled that busing, magnet schools, compensatory education, and other tools were appropriate remedies for overcoming racial segregation. But, by 2000, the Harvard Civil Rights Project concluded that American schools were more segregated than when busing began 30 years earlier (Orfield, 2001).

Although the story of segregation has focused largely on Black students, the segregation of Native American, Asian American, and Latinx students and children with disabilities is equally heinous. And every group had to seek redress through the courts to be recognized as deserving of equal access and opportunity.

After being forced from their own land, Native American students were enrolled in boarding schools and stripped of their language and cultural identity (Reef, 2009, pp. 66–67, 87–88). Chinese students were excluded from the public schools and, as far back as the late 1800s, were suing to gain access (*Tape v. Hurley*, 1885).

In 1927, the U.S. Supreme Court affirmed that the "separate but equal" doctrine applied to schools when it said a Chinese American girl could be prevented from attending a white school in Mississippi because she was a member of the "yellow" race (*Gong Lum v. Rice*, 1927).

And, several years before *Brown*, a Mexican American family in California had won a federal court decision that segregation of school children was unconstitutional (*Mendez v. Westminster School District of Orange County*, 1947). In spite of that decision, however, California continued to find ways to limit access by Latinx students.

Discrimination has not been limited to students of color. LGBTQ+ students have experienced persistent bullying, harassment, exclusion, and discrimination at school. In 2020, the U.S. Supreme Court in *Bostock v. Clayton County* finally ruled that protections from all forms of sex discrimination extended to persons based on their sexual orientation or gender identity. A year later, a presidential executive order made explicit that these protections applied to schools and students (Biden, 2021).

We owe it to our past to honor suffering, recognize inherent inequities, and move forward.

Families and educators who want to ensure a high-quality education for all children must constantly be aware that they are working against a system that was designed for another purpose.

BECOME AN EQUITY WARRIOR

If you believe as W. Edwards Deming suggested that every system is perfectly designed to get the results that it gets (Deming, n.d.), then it is little wonder that a system of public schools that was designed to exclude large numbers of children is now failing to provide those children with a high-quality education.

Anyone who wants to advance equity within public education must acknowledge the power of the existing structures and systems and learn to leverage them for the benefit of students.

That requires the mindset of a warrior, an equity warrior.

Equity warriors are doers, activists pursuing a goal. They are not fighters girding for a single confrontation but are committed to pursuing and holding onto progress toward a broader, often loftier goal.

Equity warriors are, at heart, learners and visionaries.

Equity warriors do not enter an arena and insist on ensuring that the conditions are right before they engage. Warriors enter and assess the situation as it is. In other words, they study and they learn. They are strategic about the real conditions they encounter, and they respond accordingly.

They certainly do not wait and whine about what has to change before they can be successful. They deeply understand how and why each structure and system operates as it does. And then they move. They move in ways that allow them to use the system to their advantage.

Equity warriors combine the best elements of politicians, diplomats, and generals. Making change for all students requires working in three dimensions simultaneously. As we describe in this book, those dimensions are politics, diplomacy, and warfare.

- **Politics** is balancing conflicts to govern humans effectively. In other words, how does the leader corral competing groups or competing ideas so that the organization can move forward?
- **Diplomacy** is dealing with people in a sensitive and effective way by using rewards, consequences (real and perceived), and moral persuasion so that they will embrace the work.
- **Warfare** is pressuring people to stop or start acting in certain ways.

Equity warriors are strategic in using the strengths of each dimension. For example,

- Balancing conflicts is foundational. Conflicts are rarely resolved, but, through compromise and agreements, equity warriors set the direction, conditions, and parameters that allow stakeholders to act with confidence. Maintaining balance is a continuous process as stakeholders and situations change.

- Motivating stakeholders to act requires knowing people. Not all tools work in all situations, and stakeholders are motivated differently. Some value rewards such as advancement; some fear losing something they value; many seek opportunities to make a difference.

- Applying pressure is necessary when facing intractable obstacles to advancing equity. Applying pressure by itself rarely brings about systemic change. Nevertheless, there are times when hard choices need to be made. Failing to act can be interpreted as a lack of commitment, a reluctance to persevere, and an unwillingness to do the right thing. Advancing equity is too important, and has been too long delayed, to fail to use all means necessary.

The three dimensions exist at both the school level and the district level, which means equity warriors coordinate their moves both across the level and with an eye toward what is occurring concurrently on the other level. Imagine a multilevel chessboard in which the players are directing moves across three different games (or levels) at the same time.

Public school districts are composed of many systems. This book delves deeply into three systems that are high leverage and at the core of advancing equity—student data, values-enhanced leadership, and teaching and learning. Within each system, we suggest moves for equity warriors in each dimension and on both levels. Sometimes the moves are parallel across levels. For example, district- as well as school-level equity warriors use data to craft a vision and narrative for leading their organizations. Other times, the moves are specific to an equity warrior's scope of responsibility and role. Often, the moves are nonlinear, interconnected, and overlapping. For example, school-level equity warriors are dependent on the moves made at the district level when deciding on the data to use, their vision, and their narrative. The reverse is also true. Successful equity warriors make their moves in concert across each dimension depending on the local context.

Equity warriors work with the same tools available to everyone: time, energy, and resources. They think outside the box when considering how to use their tools to fullest advantage and especially to respond to challenges they may not have anticipated.

The road to improvement is long, and improvement that sticks is incremental. But moving deliberately through improvement has value. As Jim Collins (2001) says in *Good to Great*, improvement comes from momentum rather than individual acts of heroics that often fix today's problem but create tomorrow's problems. Small successes can provide the momentum that keeps improvement going. Moving deliberately, incrementally can protect equity warriors from creating tomorrow's problems.

Advancing equity depends on a critical mass of equity warriors willing to push beyond the obvious and use existing structures and systems to educate all students well. Building that critical mass is the motive behind this book. The primary audience is those of us—teacher leaders, school leaders, central office administrators, superintendents and senior district leaders, board members, consultants, external partners, community members, and policymakers—who are in position each and every day to shape and direct public education to improve the achievement of all students—no matter who they are.

Unleashing the power of existing structures and systems is our best hope. My colleagues and I have seen it happen. And we believe more educators can make it happen more often.

Join us. The moment is now. Be an equity warrior.

Prologue: Jesse's story

We begin by facing the challenge. Consider this real example from a 10-minute visit to Jesse's classroom:

As we are about to enter the 7th-grade math class, we are told to expect the worst.

The room is dark. It is a very large classroom, twice as large as necessary for the 20 students sitting at tables arranged in a U, facing the front. The teacher has turned off the lights because he is using a projector and screen to demonstrate math problems but also because he believes keeping the room dark will improve student behavior.

The teacher is a long-term substitute, the fourth teacher this group of students has had this year. Their first and "real" teacher is out on extended maternity leave. She declined to indicate that she would not return after the regular maternity period until a few weeks before her scheduled return. Two previous substitutes ran or were run out of the classroom—7th grade can be tough. This substitute has neither a teaching credential nor a degree in mathematics. He says he does not intend to be a permanent teacher and is substitute teaching for the money. Still, he is doing well. In his second month as a teacher, he has established control of the classroom, and the students no longer seem difficult. It is said that he is committed to helping students learn and believes he can.

The school's part-time math coach accompanies me. The coach is a teacher who teaches two classes of her own and is also responsible for helping several other teachers improve their teaching. For this teacher, the coach is his lifeline. She works with him often daily, answering his questions. Some of his questions are fundamental, such as "What is slope? I have to teach it today." Some require lots of time, like being in the classroom with the teacher for entire periods to establish order.

The coach's support for this teacher is essential. However, she is at the school only by chance. The school board is reevaluating the effectiveness of coaches and believes teachers need to be professional enough to take responsibility for their teaching without help. The teachers' union endorses this position—at least publicly. Privately, union leaders know teachers welcome help. The board and the union are willing to overlook this school because of the need.

The interim principal who started the year as the school's vice principal joins us. He is new to the school and, in addition to getting to know the students, teachers, and staff, he is learning all that he needs to know to be the school's principal. The former principal, very bright and experienced, walked out one day because she didn't want to be a principal anymore. It was a good move for her, and the school. She spent most of her days in her office, complaining that no one was doing their job, that her job was undoable.

The school's central office supervisor could not replace the principal immediately. The principal left on medical leave, and several months passed before she officially resigned. The principal was respected and a veteran of the system, so everyone hoped she just needed some time off before returning. But, when she walked out of her office for the last time, she never intended to return. The principal's supervisor is responsible for too many schools to visit this school even one day a month. He, too, is in his first year as a supervisor and learning his way. He wonders whether his time is better spent working with principals in permanent positions who need support.

I enter the dark room cautiously. In addition to the students seated at the tables shaped in a U, other students are positioned in different parts of the room. The students are mostly watching the teacher, responding to his questions when asked, and referring to or taking notes on the problems. My attention is immediately focused on a student sitting apart from the main body of students, far in the back of the room, closest to the door. He is a Black student, and his desk is turned to the wall. Keeping a student away from the others is a way to control behavior, but why is this student so far away from the teacher, who is standing at the front of the room?

The student's name is Jesse. His notebook is open on his desk. There are no notes or other evidence he is participating in the lesson. I stand next to Jesse.

It is the beginning of class, and the teacher is leading a "warm-up" activity. Our visit is a month before the state academic performance exam, and the warm-up is a set of multiple-choice questions testing knowledge considered essential for 7th graders, or, rather, likely to be included on the state exam. The main point of the warm-up is to provide students with skills to be successful in taking the test so that they can show what they know. I am told that the teacher decided not to distribute the sample answer or "bubble" sheets so that the students could practice answering the questions in the way they would be expected to do so on the state test. The teacher guessed that students would make patterns from the bubbles rather than take the form seriously.

The teacher is taking too much time making sure that students know the math as well as the strategy for answering the question. Having finished the first question, he turns to the second. He asks students for the answer to the question. Several hands are raised, including Jesse's hand at the back of the room. Typical, I think. The student excluded from the circle wants to be included and calls attention to himself by "pretending" he has the answer. The teacher calls on Jesse. Again, typical, I think. I have visited hundreds of classrooms. It is common for teachers to guess what I want to see—including making sure that all students are being asked to participate in the lesson. The teacher sees me standing next to Jesse and doesn't want me to see him ignore Jesse.

Then "it" happens. Jesse gives the right answer to the problem, continues on to explain succinctly, clearly, and with confidence, in 10 seconds, how he knows his is the right answer. *All while Jesse stares at the back wall, never once turning to view the teacher.* Earlier in the day, students in a neighboring class—all sitting in groups with an experienced teacher—struggled for more than 10 minutes to select and describe the correct answer. Jesse does not have that problem. He is done and moving on. So does the teacher.

The coach describes Jesse as capable but says he has poor grades and requires a lot of attention. She believes Jesse has the ability to be successful, if he receives good teaching and support from counselors and adults at the school.

No one asks Jesse.

Jesse's story suggests some of the ways the system has failed to provide the schools ALL students deserve. Jesse's story highlights systemic challenges that prevent each and every student from having the opportunity to succeed. Consider the following:

- What do adults in the school know about Jesse's strengths and needs? Is a system of supports in place?

- What are the systemic and structural biases that create hard-to-staff schools filled with teachers who do not have the experience needed to engage and educate students?

- Why is the math coach's position structured such that she is not able to address the diverse needs of teachers?

- What support is offered to the interim principal as he learns the unfamiliar tasks of managing and leading a complex organization?

- What support does the principal's supervisor have to learn his responsibilities, to manage his time, and to know the schools and the people he supervises?

- What do the district leaders who are responsible for almost every function within the school—support, instruction, operations, budgets, and human resources, to name a few—know about the needs of Jesse's school?

- How are teacher union leaders resolving the tension between being a member services organization focused on just compensation and fair working conditions and partnering with "management" to ensure the success of students and adults?

- How do senior district leaders respond to expectations from community, state, and federal stakeholders whose views are in conflict?

- How do board members stay focused on governance and policy, while striving to understand the effect on specific individuals in a multimillion-dollar educational organization?

Creating schools that students deserve requires that district and school leaders raise and answer these and other questions for their students, families, teachers, staff, and themselves. Equity warriors use politics, diplomacy, and warfare in concert to move the system toward equity.

Keep Jesse in mind as you read on.

PART I

Build an Equity Agenda: Student Data

INTRODUCTION

The problems of the world cannot possibly be solved by skeptics or cynics, whose horizons are limited by obvious realities. We need leaders who dream of things that never were and ask why not.

John F. Kennedy, 1963

The victories of good warriors are not noted for cleverness or bravery. Therefore their victories in battle are not flukes. Their victories are not flukes because they position themselves where they will surely win, prevailing over those who have already lost.

Sun Tzu, about 500 B.C. (Cleary, 1988)

Advancing equity requires vision and strategy. Equity warriors begin by having a vision of school systems as they want them to be. The vision drives them to ask questions about *what is* in order to take themselves and others on a journey to *what can be.* Equity warriors also know that it takes more than ideals to change the world. They begin by examining and understanding the situation they face, their assets, and their challenges. They act!

> Equity warriors begin by having a vision of school systems as they want them to be.

Equity warriors use their vision as a lens through which they examine systems by collecting and using qualitative and quantitative data. They examine data that tell the experiences and reality of students—who they are, what they know, what they see, how they are treated, and what they need. Equity warriors use data as the primary tool for naming the problem or describing the current reality. Doing so helps set the direction and share the vision that equity warriors hope to achieve. The willingness to see students in the data enables leaders and others to be ready and prepared for change and to surface potential allies and

(Continued)

11

(Continued)

opponents in the journey toward the vision. Knowing the allies and opponents equips equity warriors to identify strategies that will be effective in advancing equity.

> Equity warriors use data as the primary tool for naming the problem or describing the current reality.

In naming the problem, equity warriors become more effective when they engage others in verifying the strengths of current efforts and challenges in facing existing problems. Data essentially say, "Don't take my word for it, see for yourself." Equity warriors use data to make a path and protect their vision from cynics and apathetic protectors of the current reality.

Data illuminate each situation and enable all stakeholders to understand the mission. Examining data enables educators to apply resources and talents where they will have the greatest effect, and it helps measure progress toward goals.

But getting to a place where data can play a significant role in moving toward an equitable system of learning involves far, far more than merely knowing which test scores to examine. Foolishly rushing in to erect data walls and dashboards without laying an appropriate foundation is a recipe for disaster.

There is no single vision of equity that can be applied uniformly across districts and schools. In Part I, equity warriors gather data to understand student experiences; learn how to analyze and name problems, allies, and assets; and identify tools for engaging in various contexts and assuming responsibilities. Using data effectively to assess current conditions requires knowing which politics, diplomacy, and warfare moves are available to equity warriors at the district and school levels—and to make moves in concert.

CHAPTER 1

District leaders define equity by knowing students and finding allies

☞ POLITICS: BALANCE CONFLICTS TO BUILD AN EQUITY AGENDA

Equity warriors know that to address systemic inequities deeply embedded in their organization—whether intended or not—they need to balance inherent conflicts among internal and external groups, and manage a change process. It is unrealistic in most cases to set the bar at resolving conflicts. Politics is an unending process, not a destination. We earlier defined politics as balancing conflicts to govern humans effectively. In the context of building an equity agenda, politics creates a balance that makes advancing equity possible.

Harvard Business School professor John P. Kotter (1996) studied change in large corporations and cautioned leaders to refrain from identifying solutions when starting a change process. Too often, the message is "here is the problem, and here is what we are going to do about it." District and school leaders are often assumed to know the solution and/or are expected to demonstrate leadership in order to direct the outcome. When leaders introduce the solution up front, they do not engage and do not convince. They do not build the trust necessary for those who are skeptical to think differently. They have not asked for help. They have asked for something to accomplish their objectives. They have not led—they have dictated.

Equity warriors work toward building a bold vision that may not unify all internal and external stakeholders but will set a direction for the work to move forward. Building a vision requires maintaining the "just right" balance between guiding and distancing themselves from the process. Equity warriors know not to try to impose their vision. After all, they are not solely responsible for the schools, districts, and communities where they work. They are part of a whole. At the same time, equity warriors are not seeking consensus. Too often, leaders find that waiting for everyone to be on board allows a small minority to stand in the way of advancing equity. Creating momentum with the intent of building a critical mass is enough to launch a meaningful equity agenda. Equity warriors move to a bold vision by creating the opportunity for each of us "to be touched, as surely they will, by the better angels of our nature" (Lincoln, 1861). To begin, equity warriors must understand the parameters of the situation in which they operate.

YOUR MOVE: KNOW THE DANGERS INHERENT IN USING ACHIEVEMENT GAP DATA.

Effective governance requires balancing conflicts and is key to political success. Decisions about using limited resources introduce inherent conflicts between and among groups. Nobody can have everything all the time, which means that leaders make multiple decisions about who receives resources and when.

In public education, a fundamental conflict that plays out continuously is answering the question about the best way to accelerate student success—particularly the differences in closing achievement and opportunity gaps. Equity warriors use data to shine a light on problems. But they analyze the community's readiness to receive the data and then decide where to point the light and whether the light is a spotlight (pointed at specific data) or a floodlight (examining all data). They understand the importance of crafting their message along with data to shed just the right amount of light on the right problem at the right time. Not for the faint of heart!

National efforts have failed to avoid the dangers of not balancing conflicts effectively. Starting with the enactment of the Elementary and Secondary Education Act (ESEA) in 1965, there has been a political tension around measuring the effect of federal dollars on student achievement for children who live in poverty. Congress and presidents have questioned whether federal funds—although rarely more than 10 percent of total spending on public education—yielded results. Through succeeding decades, political parties embraced either an opportunity gap or an achievement gap approach to federal policy and spending decisions. The difference is important.

Those who see *opportunity gaps* believe federal dollars would be best spent leveling the playing field for students. Students living in poverty should have access to conditions for success—instructional resources and high-quality instructors—just as much as their more privileged peers. Federal funding would provide for professional learning, libraries, school meals, and additional services to multilingual learners and students with disabilities.

Those who see *achievement gaps* believe federal dollars would be best spent identifying the problem, applying resources, and holding people accountable. Testing would identify the learning needs of students, which would enable teachers to attend to the gaps. Government would set the standards to be met, provide tools to measure progress toward the standards, and help schools—through state education agencies—use the tools to define the learning needs of students and create a plan to address the needs. Government would apply sanctions (a softer term than punishments) to schools that fail to close the gaps.

The 2002 reauthorization of ESEA that was No Child Left Behind (NCLB) brought together the opposing views by providing an additional $14 billion or a 34 percent increase in federal funding for testing, high-stakes accountability, and teacher development. NCLB made more money available for improving the conditions for learning while also ramping up accountability measures. In essence, the federal response was to forge a compromise and attempt to close opportunity and achievement gaps. Generations will live with the results of that compromise.

Certainly, NCLB cast a spotlight on schools that did not serve students well in a way that had not happened in many places previously. Around that time, the principal of the largest underperforming middle school in an urban district told me her superintendent had not visited her school once during her five years as principal. The superintendent confirmed that he devoted his time to issues at schools serving politically savvy middle- and upper-middle-class parents and communities. He knew they were holding him accountable. He also understood that NCLB changed the game by giving voice to underserved families that did not have political capital.

The NCLB compromise created many problems for advancing equity. Let's look at two fundamental political problems.

The first political problem is that closing achievement gaps pits winners against losers and creates conflicts over limited resources of attention, time, and money. Closing achievement gaps assumes the government will provide objective measures of proficiency on grade-level, standards-based work. But the achievement standard is typically set by the performance of Asian and white students. Educators can close the gap in only two ways: by increasing the performance of students at the bottom or decreasing the success of students at the top. In some places, there is real fear that equity warriors are actively contemplating the latter. That fear sometimes manifests itself in arguments claiming that resources will be diverted from those who are doing well to those who are not. Sometimes, the arguments include blaming or claims that resources are wasted on the undeserving. But, if more money is not the answer, then what is the point of arguing?

The second political problem is that identifying racial/ethnic groups at the top and those at the bottom can reinforce established stereotypes and undermine trust in data and those who provide them. Let us be clear: Exposing racial predictability in systems is critical to naming the problem to solve. Equity warriors must not back away from exposing systemic racial or class bias and must continue to name each student group by disaggregating data. Educators and policymakers must not revert to a time— as was the case before NCLB—when disaggregating data was against the law in some states. That practice was intended to hide the reality that public schools were not serving all students equally.

Equity warriors must not back away from exposing systemic racial or class bias and must continue to name each student group by disaggregating data.

Stereotyping based on performance data is present when it confirms our biases or perspectives that students of color and students living in poverty underperform, and that white and Asian students perform at higher levels. It is a stereotype consistent with what has been taught or learned. Reactions to data that confirm stereotypes include acceptance, guilt, blame, and anger—to name just a few. Equity warriors should anticipate different and multiple reactions even when results confirm accepted stereotypes.

Depending on our lens, disaggregating performance data also can result in mistrust of the performance measures themselves. If the results confirm our perspective, we accept the legitimacy of the measures; if not, we challenge the results. For example, educators express very legitimate concerns about test administration. Did students take the test seriously? Is the assessment valid? Were students taught the assessed content or skills? What is the cut score, and how was it determined? What can we do after we learn the results? Will we receive them in a timely manner and be able to act on them? In other words, educators often believe that assessments don't measure what students know.

What happens when performance results do not match our perceptions of who "should be" at the top? Psychologist Donald T. Campbell (1976) captured this idea in what came to be known as Campbell's Law: "The more any quantitative social indicator is used for social decision making, the more subject it will be to corruption pressures and the more apt it will be to distort and corrupt the social processes it is intended to monitor" (p. 49). In other words, when the target is wrong, people will game the system. In service of equitable outcomes, well-intentioned federal, state, and district leaders set targets for graduation rates, grade point averages, and suspension rates. The higher the stakes, the more likely that processes used for positively affecting the results will be corrupted. We have seen this law play out in states and districts when the results were considered wrong. Either the test is flawed or cheating occurred.

Atlanta Public Schools, a school district of 51,000 students in Georgia, exemplified these fundamental problems.

The central office of Atlanta Public Schools is housed in an exceptional building completed in 2005. Called the Center for Learning and Leadership, the building is designed to be functional and efficient. It is home to central office functions that were once scattered across the city and is a central location for professional learning. Fostering collaboration and learning are key themes reflected in the design throughout the building. Each floor contains work and meeting rooms where cross-functional teams can meet, plan, and work together. The building design is one of the symbolic ways that Beverly Hall, superintendent from 1999 to 2010, made her priorities known.

Large posters with bar graphs adorned the walls of the cabinet meeting room on the top floor of the building, adjacent to the superintendent's office. Each poster displayed information about one of the superintendent's performance targets and showed how each school in the district did against the district performance target over the past three years. This is the room where Hall met with principals and teachers and with visitors from outside the district.

These prominently displayed posters were intentional. First, the posters let all visitors, particularly those within the district, know that the superintendent valued school performance on the targets established by the district. The posters were kept up to date, which also demonstrated that the superintendent was carefully watching schools and their performance. In case visitors were not clear, Beverly Hall was known to refer to the posters to make a point during a meeting. She was conversant about each school and each performance target and expected the same from those who worked in the district—particularly those who worked in the schools displayed on the walls. Finally, the performance targets were present to remind visitors that the superintendent was being transparent. Those in the district—central office leaders and managers and principals—were well aware that their performance and their annual bonuses were tied to the performance of schools on the wall, as was the superintendent's performance and bonus. There were years in which Hall did not receive a bonus because the district's performance had not met expectations. There were many more years when she did. Improving student performance was not only business, it was personal.

Atlanta became a success story, and Beverly Hall was recognized as a champion of underserved students. She was named National Superintendent of the Year in 2009 and credited with transforming the school district. Student performance on state tests increased. Principals had three years to ensure that their schools met the growth target set by the district. If the school did not meet the target, the principal was removed.

Then, in 2011, special investigators found that 178 teachers and principals at 44 schools had cheated by changing student answers on state tests; 82 ultimately confessed to cheating during the investigation. The Fulton County prosecutor indicted 35 educators on charges stemming from the cheating scandal. Twenty-one Atlanta educators reached plea deals, and 11 were convicted of racketeering charges in 2015 (Kasperkevic, 2015).

In the beginning, Atlanta was a beacon of hope for those of us who believed in the power of standards-based systems to improve opportunities for underserved students. It was the exemplar of an achievement gap–closing district that used accountability systems to benefit students. Gains made by students began to debunk the myth that poor, inner-city Black students could not overcome conditions and achieve at high levels. The symbolism of making progress in Atlanta, so influential in the civil rights movement and the burial place of Martin Luther King Jr., was not overlooked. Its promise was that a tough-minded leader who believed it could be done with a "take-no-prisoners" approach was all that was needed for success.

The Atlanta story is sad on many levels. In fairness, Beverly Hall, who believed strongly in creating an accountability-based system in service of underserved students, passed away before she had the opportunity to defend herself against charges that she knew cheating occurred. Nevertheless, the Atlanta story and similar stories on a smaller scale in other school districts seemed to support Campbell's Law and the political pressures that can occur when groups are pitted against each other. When corruption was found in Atlanta, it further reinforced the myth that students in that district could not be successful unless cheating was involved. As we will discuss in later chapters, competition or setting the dichotomy of winners and losers does not advance equity.

Community members and parents continue to be interested in achievement data that can show a return on their investment. Yet, interest seems to be waning. Take the National Assessment of Educational Progress (NAEP), known as the nation's report card. The NAEP is administered in every state that receives federal Title I funding. The test identifies representative samples of students at random, and authorized monitors in controlled environments administer assessments that measure student knowledge against national frameworks. Nothing compares to the objectivity and comparability of these results. Nevertheless, even in districts that have shown and tried to celebrate growth compared to other districts, there is little fanfare. There are other examples. Massachusetts students have some of the highest scores on what is considered a rigorous state assessment—results that compare favorably on international metrics. Yet communities and parents continue to complain about the student performance of Massachusetts public schools.

Even though community interest in the achievement gap is diminishing, it is still a political problem for equity warriors to manage. When to use a spotlight or a floodlight depends on a calculus of anticipated reactions. Waning interest in understanding achievement data provides an opportunity for rebalancing the achievement gap conversations. We will discuss how equity warriors can reframe the conversation after we examine opportunity gaps more closely.

YOUR MOVE: DEFINE EQUITY USING OPPORTUNITY GAP DATA.

Knowing how much the community believes in closing the achievement gap or how much it believes in closing the opportunity gap is important to the equity conversation and ultimately the political survival of district initiatives.

Those who advocate for closing opportunity gaps perceive the problem as a glass half full. They believe the equity agenda for student success is achieved by applying resources where there is the greatest need. Doing so gives all students access to conditions for success. As with closing achievement gaps, closing opportunity gaps creates problems for equity warriors. Let's look at two fundamental political problems: creating consensus on what we mean by equity, and adopting strategies that advance an equity-of-opportunity agenda. Let's start with defining equity.

Defining equity through opportunity gaps is even more difficult than defining equity through achievement gaps. That's because opportunity gaps are more subjective and contextual. There is agreement on baseline conditions necessary for student success, such as teachers, learning materials, and time. Baseline conditions vary widely across the country and among communities within each state and region. So, the hard questions about closing opportunity gaps are these: What are the opportunities that matter? And how much opportunity is enough?

Equity warriors take on the challenge of answering these questions by leading the community in defining equity. Writing a definition of equity is about more than just reaching consensus about a goal. Defining is about understanding and building common language to facilitate discussion, listening, and being able to alter one's perspective. The process of writing the definition also surfaces a range of perspectives about equity. Having that information is crucial to move forward.

defini... surfaces a range of perspectives about equity.

In every district we know, reaching consensus on a definition of equity takes time. One of the great challenges in defining equity is that stakeholders who are trying to write a definition are aware of how that definition will affect the expectations for their work. In other words, people often anticipate the implications of a definition before they settle on the definition. As a result, conversations become circular—almost like having a meeting to schedule a meeting about the need to have a meeting. Equity warriors persevere to push through the definition phase. Writing a definition is exhausting work and will be doomed to failure unless equity warriors are committed to seeing it through. What hope is there to advance equity if people can't even agree on a definition?

DEFINE EQUITY FOR YOUR DISTRICT *acronymn*

The process for defining equity depends on the district context and experiences.

Use your equity lens to

- Identify a guiding coalition of key stakeholders and influencers, including students

- Deepen understanding of the system's strengths and obstacles by selecting and reviewing data that tell the story of student experience

- Name the problem to be solved and strategic opportunity gaps

- Define an equity outcome that is clear, sensible to the head, and appealing to the heart

- Name metrics as part of your definition that measure progress toward your outcome

Educators often defer to how external players define equity of opportunity. The definition that says students need more to succeed is a definition that gets more play in state and federal decision making that results in more funding for students based on income, language proficiency, and disability. Decision makers accept that it is more costly to educate students who require more time or specialized services, or who are otherwise dependent on school for learning, enrichment, or basic needs of food and safety. More funding and supports are available to students designated at-risk. Compliance with state and federal requirements is not the only reason district leaders make more resources available to designated students. District leaders recognize a sense of obligation to do the right thing for students. School board members in more affluent districts, for example, often provide additional services to students with disabilities from a sense of obligation to doing the right thing, rather than from compliance—and often in response to activist parents able to tell their story.

But, similar to our achievement gap discussion, this approach pits groups against one another. Where there is a "how-about-me" ethos, more advantaged families advocate for special considerations for their children. Sports, arts, cocurricular activities, and gifted and talented programs are the result of balancing interests. It is not just families. Educators often resent Title I schools because they have more discretionary resources than non–Title I schools. Some school boards "adjust" funding formulas to include more schools in the Title I pool, which decreases dollars for schools with the neediest populations. Fair student funding formulas that are weighted toward school-dependent students are not universally in place. Even in middle- and upper-middle-class communities, when economic times are tighter, generosity tightens too.

Equity warriors have been successful using two strategies to advance an equity-of-opportunity agenda. Both strategies begin with gathering data on opportunity gaps, and both propose outcomes that are measurable. Implicit in each is how they define equity of opportunity.

The first strategy is universal access. To counter the resentments and increase the odds for sustainability, opportunity gaps measures are more likely to remain in place when there is universal access. Federal and state laws and regulations and local programs providing supports to students with disabilities are sustained even though the costs continue to consume higher percentages of district budgets. Of course, there is pushback on increased spending that affects opportunities for general education students. Opponents of increased spending focus on controlling expenses, improving efficiency, and demanding full funding from state and federal governments—they rarely say they want to deny services.

Similarly, universal pre-kindergarten (preK) programs, like those in New York City, are built on the political reality that sustainability is more likely if all parents have a common interest, even those who could afford such programs. It makes sense that children, particularly those whose first language is not English or who do not have access to enrichment activities, are better prepared for success in kindergarten if they have attended a preK program. Making pre-kindergarten available to all increases the odds that it will be considered a right, not a privilege, and will be available to those most in need.

The second strategy holds harmless and advances opportunities for more advantaged families while providing additional supports to school-dependent students. The Montgomery County (Maryland) Public Schools (MCPS) *Our Call to Action: Raising the Bar and Closing the Gap* provides an example.

Our Call to Action took a comprehensive look at the academic performance of students and showed the disparities within one of the wealthiest and largest school districts in America. As Superintendent Jerry Weast framed the question:

> [W]hat do you do if 75–80 percent of all [Black and Latinx] students live in a well-defined geographical area, 75–80 percent of all poverty is in that same area, 75–80 percent of all students learning English are in that same area, and disproportionately lower student performance occurs across the same geographical area? What do you do when that same geographical area includes more than 67,000 students, the equivalent of the 53rd largest school district in the nation, and the poverty rate of kindergarten is 50 percent and growing? (Childress et al., 2009, p. 34)

One part of the strategy was to structure a win-win situation by setting a universal target that resonated with the community. The target, referred to as the North Star, was readiness for college and high-wage work. While many leaders frame aspirational goals, Weast and his colleagues defined the milestones along the way that students would need to meet to be ready. The milestones, *Seven Keys to College Readiness*, were

- advanced reading in grades K–2;
- advanced reading on the Maryland State Assessment in grades 3–8;

(Continued)

(Continued)

- advanced mathematics in grade 5;

- Algebra 1 by grade 8, "C" or higher;

- Algebra 2 by grade 11, "C" or higher;

- 3 on AP exam, 4 on IB exam; and

- 1650 SAT, 24 ACT (Childress et al., 2009, p. 128).

This part of the strategy was intended to increase accountability vertically and horizontally across the district. Being explicit about the benchmark served to arm parents—those able to be more actively engaged in supporting their children as well as those who are more school dependent—with knowledge that can push conversations with educators about whether students are on track for success. This approach assumes that more actively engaged parents would push their children's schools, and that teachers and schools would push accountability vertically. For example, if a district expects all students to participate in advanced mathematics in grade 5, grade 5 teachers are more likely to push vertically to ensure that teachers prepared students to be ready for advanced work. Counting on parents and more effective schools to do their part, district staff could focus attention on schools that served school-dependent students.

Another part of the MCPS strategy was the superintendent and board's guarantee that district per-pupil spending levels would remain the same for students outside of the high-poverty areas (Green Zone). While schools in the Green Zone would be in effect held harmless, the district would increase per-pupil spending to schools in the high-poverty area (Red Zone), along with increased accountability. At least in the short term, the district had addressed the fear of loss among more affluent families.

Reaching consensus and acting on resource distribution so that students have what they need to be successful is not enough. It is not enough because that approach operates from a deficit model: It suggests that district leaders are doing for students who can't do for themselves. Of course, students need support. Students who don't enter kindergarten able to read need more support than students who do. Students who live in temporary housing need more support than students who do not have obstacles preventing them from attending school each day.

However, equity warriors must be vigilant in defining equity to challenge the implicit and explicit messages that students and their families who attend our schools are "less than"—that we are here to take from ourselves in order to save them from miserable and horrible conditions, and give them a chance. Although well-intended, those of us who entered the field of education—as we did—to provide all students the same opportunities we hoped to provide for our children miss the point that students need to be understood for who they are, not who we want them to be.

This is a tricky proposition. K–12 education may be the only social system Americans experience in common across our nation. Its intent from the beginning is to inculcate—some say indoctrinate—generations of Americans into a common culture by providing opportunities to encounter, respond to, and be appreciated by others. Schools articulate what we should know and how we demonstrate our knowledge and skills, and they reinforce behaviors appropriate to living in a democratic society. Educators and everyone else have argued over who should control learning, but communities still end up in control by default.

Defining equity is about how the district chooses to talk about students. District-level equity warriors recognize that any deficit model creates winners and losers and therefore is not sustainable. Equity warriors recognize and celebrate each and every student—and mean it. Yet, that is one piece of the puzzle. Actions matter. Leading the community through the process of defining equity creates an opportunity for educators, families, and students to learn together as they develop common language.

Equity warriors recognize and celebrate each and every student— and mean it.

It is not easy, in the day-to-day of teaching and working with students, for educators to reflect on biases—everyone has them—and to engage others. Yet by doing so, students and families have the opportunity to be partners in learning and in advocating for a system that works. By valuing students and families, we know them.

YOUR MOVE: CREATE METRICS THAT MATTER.

There is a lot to learn from the successes and stumbles of other equity warriors. Our starting point included a heavy emphasis on achievement data. We used data to ask questions about the data and hoped the answers would yield solutions. District and school leaders, over time, convinced us that while data are important, they really did not want to spend a lot of time on naming the problem. They thought they knew the problem. They certainly knew they had a problem, or we wouldn't be talking.

We have come to understand that the right data set the direction, and we should focus on programs and practices that are yielding the results we desire. Frankly, we know that many of the programs and practices employed to address achievement gap measures do not have the desired effect. Yet, we keep doing them. What is the reason? There is no simple answer. Maybe we are pleased with the results because they align with our expectations, although they are not the results others are measuring.

Before NCLB, Hayes Mizell, a friend and mentor, once asked a room of Corpus Christi, Texas, educators, if there were no state assessment, what measures would they use to demonstrate student progress to the public (Mizell, 2002). Across the room, you could hear anxious muttering. Mizell went on to ask, would educators ever do the right thing for the right reasons? The room was tense. He went on to explain that schools and districts would need to begin to accept responsibility for student outcomes if they wanted to be free of external agents setting the outcomes and the measurements. In addition, schools and districts would need to make tough choices and take action when they failed to make progress toward the outcomes. Only when schools were responsible and showed they would take action would educators gain public confidence.

Can equity warriors rally the community to support an equity agenda?

Mizell's question came from one who was well informed. As a civil rights leader, he operated with a moral compass evident to everyone he touched. As the education program officer for the Edna McConnell Clark Foundation, he directed the spending of nearly $90 million in a few large urban districts for more than a decade to promote middle-level school reform. He spoke with confidence of leading a major initiative over time in different urban districts. But, after a decade of helping schools with large percentages of underserved students, he was also frustrated that educators were not taking the lead to be responsible.

This remains the question. What metrics and data will convince the public that public schools are successful? For equity warriors, the politics of determining the measures is the nub of the question. District leaders know that with community planning and a clear strategy, they can rally the majority of voters to support funding for school building or technology upgrades, even in tight economic times. Can equity warriors rally the community to support an equity agenda?

This all points to the role of district leaders in creating the narrative by framing what is most important for the district and why. Rather than telling the story in student performance data, *equity warriors tell the story in terms of conditions of success.* What messages are compelling to parents and the community? What promises is the district willing to make to each and every student about the outcomes of a preK–12 education? What data can best tell the story? Here is where elevating student data is most effective.

We learned a lesson several years ago, in working with district leaders to create data dashboards to show students' progress on multiple measures. We convened a group of politically active parents who were engaged in the district. These were the go-to parents. We demonstrated the dashboard and how the community and families would access data on several indicators. We were convinced that we would build confidence in the district's agenda. The parents were engaged, respectful, and quiet. At the end, we pulled a parent aside and asked for her candid reaction. She said the data system was "nice," but all she really wanted to know is whether her son was on track to graduate and be prepared for college. The dashboard could not answer that question for her.

Similarly, when we were interviewing parents for a candidate in Boston's mayoral election about a contentious issue— expansion of charter schools—we heard clearly that charter schools were not an issue for families. Families wanted their children to attend a good school, but they didn't care whether the school was a charter school or a traditional public school or whether they needed to transport their children to another part of the city. They preferred to have their children in a neighborhood school, but "good" trumped distance or structure every time.

For too long, actually starting in 1983 with *A Nation at Risk*, many players have approached change by creating disequilibrium. These players suggest that public education is a problem to be solved and that they have a solution to fix it. Proponents of various sorts of change have successfully generated significant increases in federal, state, and local dollars for public education. They have encouraged alternatives to traditional public schools. This strategy has not made us feel any better about our public school system, and it hasn't produced substantial or sustainable change. That is a shame.

Equity warriors know that they must be successful in balancing conflicts if they want to lead their community's equity agenda.

Equity warriors know that they must be successful in balancing conflicts if they want to lead their community's equity agenda. To do so effectively, equity warriors understand the conflicts that arise through attempts to close achievement and opportunity gaps; they build strategies that are right for their communities and their agenda; and they create metrics and a narrative that is personal, relevant, and honest for their communities.

REFLECTION: *What are the conflicts you, as a district equity warrior, confront? What are the parameters in surfacing your community's achievement and opportunity gaps? What is your definition of equity based on your context and data?*

_____

_____

_____

_____

_____

_____

_____

_____

_____

 ## DIPLOMACY: BUILD A CRITICAL MASS OF SUPPORT FOR ADVANCING EQUITY

As important as it is for equity warriors to identify and collect the most compelling data and to resolve conflicts to frame the narrative, diplomacy—the processes of dealing with people in a sensitive and effective way—is essential to preparing an organization's culture to achieve the vision.

Diplomacy is the process through which equity warriors ensure that meaningful, long-term change happens. Two of the three tools of diplomacy—rewards and consequences—are fundamentally transactional. For example, district leaders use rewards of promotion, funding of initiatives, and access or preferential treatment to entice others to act in ways consistent with their wishes. Likewise, some leaders imply that consequences such as the loss of rewards, change in position or status, and even terminations will result from failure to behave in a particular way. These tools can be effective and sensitive ways to change behaviors when the transaction offers something of value to the people involved. Rewards and consequences are effective in the long term when the people involved see them as an agreement or a "contract." District leaders rely on these tools to effect change. They work well as long as the rewards and consequences are applied consistently and as long as they remain in place.

Diplomacy is the process through which equity warriors ensure that meaningful, long-term change happens.

Diplomacy is the process through which equity warriors ensure that meaningful, long-term change happens. Equity warriors have three tools in their arsenal for diplomacy work:

Rewards: Transactions that may be intangible or tangible such as access, status, recognition, preference, and autonomy, as well as promotions, extra pay, reduced workload, and improved working conditions.

Consequences: Real or perceived transactions that harm or damage another. Transactions can be the opposite of rewards (e.g., exclusion from activities) that are valued, or they can create fear that a threat will take place in retribution for action.

Moral persuasion: Convincing others to take action because it is the right thing to do. Just saying that advancing equity is the right thing to do doesn't convince or move people to action. Moral persuasion aims to transform people through processes that identify motives, aspirations, and values; that seek to satisfy higher needs; and that engage others in making a commitment and taking responsibility for implementation. Effective processes recognize that individuals have options and must be convinced of the "right" option before making a commitment and taking responsibility.

The third tool of diplomacy—moral persuasion, which is convincing others to take action because it is the right thing to do—is a process that rarely yields results in the short term when sensitivity and effectiveness are at odds. For example, there are effective, well-known, and well-respected protocols for teaching about racial identity and engaging educators and other adults in interracial conversations. Districts across the country adopt and use these protocols. Nevertheless, few places use these protocols consistently. White leaders—board members, community members, and educators—push back from uncomfortable conversations for multiple, complex reasons. Just agreeing to use a protocol is not enough.

My personal journey in confronting our awareness of race and privilege has been very well-intentioned and has been one of continual exploration of feelings and reflections. I am far from finished. Through experience, I recognize the importance of creating conditions so that participants—those internal and external to the organization—engage in hard conversations. Sensitivity and a willingness to understand initially rather than blame are critical to moving beyond superficial and reactive conversations.

YOUR MOVE: EMBRACE EXTERNAL PARTNERS AS YOU STRIVE TO ENACT AN EQUITY AGENDA.

Equity warriors persuade others that an equity agenda is in their interest.

Equity warriors persuade others that an equity agenda is in their interest. Persuasion, rather than telling, is an integral part of the change process. The audiences for these messages are both educators within the system and parents and community members who are outside the system.

Building on a foundation of data enables equity warriors to engage others in understanding the current reality and seeing progress toward prescribed goals. Embracing a change mindset enables equity warriors to engage internal and external stakeholders. Building trust is essential to building support. That means bringing stakeholders into the process and helping them verify the problem and develop a solution, not imposing a solution on them.

If others can verify for themselves that the problem exists, they begin the process of sharing ownership in solving the problem. Sharing data about the current reality also becomes a sorting activity because it will identify who will be leaders, allies, and blockers. When people who are considered objective or at least not obligated to toe the district line verify the problem, then the fence-sitters also are likely to become allies.

Not everyone, of course, will be persuaded. But knowing who is not convinced—and particularly who will be blockers—is valuable information, especially when identifying those individuals early in the process. Knowing the nonsupporters provides the opportunity to include their perspective at every stage of the process—an essential element for building trust in the process and the goal.

Helping people see the problem for themselves means embracing transparency. Those examining the problem need access to most of the information available to leaders so that exploration of the problem is real. There are obvious lines that cannot be crossed, such as personally identifying personnel and students, even if pushed. Too often, though, the overriding concern is that sharing too much of the problem will lead people to lose faith in the system. However, setting conditions for releasing information is perfectly acceptable. Bear in mind that releasing information to anyone means releasing information to everyone. Failing to be transparent about what information will be shared can jeopardize your efforts to build trust among various groups.

District leaders control how information is shared and with whom. Districts typically have processes for researchers to access district and school data. Granting access to data to build critical mass could begin by reviewing normal operating procedures for doing so. Nevertheless, it is common to claim transparency and then not share information that people have access to anyway. Family members walking through a school will notice student populations and staff diversity and make judgments about the school's policies regarding students of color. With very little effort, family members can learn from friends, siblings, social media, websites, and ZIP codes which middle schools are safe, which high schools are preparing students for postsecondary success, and which elementary schools have a welcoming environment. Keeping data from them does not build trust.

Charlotte-Mecklenburg in central North Carolina offers an example of a community that responded to an external prod to look at itself and developed its own response to its discoveries.

In 2016–2017, community members in Charlotte-Mecklenburg formed a task force to study the effect of low-income neighborhoods on future economic opportunities. The impetus for the task force came from two places: The first was a Harvard University/University of California at Berkeley study that showed Charlotte-Mecklenburg was 50th out of 50 cities for upward economic mobility for children born into the lowest income quintile. The second was the killing of a Black father by a police officer in 2016.

Over 18 months, task force members examined three determinants with the potential to influence the opportunity trajectory for individuals: early care and education, college and career

(Continued)

(Continued)

readiness, and child and family stability. They also examined two factors that cut across each determinate: segregation and social capital. They analyzed segregation through three different lenses: wealth, poverty, and race/ethnicity. They defined social capital as the relationships and networks that connect people to opportunities.

The task force's report, *Leading on Opportunity*, is a bold and unvarnished uncovering of the conditions of their community. For example, the report showed that one-third of the schools are segregated by poverty, half of the schools are segregated by race, and one-fifth are hypersegregated, meaning 90 percent of the school's population is of one race. The task force looked at policies related to housing, early care, and incarceration as well as family structure. The report begins with a call to "acknowledge the significant roles segregation and racialization have played in our current opportunity narrative and commit to becoming a more inclusive, fair, and just community." Among the task force recommendations are a heavy investment in early childhood care and education, college and career pathways, and nine strategies to address "interrelated factors that have the greatest impact on child and family stability" (Charlotte-Mecklenburg Opportunity Task Force, 2018, p. 15).

Formed in 2018, the nonprofit Leading on Opportunity—whose staff reports to a board comprising civic, government, nonprofit, and business leaders—continues to influence the community in implementing the strategies, key recommendations, initial implementation tactics, and policy considerations with the critical partners identified in the report.

District leaders have opportunities for action when they embrace external partners and seize the moment when the community recognizes the importance of addressing the vestiges of systemic racism and structural equities. Such moments and the interests of external partners can be fleeting. External partners who may have limited time to focus on complex and resistant systems can help start to build the structures necessary to sustain change. The rewards and the progress made in advancing the equity agenda need to be clear in order to sustain the moral imperative a moment launches.

YOUR MOVE: BRING THE
BOARD AND PUBLIC WITH YOU.

Equity warriors have a sense of urgency to advance their equity agenda. Some superintendents are hired by the board with a specific charge to advance equity. There are those who bring their passion for advancing equity to new situations. There are times, as was the case in Charlotte-Mecklenburg, that events spark urgency. Since decisions to advance equity are made in a public arena, equity warriors can use telling the story to generate public awareness and support their equity agenda. Telling the story must be handled carefully or it can be counterproductive, even jeopardizing the success of an equity agenda.

Superintendents who have been hired specifically to address equity challenges begin by surveying the situation while not backing away. The first questions to consider are: What is the evidence the board and community support the equity agenda? What is the status of previous attempts to move the agenda? Having the board just say to the superintendent that she has board support is inadequate. Interest in and support for equity should be evident in community and school board conversations during a superintendent selection and hiring process. If there is no evidence, that should signal caution.

What problems are we trying to solve?

There are multiple examples of equity warriors who have found they did not have the support they anticipated for the equity agenda or were out ahead of the readiness of their board and community. Sometimes, the intentions of the board and community are misleading or misread. Other times, the board and communities back away because the stakes are too high or higher than they anticipated.

High-stakes challenges to advancing equity are those where the most obvious solution is that a group will lose something it values. High-stakes challenges are particularly difficult for equity warriors because knowing the outcome limits the use of strategy and effectiveness of engaging the public. Unless there is a critical mass and momentum behind the challenge and the number of people receiving the benefit are greater than the number losing, there is rarely the political will to make significant and lasting structural change in the short term.

Take the high-stakes example of challenging the common practice of traditional public school districts that have entrance requirements and admit students to select schools or programs within schools. By law and court decisions, schools can have entrance requirements that do not discriminate against a protected class while allowing students access to public education. Schools are considered not to discriminate even when the entrance requirements yield very small numbers of Black students admitted to select schools. District leaders who question these practices do so on behalf of disenfranchised families who are not able to challenge the system on their own.

Pushback can be considerable when a statement of the problem is accompanied by—implicitly or explicitly—the solution.

In New York City, Chancellor Richard Carranza went on the offensive in June 2018 and publicly challenged the makeup of the city's selective high schools, where students are admitted after acing a single high-stakes exam that tests their mastery of math and English. Although Black and Latinx students make up nearly 70 percent of New York City's public school enrollment, just over 10 percent of students admitted into the city's eight specialized high schools were Black or Latinx. Stuyvesant High School, for example, which is the most selective of the specialized schools, admitted only 10 Black students in 2018. White and Asian American students are the majorities at all eight of the specialized schools. At Stuyvesant, three-quarters of the students are Asian American.

Changing the makeup of the student body at the exam schools means changing the way that students are admitted. Asian American groups immediately saw this as a threat and launched a campaign to retain the current policy, quickly raising dollars to lobby state lawmakers for retaining the test-based system (Harris & Hu, 2018).

Challenging high-stakes practices is not for the faint of heart! Even much lower-stakes practices, such as removing a principal, are political and come with consequences. Nevertheless, the most difficult challenges can be met given a public relations strategy, time, and perseverance. Equity warriors use a public relations strategy to tell their story. When there is clear evidence of growing support for an equity agenda over time, we have watched as superintendents frame the district's story and advancing equity as being part of its good-to-great journey. They show how previous administrations brought the district to a certain level. They engage the board and members of the public involved in selecting the new administration to share their expectations to move forward an equity agenda. They fight the urge to be the face of the equity agenda and the teller of the story. It is the board and community story, so they should be helped to tell it.

District leaders can also seed the story. Rather than having all messages about a problem or a solution come from district leaders, leaders will sometimes openly and sometimes quietly encourage others to speak out. Sometimes seeding the story is as simple as encouraging external partners to share their stories more publicly. Other times it involves encouraging or planting stories that others can tell on the leader's behalf.

Another way to seed the story is by hiring external consultants to audit finances, facilities, curriculum, and/or programs and publicize the findings to call attention to a desired situation. There is an inherent danger in this strategy: If public funds are spent to create a report, then the report must be shared even if the results are not in line with the desired outcome. Proceed cautiously when embracing this option.

YOUR MOVE: ENGAGE STUDENTS AS VITAL STAKEHOLDERS IN THE GUIDING COALITION.

A key element of diplomacy is engaging students along with other stakeholders as partners in each step of the change process. Using compelling student data to tell stories is one part. Having students verify and communicate the problem can help build confidence that the district is genuinely interested in defining and solving problems.

Equity warriors, ourselves included, do not include students often enough. When included at all, students are invited to testify or have a spot at the table. They are sometimes invited to be panelists to open a session. We are often afraid to hear student stories about the quality of the education they receive because we are uncertain what they will say. Yet, we are moved by students telling authentic stories. Even more to the point, students know what inequity looks like and how they are affected by it. They know the expectations adults have for them. Building their skills and engaging them as partners can enable them to become effective spokespersons for equity. After all, it is about and for them!

We are often afraid to hear student stories about the quality of the education they receive because we are uncertain what they will say.

As an advisor to high school students, I learned that students could make significant contributions to policy conversations when they understood how education systems worked. Their contributions were unvarnished and authentic. They could portray the reality of schools and provide a lens into the experiences. More often than not, students could identify issues based on their experiences well before adults became aware of the issues.

Equity warriors engage students as partners alongside other stakeholder groups. That means creating a guiding coalition that gathers information and identifies alternative solutions. Kotter (1996) describes guiding coalitions as agreeing on approaches and communications that are sensible to the head and appealing to the heart (p. 66).

We recommend that guiding coalitions include no more than 20 people—large enough to represent the different roles and perspectives, yet small enough to allow for team building. The guiding coalition should include supporters and skeptics—those who believe in and drive the work and those who are not initially supportive but in positions of authority that can block progress. We have used guiding coalitions in different ways. Here is one example in which students as stakeholders and student stories were used to shine a spotlight on a challenge.

Norfolk Public Schools is a district of 33,000 students and 42 schools in Virginia. John Simpson, superintendent from 1998 to 2004, created a guiding coalition of about 20 influential parents and community, school, union, student, and district leaders to examine student literacy. His first step was to engage the coalition in reading and discussing research and articles on the effect of illiteracy on students' academic and social well-being, as well as programs and initiatives shown to improve literacy. The selected readings helped participants become empathetic to those who were not literate and outraged that system failings, not intellectual capacity, were often the cause. Once Simpson had consensus that a problem existed, he turned to the guiding coalition to determine next steps. The guiding coalition settled on creating an initial target of having all students reading at grade level by 3rd grade.

Before the guiding coalition, Norfolk's educators agreed that 3rd-grade literacy was an important education performance target. Although they worked on the issue internally, the problem persisted. What they needed was the push and support from outside the system.

The guiding coalition became a game-changer in Norfolk. The process of educating the public and sharing ownership for low literacy created a movement within the city. City government, community organizations, and business partners contributed resources, time, and energy to create an alternative reality. Community leaders turned to professional educators for their expertise in identifying which reading programs were already successful with

Norfolk students, settling on the few that best met student needs, and finding reliable assessments for reading comprehension.

The focus on literacy remained in place in Norfolk long after Simpson retired. Years later, the teachers union president, who had been a member of the guiding coalition, continued to advocate for a focus on 3rd-grade reading comprehension and to call attention when progress was not made. The story of the guiding coalition was folklore for a while—the good ol' days when the community banded together in common cause around a moral imperative.

Social media and technology provide new opportunities to engage stakeholders in contributing to decisions that impact their lives. Accessing these tools provides ways to channel creative energy and foster understanding and trust. In particular, not engaging students leaves them with no alternative than to be recipients, not participants, in the equity agenda.

YOUR MOVE: CREATE INTERNAL MUTUAL ACCOUNTABILITY BETWEEN DISTRICT AND SCHOOL LEADERS.

Advancing equity always starts and ends with student academic success. Equity warriors know that strategies and actions have a through-line to student success. However, strategies and actions are often disconnected. District leaders must avoid the tendency to slip into the wrong question—and wrong questions lurk around every corner. For example, in a conversation with area superintendents about the rollout of a new instructional framework, they voiced frustration that district curriculum leaders had not given them a clear definition of what success looks like. Is it implementing this or that instructional strategy? What is the sequence? How many teachers? What is the frequency? How do we know we are doing it correctly?

Advancing equity always starts and ends with student academic success.

These important questions need answers at various points in the implementation process. Yet, the questions need nuance for an equity agenda. Equity warriors ask questions that begin with, "Given the needs of our students . . ." or "Given the student outcomes we seek. . . ." For example, given the needs of our students—language proficiency, reading level, access to materials, instructional time—what instructional approaches should we use? Or, given that we want to increase student reading levels for multilingual learners by two grade levels in a year, what approach and structures should we use?

These questions reflect an interest in clarifying who has responsibility. The person asking the question holds part of the responsibility for the answer. She is responsible for representing the needs and outcomes or bringing clarity around a definition. My role may be to know my students. Your role is to match the resources and experiences to help me be successful with my students. Equity warriors need to be clear. To borrow a phrase from Brené Brown, clear is kind (Brown, 2018, p. 44).

It is easy to deflect responsibility for valid reasons—such as not having the support, resources, or time to address equity issues. Saying everyone is responsible for student success is easy. But the preponderance of evidence suggests otherwise. The reality is that when everyone is responsible, no one is responsible. It is much less easy to achieve accountability in the absence of a through-line from the board to the classroom that articulates responsibilities and the particular role participants play in students' ultimate success.

One way to use the tools of diplomacy is to understand the difference between adaptive and technical challenges (Heifetz & Linsky, 2002, p. 13). Based on the work of Ron Heifetz and Marty Linsky, technical challenges are those things we can apply known solutions to remedy. That does not mean that technical challenges are easy to address. In fact, some technical challenges are remarkably complex—for example, textbook adoption takes a great deal of time, involves many people, and requires approvals at many levels. The key criterion is that technical challenges can be addressed using existing or available expertise.

Adaptive challenges are those based on fundamental beliefs held by individuals or the organization. Adaptive challenges require thinking in different ways, to view a problem from different perspectives and lead from the balcony, not from the ground, in order to change beliefs that are obstacles to acting to meet new or different expectations. There may be strategies and experiences to guide us; however, the ways to address adaptive challenges may not be known to others or us. There is no guidebook or manual to help. Let's consider one strategy.

Long Beach Unified School District, the fourth-largest district in California and located south of Los Angeles, serves a diverse urban and suburban student population. It also long had a strong culture, referenced in numerous publications as the "Long Beach Way." One of the key strategies in the district has been its use of *Key Results Walk-Throughs*, which offer an approach to adaptive challenges.

Many districts use walk-throughs or learning walks as protocols for district teams to learn about school programs and/or advise school leaders on ways to strengthen practices. When these visits are more about district leaders telling or giving advice to school leaders rather than learning, the visits have little value because they are neither sensitive nor effective in changing practice. When visits are not repeated or are done infrequently, they become more like events than continuous learning opportunities. As there is limited time and resources, the visits often "help" by monitoring progress of schools.

Too often, visits suggest that district leaders have answers to the challenges facing school leaders. District leaders feel obligated to have an effect as a result of their visits. It rarely happens. Typically, one of the following occurs:

- School leaders learn more about their challenges from preparing for the visit than from the exchange of ideas with district leaders. The school benefits and moves forward.

- District leaders filter the school visit through their own past experiences and give advice based on what worked for them as school leaders. There is no application or change.

- District leaders agree or insist on providing resources or professional learning they have at their disposal. School leaders appreciate extra resources; however, the resources aren't tailored to their needs or school leaders do not know how to use them effectively. The challenges worsen as school leaders lose focus.

- School leaders are unprepared for the visit or make a poor showing. District leaders are angered and/or frustrated and decide to change school leadership or, uncertain what to do, they do not visit again.

In each scenario, the visits were not tailored to wrestle with the adaptive challenges facing the schools and the district. If district leaders believe these visits are sensitive and effective, then they are not clear about how to exercise their roles to support schools. Lack of clarity leads to blaming others. Blaming leads to frustration, negativity, and shutting down. School leaders don't seek support from district leaders because it is clear they don't know what to do.

(Continued)

(Continued)

Long Beach Unified had a different approach. District leaders used Key Results Walk-Throughs as a key element of their high school reform efforts. At the time, the district's six comprehensive high schools enrolled 25,000 high school students. Since there were only six high schools, district leaders could visit each school three times a year. The district team included the assistant superintendent who supervised high schools, curriculum specialists from all content areas, and principals from each of the other high schools. The school teams included all administrators and teacher heads of each department. Each visit started with an overview of the schools' data since the last visit, followed by classroom visits by department, discussion of next steps, and a debrief that described agreements on next steps by all parties before the next visit.

The visits were intended to focus on the adaptive challenge of clarifying role responsibility among the district and school leaders. Specifically, Long Beach Unified had a central curriculum team that had strong knowledge about standards-based instruction. The team offered and conducted professional learning for teachers. The professional learning was thought to be well designed and rich in best practices in all disciplines. The department heads were responsible for professional learning at their schools, which they coordinated with the assistant principal or principal who supervised the department and the central curriculum team for that content area. The question was this: Are we able to see a throughline from the expectations and professional development to classroom practice?

This question is a fundamental adaptive challenge for many districts. District and school leaders and teachers make choices about what they do based on limited time and resources and competing demands. Those choices often appear as parameters around their work that are disconnected from others—for example, district leaders plan workshops, others develop or select curriculum, school leaders are responsible for all aspects of the school day, and teachers deliver instruction while maintaining discipline. Each of these areas of work has its own technical challenges. At the same time, there are adaptive challenges that grow out of fundamental beliefs and values.

Long Beach district leaders faced those adaptive challenges. They understood that if a curriculum is technically outstanding, but teachers don't understand it, then it is of limited value. If teachers are able to connect with students but do not know what academic excellence looks like, they cannot prepare students for success. If administrators do not have a vision for how to use resources effectively to support the specific needs of their school—and stand up for what they need and push back on resources that derail their efforts—then we are wasting precious time. Vertical collaboration based on a shared sense of interdependence and collective responsibility is an adaptive challenge. It was a challenge worth facing.

It was rough going. Central curriculum specialists were not accustomed to the suggestion that they be accountable for changes in teacher practice. They had their responsibilities and work—creating curriculum units, keeping current and participating in standards development and changes, planning professional development. They really did not have time to redirect their efforts and follow their work into classroom practice, unless it was to work with individual, struggling, or new teachers in response to a request. The school leaders were not comfortable sharing their school's data with colleagues and/or admitting they were not clear about how standards-based instruction should look in content areas outside of their teaching experience. Department heads were not willing to judge their colleagues' teaching practices or willing to hold teachers accountable for what they recognized as poor instructional practice. While there may not have been tears, there was a lot of angst.

Yet, over time, Long Beach developed a strong culture that supported doing the right thing so that educators could have honest conversations about how to affect instruction so student learning would improve. Central curriculum specialists began to learn how to better design programs and support teacher learning. School administrators recognized their role as instructional leaders—not as curriculum experts but as those responsible for making certain that resources were not only gathered and used but that they were effective. Teachers felt pressure and support across the system.

Equity warriors know that the tools of diplomacy—rewards, consequences, and moral persuasion—can be helpful in fostering community engagement and critical school district conversations to advance equity. For conversations to be successful, they need to fulfill a couple of conditions. First, there must be a clear purpose and a goal (e.g., affecting student data that matters with milestones). Second, stakeholders must believe in interdependence and shared accountability. We will address the contributions of explicit values in Part II. For

Equity warriors know that the struggle for justice is a long road. Nevertheless, there are times when conflict cannot be avoided.

now, the point is that school districts do not have to be places where differences in perspective are resolved with winners and losers. Equity warriors know that the struggle for justice is a long road. Nevertheless, there are times when conflict cannot be avoided.

REFLECTION: *Can you name the external and internal stakeholders who hold the keys to establishing your community's equity agenda? What processes have you used to bring student experiences into the equity discussions? What tools of diplomacy—rewards, consequences, moral persuasion—are at your disposal?*

_____

_____

_____

_____

_____

_____

_____

_____

WARFARE: USE STUDENT DATA TO CONVINCE, QUESTION, AND TEACH

In the district-level politics and diplomacy sections, we discussed the options and challenges facing equity warriors in determining direction, readiness, allies, and strategy. We named and considered processes and approaches to bring people together around a common cause.

Nobody should charge directly into warfare. Politics and diplomacy should lay the groundwork and often can be sufficient. But equity warriors are well aware that sometimes adults do not want to participate in processes, or, worse, they stall and undermine the work. The success of equity work is so important that equity warriors cannot give up in the face of opposition. When we are certain that we are not gaining traction, the warrior takes over.

Equity warriors cannot give up in the face of opposition.

We define warfare simply as pressuring people to stop or start acting in certain ways. Direct warfare happens when individuals with position authority stand in the way. Those who hold position authority include school board members representing more affluent communities and stakeholders within the district, elected officials having direct control or budget approval, media influencers, opinion makers, and other power brokers. It can also mean coalitions or individuals able to exert influence over those who have position authority. All politics are local. In some communities, power brokers change over time. In others, they remain.

Effective equity warriors know who might stand in the way or attempt to divert funding to a different agenda. Equity warriors make judgments about the appetite for the changes, timing, and seriousness of the opposition. Being strategic is knowing how far to push, when to push, and who to push. Some equity warriors prefer to sacrifice themselves for the cause by reaching well beyond the limits of acceptance and refusing to compromise. It might seem heroic to do so. Be bold or go home! Most often, it means the end of their effectiveness and/or their position. The worse outcome for a failed attack is to undermine efforts for the future.

Equity warriors make judgments about the appetite for the changes, timing, and seriousness of the opposition.

We approach conflicts not to vanquish opposition but to achieve our equity agenda and build and sustain changes to the organization's culture. Equity warriors know that opposition is likely to occur on two fronts—with internal and external audiences—and that not all fights are the same. As we know, warfare is about reciprocal actions, and anticipating and disarming the opposition. Sometimes a show of force and unity will be enough to eliminate any serious opposition. At other times, fleeing is an option. Data that reveal the lived realities of students are among the equity warrior's most effective tools. The following moves show how.

YOUR MOVE: USE DATA AS A WEAPON WITH EXTERNAL AUDIENCES.

Equity warriors use data as a weapon sparingly, judiciously, and strategically to correct clear injustices and send messages. Like all warfare, conflict in addressing inequity results in collateral damage and unintended consequences. So, exercise caution!

For example, a superintendent in a high-poverty Midwestern district serving almost exclusively Black students discovered, in reviewing district data, that the small population of white students in the district were overly represented in gifted and talented programs. The superintendent convinced the school board to eliminate gifted and talented programs and adopt universal heterogeneous grouping of all classes. Before the next school year began, almost all students—Black and white—who were in the gifted and talented programs moved to other districts. While acting on principle is laudable, the consequences to the district were a disaster. Losing students and the associated funding was only part of the result. Parents did not understand and/or lost confidence in the administration, and the district lost the opportunity to choose other options, such as targeted heterogeneous grouping, to integrate students and improve learning. Charging into conflicts without anticipating the reciprocal actions is a mistake, no matter how morally right the action might be.

Equity warriors know the best avenue to success in advancing or protecting the equity agenda is to use data that matters to gain broad community support. Returning to the example of Montgomery County, Jerry Weast was effective in using performance data to show the widening gaps among economic, racial/ethnic, and native English-speaking student groups. He used the data to create a strategic response based on residential patterns. Achievement in the Red Zone was predictably lower based on the demographics of its neighborhood. The strategy met with resistance initially. Nevertheless, the use of moral persuasion and holding funding levels for high-performing residential areas in place prevailed.

Community support results when residents are convinced it is the right thing to do for their community, and it is the right thing to do for themselves. The strategies mentioned previously— universal preK, promises to hold harmless—are examples of how districts can gain broad support for initiatives. Convincing external audiences requires a strong narrative, compelling data about effect, and a critical mass of people able to influence their opinions. It means making moves in the other dimensions that are necessary to set the stage for reasoned confrontation. Then, conflicts are perceived as only one strategy or arrow in the quiver.

YOUR MOVE: TAP EXTERNAL AGENTS AS ALLIES IN ADVANCING EQUITY.

Equity warriors depend on allies. Superintendents have often used external partners to bring attention and/or pressure to advance an equity agenda. External partners can quell external opposition or disrupt internal resistance.

Equity warriors depend on allies.

One potential external partner is the state education agency. State education agency leaders have a bully pulpit and sometimes can be seen as objective actors. We are not sure how many local leaders actually join in alliance with state education leaders. If they do, they don't publicize their efforts to do so because state and local relations are typically adversarial. However, support from state leaders is exactly the kind of alliance that equity warriors need.

I learned this lesson early on. A school that proposed major changes for underserved students received a small award from a state grant program I was managing. In confidence, I asked the principal why he would propose to do so much more than the grant required. He said he was facing resistance within his district and school and was using the grant to "require" him to make changes that he had been unable to make.

In our work leading state intervention teams, we regularly consulted with district leaders about how, as an external partner, we could support their work in the district. When a school was designated as underperforming, the state would often require the school to collaborate with an external intervention team to develop an improvement plan. A program improvement designation can cause fear and resistance at a school. We hoped that approaching the school as a partner and listening rather than telling would support positive change. Our team would conduct a two-day assessment of the school and develop a multi-year plan based on guidelines from the state. The state wanted to see improvement in student performance, and we knew the best way to achieve improvements was to have district and school leaders buy into the action steps and hold themselves accountable for implementation. So, even before we visited, we met with district and school leaders to ask for their thinking about potential recommendations. In most cases, they knew what needed to be done and were eager for the push to do so. As we gathered information from the site visit and drafted recommendations, we incorporated their recommendations. It worked! With regular visits and constant reminders to stay focused on the recommendations, and making adjustments along the way, each of the schools we supported improved student achievement and performance over time.

Philanthropy is another potential external ally. We have known district leaders who partnered quietly with philanthropies to call attention to a challenge or advance an idea that would create pressure to respond. Philanthropies advance their agendas in different ways. Some provide grants to districts that propose or agree to participate in projects that are consistent with the philanthropy's agenda. Others have a close relationship with district leaders and are able to provide flexible funding and other resources. We have partnered with districts on behalf of philanthropies that have contracted directly with us. The following is a rare example from a national philanthropy that exemplified the ability of an external partner to help district leaders further their agenda.

From 1985 to 2018, the Panasonic Foundation partnered with public school districts interested in sharing its equity agenda. The foundation's mission, which evolved during the tenures of its two executive directors, Sophie Sa and Larry Leverett, was to partner "with public school districts and their communities to 'break the links' between race, poverty, and educational outcomes by improving the academic and social success of ALL students: ALL MEANS ALL." Instead of providing grants, the foundation entered into long-term partnerships—in some cases lasting beyond 10 years—with school districts that made a commitment to furthering an equity agenda. Its approach was to strengthen the district's leadership capacity—school boards, superintendent and cabinet, and association/union leaders—to collaboratively further the district's equity agenda. Once a partnership was launched, the foundation matched a team of senior consultants with the district in a whole-system approach fostering system-level and systemwide changes to improve learning for all students. Teams were provided at no cost to the districts.

Teams provided technical assistance through monthly visits and support for districts on initiatives specific to their equity agendas. In some cases, teams would help the district define its equity agenda. At other times, teams would introduce and/or link districts with resources and examples from other districts to prompt or augment their equity journey. Teams helped district leaders improve their capacity to collaborate by planning and facilitating quarterly or semiannual board/superintendent retreats and convening semiannual, three-day working conferences for partner districts.

The foundation engaged in more than 20 partnerships during this period. Since the team did not have a program or product that districts were obligated to accept, the initial phase was a period of negotiations and relationship building. Like all relationships, the partners learned about each other through having experiences together. The teams lived outside the district's organizational structure. They provided district leaders with an objective, honest sounding board for their ideas and often carried messages to and among board members, superintendents, and union leaders that people internal to the chain of command were unable or unwilling to offer. Most of all, the teams' regular visits and the longevity of the partnerships allowed teams to hold up a mirror to the district leaders on their progress on their equity agenda, push and prod when necessary from the inside, and become trusted critical friends. Teams helped districts organize through transition periods. Teams sometimes became the institutional memory as the partnerships lasted longer than the tenure of two—sometimes three or four—superintendents and all of the school board members. (*Note:* In 2018, the Panasonic Corporation changed the foundation's approach to be more closely aligned to the corporation's mission. The foundation began awarding grants and closed its partnerships.)

The independence of philanthropies can help district leaders think through the strategic moves necessary to advance their equity agenda. Increasingly, philanthropies have a targeted agenda that can be at odds with the district's interests. As it is with leaders internal to the organization, philanthropies that approach partnerships knowing the answer to a challenge may force their solutions on district leaders through the promise and obligation of money. We learned the lesson that not all money is good money. Being obligated to the wrong partner is worse than not having a partner at all.

Winning support from an external partner, however, requires a willingness by the district to engage in a win-win relationship with the partner. External partners will want access to data and information. They want to be in the inside. They want to know there is a chance of success. They need to know the district is really committed to the goal. The executive director of a large community trust explained it this way: "We need to know the objective and be part of the game." With access to data and plans, he was willing to allow his organization to be a player.

As we discussed earlier, providing access to data comes with risk. The strongest approach to building allies is to be clear about the assets. What part of the equity agenda are we doing well and shows the promise of expansion? Equity warriors build confidence by having command of the strengths of the organization, clearly defining the challenges, and providing access to supportive data. Allies who are convinced of the commitment and clear about the purpose are able to partner in creating the narrative and counternarrative to external pressures.

This approach to leadership may sound Machiavellian. It can be so, which is the reason to be cautious and thoughtful. Most of all, the approach must be anchored firmly in the equity agenda. If external partners sense that the approach is used for personal gain or to cover for the leader's inadequacies, they either will not join or could turn against it. However, we have found that external partners who share an equity agenda are waiting to be invited. They look for impact that adds value.

YOUR MOVE: ESTABLISH INTERNAL DATA PROTOCOLS TO UNDERSTAND EACH SCHOOL'S ASSETS AND CHALLENGES.

Superintendents and district leaders can use data in a direct way with internal stakeholders. Typically, district leaders assume good intentions until they confront a situation that offends them. When incidents happen, district leaders are quick to react internally to correct the situation and send messages to the broader community that they won't tolerate certain actions, and they have handled the situation. District leaders follow well-established protocols and accepted practices to investigate complaints or respond to incidents. If the situation suggests a widespread problem or where the school community—students, adults, or both—has been complicit, district teams or partnership organizations are equipped to respond to acts of bias, racially motivated actions, assault, or violence.

Equity warriors are proactive. District equity warriors have many data protocols for learning about their schools' assets and challenges. We will consider three that have been effective in strengthening district leaders' ability to identify and call attention to data that give students voice:

- Equity visits
- Root cause analysis
- Deep data dives

These protocols share two characteristics: They are intended to uncover the assets and challenges facing underserved students that aggregated data may hide, and they inform district actions specific to schools based on a deep understanding of student needs.

DATA PROTOCOLS FOR EQUITY WARRIORS

Equity warriors use data protocols that uncover the assets and challenges facing underserved students that aggregated data may hide, and inform district actions specific to schools based on a deep understanding of student needs.

- **Equity visits:** Focus on a specific equity goal as the problem of practice, using the instructional round structure of problem of practice, observations, and decisions/actions.

- **Root cause analysis:** Engage in inquiry about the underlying causes for performance or achievement and using the analysis to devise responses.

- **Deep data dives:** Explore a question about performance or achievement with a focus on a defined group of students by collecting and analyzing data specific to those students.

[handwritten note: 5 whys protocol]

YOUR MOVE: INTRODUCE PROTOCOLS FOR EQUITY VISITS TO SCHOOLS.

Equity warriors shine a spotlight on two types of schools: Schools where most students are successful and schools where most students are not. That is to say, all schools should be on district equity warriors' radar.

District leaders tend to give schools where most students are successful a pass because other more pressing challenges need attention or the compliancy and resistance is so strong that it is not worth the effort. At the same time, schools where most students are not successful are treated as though they have few strengths and challenges that are overwhelming. The response is to dump services and resources without regard for how the supports knit together.

Equity warriors know that a successful equity agenda depends on all schools being part of the agenda. Administrators and teachers know there is no perfect school. Even in schools where 85 percent of the students are proficient, there are underserved students. The voices of these students cannot compete with those of the majority. Are these schools able to marshal their assets to help all students? They should be able to do so.

Equity warriors know that a successful equity agenda depends on all schools being part of the agenda.

Not including all schools in a districtwide equity agenda reinforces a deficit message, one that says only troubled schools need worry about equity. Teachers across the system know that no school is perfect, and some teachers are under higher scrutiny. Complaints about fairness mask the underlying concern about lack of appreciation for teaching school-dependent students. Teaching students who have not experienced success in school is different and, in many ways, more difficult. Leaving some schools out of the work creates resentment and limits equity warriors' effectiveness.

Equity visits and root cause analysis are two data-collection protocols that district equity warriors use. These two protocols are appropriate for all schools, although the application is different. We describe each in turn.

Equity visits. Developed by Richard Elmore and his colleagues (City et al., 2009), instructional rounds are based on medical rounds through which physician teams gather evidence and confer on their diagnoses and treatment. Instructional rounds are intended to gather evidence as objectively as possible on a predetermined problem of practice. The key to successful instructional rounds is objectivity. The evidence collected must be observed and the description specific. There is a time for interpretation after the evidence is reported without bias or professional judgment. Providing just the facts creates a level playing field for the team so that everyone can contribute, and agreement on the evidence can precede decisions. Learning to be objective is easier to say than to do, and preparation for objective evidence gathering takes time.

Equity visits are a variation on instructional rounds. Using the instructional round structure of problem of practice, observations, and decisions/actions, district leader equity visits focus on a specific equity goal as the problem of practice. The New Jersey Network of Superintendents developed equity visits during a 10-year journey that started with instructional rounds and morphed into an approach to build and support superintendents in creating an instructionally focused equity agenda for their districts (Roegman et al., 2009). Twenty-five school districts, with student populations of 300 to 30,000, averaging 6,400 students, participated in the network. Over time, the superintendents created problems of practice and look-fors that were specific to instructional improvement and equity. Consider the following example of a problem of practice and its associated look-fors:

Problem of practice: Do we have effective practices to support equity and access to learning goals and increased achievement of every student? Are our coteaching classes (heterogeneous classes with one special education teacher and one content area teacher) effective?

Look-fors:

- What types of coteaching models are teachers using?
- How are both teachers differentiating instruction for individuals or small groups?
- What does it mean to effectively coinstruct in coteaching classrooms?
- To what extent do both teachers have an established role and contribute to instruction, management, assessments, and planning?
- To what extent do students respect each teacher's role in the classroom? (Roegman et al., 2019, p. 25)

This problem of practice and the associated look-fors are applicable to every school we have visited. Each school has room to grow in creating effective coteaching classrooms. While these questions may be helpful for school leaders to consider, the purpose of the equity visit protocol is for district equity warriors to better understand equity and instruction. The authors of *Equity Visits* describe a three-step protocol: identify an equity focus such as the one above, collect and analyze evidence through an equity lens, and reflect on the next steps of district equity-focused work (Roegman et al., 2019).

District leaders, not school leaders, drive each step in the process. Schools are the context in which the evidence is collected that enables district leaders to consider systemic responses. School leaders do not identify the equity focus and do not participate in the visit except to arrange logistics, provide background, and answer questions. The visit is not about one school. Responses to challenges must apply to all schools and every student. Therefore, equity visits are conducted across schools in order to objectively collect data to inform the solution.

Equity warriors who make a genuine commitment to tackling complex equity challenges will not achieve their objective overnight.

The problem-of-practice example above introduces a depth of focus and scrutiny that may make district equity warriors uncomfortable. The journey to developing the focus and scrutiny is important. Although it should not take 10 years, district leaders need to build relational trust, be reflective, be willing to confront their own biases about what is possible, be willing to learn by using multiple data, and be accountable to each other. The benefit of a bold goal is that it is not easily attainable and blame cannot be laid on one person or one part of the organization. Therefore, engaging district equity warriors in understanding and sharing responsibility for solving an equity challenge is possible. Equity warriors who make a genuine commitment to tackling complex equity challenges will not achieve their objective overnight. They will make progress toward the objective when district and school leaders see that efforts are being made to address the real work.

Root cause analysis. Using an equity-focused problem of practice and conducting equity visits to every school allows equity warriors to pressure all schools to examine their practices. Some schools will not be able to wrestle with the challenge posed by the coteaching problem of practice. There are too many levels of dysfunction. Nevertheless, schools where the majority of students are demonstrating success should be pushed to join in the equity agenda. They, too, have work to do.

Root cause analysis, a process used across industries, is a tool that district equity warriors use with school leadership teams to know their students. The San Diego Unified School District's board of trustees, superintendent Cindy Marten, chief of staff Staci Monreal, and the district leadership team are equity warriors, as the following example shows.

San Diego Unified School District, the second-largest district in California and located just north of the Mexican border, serves 124,000 students, of whom 46 percent are Latinx, 23 percent are white, 8 percent are Black, 9 percent are Asian, 21 percent are English language learners, and 58 percent qualify for free or reduced-price meals. As part of their equity journey, San Diego Unified district leaders required principals to lead their instructional leadership teams in a modified root cause analysis to deepen their schools' understanding of the conditions that contribute to student achievement. Each school team was required to participate in the analysis and prepare an action plan for the year. The action plan was intended to supplement the comprehensive school plan required by the district.

The analysis process included five sets of questions:

- **Data analysis:** What is the current reality around student performance or achievement gaps? What do trend data tell me about student needs at my school?

- **Identify possible root causes:** What are possible root causes of student underperformance or achievement gaps? What observations will I have to conduct?

- **What needs to change:** What must change for students to achieve at higher levels? What is the desired state?

- **Why change:** Why is the change important? Why is this change necessary right now for my students?

- **Call to action and leadership considerations:** How will I shift schoolwide culture, curriculum, and instruction to create the conditions for change?

District leaders provided opportunities for principals to learn the analysis tool and discuss and plan for how they would engage teachers in the analysis. The best situation is when teachers feel ownership for the data and selected solutions. Teacher involvement in the analysis is critical since teachers' beliefs affect student learning. To move beyond the preliminary and often superficial review of performance data—particularly for schools at the extremes of student performance—teachers need to be honest in answering questions about the possible root causes. To do so requires that there exists a trusting relationship among teachers and administrators and a willingness to honestly share their beliefs.

Root cause analysis was stronger when external facilitators participated. Even when trust is not an issue, teachers with strong opinions tend to overpower and fill the space vacated by teachers who are reluctant to share because they are uncertain or worry how their opinions will be received. External facilitators who are trusted or come at the request of the team help by enforcing norms and asking questions to push conversations deeper.

Some principals took ownership of the data and root cause analysis steps. They presented their analysis to the team, asked for their acknowledgment, and then proceeded to engage the team in discussions about what needs to change and, most important, why it needs to change now. Here is the opportunity for the school's leadership team to create a compelling narrative about its equity agenda. We will say more about this critical step in the next chapter.

Principals presented and discussed their plans with their area superintendent. The discussions provided opportunities to challenge assumptions and examine alignment between root causes and the changes proposed to address the causes. They also

(Continued)

provided opportunities for school and district leaders to strategize and work collaboratively on ways to address the causes. For example, if a probable root cause was high student mobility, could the school identify mobility patterns? If so, could the district develop systems to improve how student information was shared and align curriculum so that students would recognize the content they are expected to learn? It was rare that conversations led to more complex strategies. More often, discussions were about support that district leaders could offer schools.

One of the key outcomes from the process came from the school leaders' answers to the call-to-action question. The response to the question helps district leaders assess whether school leaders are equity warriors. The expectation is that the analysis and examination would lead to specific steps that would improve student learning. If school leaders were not passionate about the steps, they probably were not ready to do the hard work required to make it happen. It would be incumbent on the district equity warriors to have difficult conversations.

Equity visits and root cause analysis are two tools that can engage all schools in a district in collecting and analyzing data that are at the core of knowing students well. When equity warriors apply these tools, people can become uncomfortable. These protocols ask hard questions, and they are intended to uncover real challenges and to assess which leaders are ready to advance the equity agenda. The third tool is doing a deep data dive with a specific focus.

YOUR MOVE: DO DEEP DATA DIVES AND PUT THE FACE OF STUDENTS ON SYSTEMIC PROBLEMS.

Equity warriors make the equity agenda personal and hard to ignore by discussing the experiences of individual students.

Equity warriors make the equity agenda personal and hard to ignore by discussing the experiences of individual students. Putting a name and face to data that reveal the system's failures to educate students to high expectations yields powerful results. Equity warriors use protocols for deep data dives that can spotlight student experiences and generate momentum around systemic actions. We have partnered with districts that do deep data dives to understand the experiences of specific groups, such as Black male or Latinx students. The learning from these protocols helps us understand some of the underlying institutional barriers that result in persistent under-performance of group members. Deep dives allow equity warriors to become more specific in identifying where actions to address the barriers have been successful and where they were not, and they provide direction for powerful conversations to hold leaders accountable for their actions.

For example, in our work with partner districts, we have often been remiss in not taking on the challenge of looking at special education. We have many excuses for doing so. Federal and state laws and regulations and court decisions fill volumes. No other part of the education system is as highly regulated, monitored, and prescriptive. District leaders responsible for the special education system are well steeped in the system and have specific knowledge about the laws and parameters within which they operate. Reciprocal actions to inquiries into practices, protocols, actions, or costs include citing regulations, calling in state and federal offices and advocates, and threatening court action. Those outside the special education system tend to stay away. As a result, students with disabilities become someone else's responsibility.

Yet, a deep data dive into the special education system often shows a disturbing reality. Our first experience with this was when a high school literacy coach explored the background of Black and Latinx students who were reading below grade level and had been receiving special education services since the primary grades. Her dive into the students' individualized education programs (IEPs) showed that services were inconsistent, and there was no continuum of support from year to year. Students received services every year, with no evidence that any service was improving their reading levels.

Equity warriors struggle with knowing where to begin to address the disturbing reality within their equity agenda. There is so much work to be done for the 85 percent of students who are not identified as students with disabilities. We educators justify our limited ability to address the needs of students who are the most vulnerable among us by tinkering at the edges. We try to improve support for teachers and help them develop the skills and temperament for dealing with student behaviors in classrooms with too many students. We try to integrate students with disabilities into classrooms with general education teachers and students. We try to forge closer cooperation and collaboration among central teaching and learning and special education staffs. We try to convince state and federal regulators not to impose well-intended regulations that do not fit the reality of our student and teacher populations. While we tinker, students are lost. A good friend continually cites an African proverb: When the elephants fight, the ants suffer.

There is no easy or good solution to the challenges of our special education system. There are thousands of smart, passionate, committed people far more knowledgeable than we who are working on the system. They haven't been able to build an equitable system for all. To use another pachyderm analogy, the way to eat the elephant is by taking one bite at a time. The bite is that equity warriors can begin by doing all that is possible to ensure that the only students who enter into the special education system are the ones who truly need the services.

One district took a bite of the elephant in this way.

Taking a data dive into its special education system was the topic for the district leadership team retreat. Present at the retreat was a team of 10, the superintendent's cabinet that included the executive directors who supervised schools. The special education division director decided to start the conversation about needed improvement by reviewing some existing IEPs. To prepare, she reviewed 50 randomly selected IEPs and chose a few that would help make her point. She was stunned and disappointed that many of the IEPs, selected at random, would have been suitable. She reached into the pile, selected two, and asked staff to redact information that would identify the schools or students.

The special education director introduced the session, told staff the two IEPs had been selected at random, and asked cabinet members to read the information and offer their opinions on whether the placement and services matched the needs of the students. The members silently read the assessment data and the evaluation team's determination. The first student was a 2nd-grade Black girl. Her reading level was at the low end for 2nd grade, but she was on grade level in mathematics. She was referred for evaluation because she was not fully engaging in lessons, and her teacher wondered if she had developmental issues. The assessment showed that her single mother had moved residences twice in two years, which necessitated a school change each time. There were no signs of developmental delay. Nevertheless, the evaluation team recommended and her mother approved supplemental services that would pull the girl from her teacher and classmates for an hour each day. The second IEP described a similar situation.

The discussion that followed was filled with passion. There was consensus, based on the IEP data, that the 2nd-grade student was doing well, particularly for one who had changed schools twice. The data indicated that she could learn, especially given that she was able to remain at grade level when changing schools and potentially reading and mathematics programs. But pulling her from time with her peers would further isolate her and possibly hinder her learning of the core curriculum. So, what was the rationale for the supplemental services? Since we did not know the school, we could only speculate. Lack of knowledge, neglect, overprotection, good intentions, or bad intentions were raised as possibilities. One thing was clear: The school administrator's signature was needed to move the recommendation. Targeting the principal emerged as a districtwide approach.

The cabinet members repeated the exercise using the same IEPs with the district leadership and reached the same conclusions. The next step was a districtwide professional development session with principals. The principals' reactions to the exercise surfaced systemic issues that prevented them from making decisions that were in the best interest of students. Unfortunately, although district leaders stressed an objective review of the data and the importance of honest conversation, there was too much blaming and shaming by principals about the faults in the system.

At the core of the discussion is that principals want to support all students. Providing extra supports to teachers whose class sizes are too large and whose students are school dependent is one way to help. Cuts in administrative staff mean special education teachers are conducting IEP evaluations. Teachers are unable to push back on teachers and families who demand supports. Administrators are doing the best they can.

Putting the face of students on systemic problems is a form of warfare. Similar processes can analyze data from any student group. Using data in this way can motivate individuals to take steps to improve opportunities for student success. It can also open a can of worms. Equity warriors increase their chances of success by having clear expectations for the next steps once awareness is created. Surfacing a problem without addressing it can do more harm. There needs to be an exit strategy.

Putting the face of students on systemic problems is a form of warfare.

REFLECTION: *Which data are the most powerful in creating a sense of urgency about equity? What protocols will you use to engage external and internal audiences to see the real story? What reciprocal actions do you expect?*

_____

_____

_____

_____

_____

_____

_____

_____

_____

CHAPTER 2

School leaders center the equity agenda on student experiences

Equity warriors use data to let others visualize student experiences as they create a vision and equity agenda. As it is for superintendents and district leaders, student experiences are the best assets for a principal and other school leaders. School-level equity warriors seek data that tell their school's story within the larger context of the district. At times, the interests of the school are in conflict with the district's interests. The school's smaller size can allow equity warriors to reach quicker agreements and act faster than their district colleagues. The opposite is also true. Data comparisons across schools often contribute to a school community's complacency in maintaining the status quo or its hopelessness at not having the scale and resources to generate momentum for change. School-level equity warriors learn to navigate their ship, conscious of the district's winds and currents, and the other ships around them.

Equity warriors at the school level operate with awareness of their actions across politics, diplomacy, and warfare, as do their district colleagues. Like district-level equity warriors, they coordinate their moves for maximum affect. School-level equity warriors have the advantage of knowing their students in a way that their district-level colleagues cannot. School-level equity warriors have the advantage of freedom to act within their sphere of influence and the disadvantage of being dependent on their district colleagues for encouragement and support. In this way, successful school-level leaders balance not getting too far ahead of the district or their school community with not lagging behind the momentum and interests of either. Relying on data and telling their students' stories is a way to find the balance point. For all equity warriors, especially at the school level, knowing and responding to the needs of students is always the right thing to do.

POLITICS: ENGAGE THE SCHOOL COMMUNITY IN SHAPING AND TELLING THE SCHOOL'S STORY

Equity warriors engage with their school community in creating a vision of what they want their school to become. They build from their knowledge of students and the stories told by the data to create a vision for the school that is sensible to the head and appealing to the heart. They package that with a plan to deliver on the vision.

The ubiquitous access to and communication of information creates opportunities and challenges. In the past, schools were treated as closed systems, as if only the teachers and principal knew what went on in school every day. Operating with that belief, the principal was the primary link to anyone outside the school doors. Today, we know that schools are not closed systems. External stakeholders have multiple ways to learn about schools. States are required to make available volumes of data about school performance, and websites abound with information about test results, discipline reports, funding, and teacher performance. Students post video and photos. With social media, families and community members no longer need to rely on talking with teachers in grocery store lines to obtain informal data about schools. We are, in fact, awash with data about individual schools.

All of this means that principals must work to shape the school's story while understanding and balancing conflicts that may occur when external stakeholders use school data.

YOUR MOVE: UNDERSTAND THE ASSUMPTIONS ABOUT YOUR SCHOOL.

On the surface, schools are more alike than different. Scratch the surface and you'll see that schools are complex webs of human and social networks. No matter the size—and we have worked in schools with as few as 11 teachers and as many as 200—schools are not what they appear to be. Those within the school walls have different experiences. Teachers are often surprised by the experiences students have outside their classrooms. The further away from the school, the less likely one is to know the school. Assumptions are based on the data available or the data and stories told. Often the data are anecdotal and from a single moment in time long past. Equity warriors know that the politics of student data—how conflict is balanced to govern effectively—determines the school's story and defines how the school is perceived.

Each school's story either builds on or challenges assumptions. Assumptions do not change easily or quickly. School leaders must be able to marshal data in support of the story they want to tell about their school.

Families make assumptions about schools. If a school is in an affluent neighborhood or affluent community, families assume it is a good, safe, and happy school. Families in large urban districts that have school choice often make this assumption and are willing to have their children commute an hour or two each way to attend a school that they consider desirable. Families may make enrollment decisions without ever visiting the school, relying solely on what they hear from others because they feel unwelcome or may not have the time or resources to visit during the day and visiting at night may not be safe.

No family wants to send their child to a school they consider inferior, so they may selectively use data that support their own assumptions about a school, not actively seeking data that might challenge their personal assumptions. A school often becomes "good" because families have chosen to send their child to the school. After all, no family wants to be responsible for sending their child to a "bad" school.

Assumptions may be self-fulfilling. Students who travel roundtrip to school three or four hours a day must be committed to attending school and more motivated to learn. However, when we disaggregate performance data for students within the attendance zone and those from outside the attendance zone who choose to attend the school, we may find the assigned students mask the performance of students who do not live within the attendance zone.

Equity warriors get ahead of the story that others tell about their school and also engage others in the storytelling process. State education agencies, district leaders, school leaders, teachers, families, and students all may tell different stories about the school. Think of the story that is told about each school whenever test results are released. The data shape the school's public image. That image may be right from a certain perspective. Often the data presented tell conflicting stories. Assumptions made from a particular perspective do not change easily or quickly. But, if equity warriors are proactive about ensuring that the public has access to a broader set of data that tell the stories of their students, then families and the public will consider test results as only one factor in a broader picture about the school.

YOUR MOVE: CREATE METRICS THAT MATTER TO YOUR COMMUNITY.

Equity warriors are able to build the confidence of the families in their schools by showing leadership and marketing their schools. This move has two parts. The first is having a vision for the school that is sensible to the head and appealing to the heart; the second is having a plan to deliver on the vision. Equity warriors seize the opportunity to select metrics that give credibility to their story. Claiming the metrics that are important to the community can drive the telling of the story and guide the development and execution of the plan. Equity warriors balance

Equity warriors are proactive about ensuring that the public has access to a broader set of data that tell the stories of their students.

metrics that tell the story of closing achievement and opportunity gaps. And, they realize that they need to engage families in a way that builds relationships and recognizes the shared responsibility for student success.

Schools whose students do not perform well on state assessments face the challenge of closing achievement gaps. State or district leadership may dictate the metrics that must be used to evaluate success on closing achievement gaps, which puts this factor outside the school's control. However, even though it might not seem so, how school leaders react to information about closing achievement gaps is within their control. Equity warriors ignore achievement gap data at their peril.

Equity warriors identify which students are struggling learners and the specific barriers to their learning. For example, one instructional strategy for improving student performance focuses on expanding students' familiarity with the academic language used in state assessments. When working with middle and high schools, we found that students were not familiar with the common academic and content-specific vocabulary in the test items. Teachers learned that introducing academic vocabulary enabled students to better understand the prompts and respond with what they knew. Closing achievement gaps is not typically as simple as introducing academic vocabulary and/or vocabulary used in the state test questions, however, we have seen student performance increase by improving their familiarity with common vocabulary, which we take for granted that students will know.

School leaders and teachers may resist a focus on instruction they perceive to be "teaching to the test," thinking it is dishonest or not in the students' best interest. Frankly, students who are underserved deserve to have the opportunity to demonstrate proficiency on state tests just as other students do. Even more to the point, knowledge of academic vocabulary will serve students well beyond the test as vocabulary is essential to understanding subject-specific content. Further, going through the exercise of understanding where students are struggling, as in the specific needs of multilingual learners, is vital for teacher efficacy. For example, we worked with a team of 6th-grade humanity teachers who are among the best teachers we have observed. We would be grateful to have our children as students in their classes. Although their instruction was purposeful and students grew academically and in confidence as learners, they did not perform any better on state assessments than they had under their former teachers. Teachers and students became discouraged by the lack of progress. Their first

> *Equity warriors are able to build the confidence of the families in their schools by showing leadership and marketing their schools.*

reaction was to discard the state assessment results as unimportant. With encouragement and with full confidence in their ability, they dug deeper into possible disconnects between the content they were teaching and state standards. They soon saw that students were learning, but they were missing key areas of content knowledge expected by the state standards—and thus measured by the state test.

Equity warriors propose metrics about the conditions that affect student learning. That includes the well-being of students and adults. For example, schools have become increasingly aware that students, teachers, and staff suffer from trauma in their lives outside of school. Every community, not only those in high-poverty areas, are considering the social and emotional preparedness for learning of their children and adults. Increasing pressures for academic achievement from preK to grade 12 are resulting in stress-related illness. Economic pressures on families, teachers, and staff are prevalent across communities. A few years ago, we began the school year with a values exercise with about 25 teacher leaders from a high school. We gave them a deck of 60 cards, each with a value statement. They worked through a couple of rounds to select five values that were most important to them. Securing their financial future was among the top five for more than two-thirds of the teachers. They talked about the stress they were under as rents were rising, gentrification was driving up home prices in a historically lower-middle-class urban neighborhood close to the school, and with their salaries not increasing, they and their families were being forced to move farther away from their school. Teachers who live in the community share and understand the pressures on students and families.

Clearly, schools must consider the needs of the whole child, which means including the needs of their families. Analyzing opportunity gaps extends beyond providing book bags and pencils to students. Using Maslow's hierarchy of needs as a guide, equity warriors use root cause analysis to consider the physiological, safety, love/belonging, esteem, and self-actualization of students, teachers, staff, and the families they serve. Doing so helps create the aspirational vision and action plan that will be necessary to earn the community's respect and trust.

San Diego Unified School District tackled the idea of creating metrics that truly captured achievement and opportunity gaps to define a quality school. The following example describes how they worked collaboratively to support school leaders as they wrestled with metrics to tell the story of their school.

In 2009, the San Diego Unified Board of Education adopted its mission statement and Vision 2020 for Student Success. In Vision 2020, the board challenged the system to create a "quality school in every neighborhood" within five years. In hearing the challenge, school leaders asked, "What makes a quality school?" District and school leaders were invited to develop indicators of a quality school. The emphasis on indicators was a shift from more traditional attempts at defining school quality by the implementation of district initiatives, by the programs and services schools offered, or by single measures of school performance. By focusing attention on indicators, schools would be able to know their destination and identify progress in reaching their destination. Schools also would be able to identify and learn from exemplary practices in other schools.

The school and district leaders identified 12 quality indicators:

- Access to a broad and challenging curriculum
- Quality teaching
- Quality leadership
- Professional learning for all staff
- Closing the achievement gap with high expectations for all
- Parent/community engagement around student achievement
- Quality support staff integrated and focused on student achievement
- Supportive environment that values diversity in the service of students
- High enrollment of neighborhood students
- Digital literacy
- Neighborhood center with services depending on neighborhood needs
- Safe and well-maintained facilities (San Diego Unified School District, 2012, p. 11)

Each indicator had a destination statement, objectives, and possible evidence/data sources. For example, the destination statement for closing the achievement gap with high expectations for all was: "All schools are places in which high expectations for success in meeting the requirements of a broad and challenging

(Continued)

curriculum are held by ALL students and the adults who serve them" (p. 20).

The measurable objectives, such as close the achievement gap, were accompanied by specific evidence to be used to measure progress toward closing achievement gaps.

The San Diego Unified example, particularly for its time, was a novel asset-based approach to use metrics to define a school's vision. It allowed school leaders and their communities to shape conversations to see the complexities of the schools, to determine what they did well, and to focus more attention on areas in need of improvement. Most important, only one indicator—closing the achievement gap—was directly connected to state assessment data. School leaders could broaden the conversation, which was welcomed by teachers, staff, and communities.

The San Diego Unified process informed the ways that California state policy makers designed future iterations of state accountability systems. However, its influence on school-based conversations was limited by a missing key ingredient: the engagement of families.

YOUR MOVE: ENGAGE FAMILIES AS PARTNERS IN DETERMINING THE VISION AND METRICS FOR THEIR SCHOOL.

School leaders, particularly at the secondary level, describe the conundrum of needing family support as partners in their child's learning and the difficulty of engaging families. We have mentioned some of the reasons given for the lack of engagement. There is no denying that some families face barriers. Nevertheless, part of the problem is that many educators do not know how to engage families.

In almost every district and school in which we have worked, family engagement is among the lowest priorities for educators. Almost everyone points to the critical role that families play in their children's education, and yet very little is done to engage families as partners. The role of families is often limited to fundraising; participation in events to appreciate teachers, staff, or students; and attending district, state, or federally mandated meetings to approve site or district plans. Family engagement is something to do when time is available or when a situation has gotten out of hand.

Schools that serve middle- and upper-middle-class families often complain about too much family involvement. Families in these communities are often more actively involved in selecting and participating with school leaders. School leaders are chosen because they can foster positive relations with families and know how to navigate the politics of privilege. In an ideal world, school leaders use families as assets, storytellers, advocates for resources, and influencers to protect the school, to a degree, from having to implement district and state directives that are inconsistent with their vision.

Equity warriors also know families are an asset. They are able to share and shape the school's narrative within the social networks in their communities. That family engagement has not worked is a system failure. Nevertheless, positive and meaningful engagement has occurred in schools when educators and families are willing to learn together how to engage around the needs of their school. Here is an example of how it can be done.

Under the Obama administration, the U.S. Department of Education promoted Karen Mapp's dual capacity-building framework (Mapp & Kuttner, 2013). The framework grew out of Mapp's work building family engagement systems in Boston Public Schools. That work taught her that families are not involved because educators don't know how to engage them. She also learned that both educators and families needed opportunities to learn how to work together effectively. Both sides of the equation had to work simultaneously to achieve true engagement.

The dual-capacity framework identifies the conditions necessary for both sides to learn and apply what they've learned and to sustain the relationships that are created as a result. According to Mapp and Kuttner, the following types of opportunities are most likely to enable families and educators to improve their ability to work together:

- **Linked to student learning:** Initiatives are aligned with school and district achievement goals and connect families to teaching and learning goals for students.

- **Relational:** A major focus of the initiative is on building respectful and trusting relationships between home and school.

(Continued)

(Continued)

- **Developmental:** The initiatives focus on building the intellectual, social, and human capital of stakeholders.

- **Collective/collaborative:** Learning occurs in group rather than individual settings and is focused on building learning communities and networks.

- **Interactive:** Participants have opportunities to test and apply skills. (Mapp & Kuttner, 2013, pp. 9–10)

Mapp and Kuttner identify the skills and knowledge that educators and families need to develop in order to work together successfully. They cluster those into four components:

- **Capabilities:** Educators need to identify and learn about the assets available in their communities. To do so, they need cultural competency skills and help in building trustful relationships. Families need to know about student learning and how school systems work, and they need to develop skills to advocate for students.

- **Connections:** Educators and families learn how to create meaningful networks to build relationships between families and their school, among families, and between families and their community.

- **Confidence:** Educators and families gain confidence to express themselves and their interests and to work across cultural differences.

- **Cognition:** Educators and families should share assumptions, beliefs, and a worldview that staff and families are partners. (Mapp & Kuttner, 2013, pp. 10–11)

Equity warriors encourage partnerships with families to signal that educators aren't the only ones responsible for student success.

The framework ends by describing the outcomes that partnerships will foster in building staff and family capacity to improve student learning and improve schools.

Equity warriors encourage partnerships with families to signal that educators aren't the only ones responsible for student success. Building the capacity of staff to engage as partners with families provides opportunities for staff and families to learn together about the ways the school is vital to the lives of families. Families can learn to navigate through the education system, and teachers and families can support each other in achieving agreed-upon metrics. Equity warriors understand that building capacity of staff and families, particularly for school-dependent students, is not easy, but necessary.

YOUR MOVE: FOCUS ON ASSETS. BE ASPIRATIONAL.

After metrics have been determined in partnership with families, equity warriors have a context for determining how well the school is positioned to move the needle on the metrics. Resolving conflicts in the narrative about the school depends on constructing a story that highlights the school's assets and is aspirational. Telling a compelling, aspirational story is easy when the school is generally successful. For example, during the NCLB years, we worked with a Kansas high school at which 90 percent of the students were at least proficient on state assessments. The principal was able to use data with his instructional leadership team to identify students who were falling behind, primarily students with disabilities, and organize efforts to focus on the 10 percent who were not proficient. Teachers found that all students benefited from instructional strategies designed for students with disabilities. Instructional strategies—particularly the use of learning goals—became an asset they could use in the school's story about creating success for all students. Telling the story of a successful school may seem easier. Nevertheless, demonstrating that the school is committed to the success of all students speaks volumes about a school's expectations and offers great hope for families.

Equity warriors demonstrate courage, leadership, and focus, even in schools that work for a high percentage of their students. In largely successful schools, the adaptive challenge is not one of complacency or efficacy but one of convincing adults to stop doing some of what they are still doing and take on responsibility for new challenges. Reactions among teachers are often interpreted as a personal attack. A teacher explained it to me this way:

> I am tired of people not valuing the work I am doing and my work load, and telling me to do something else. It is not whether I think the suggestion is a good idea or not. What I do should be valued.

When schools are not known to be successful with students, aspirational stories are more difficult to tell. In leading state intervention teams into schools designated as failing, we have seen first-hand the results of critical story telling. No one wants to be part of a sinking ship. Students and families who can exercise options to leave do so. Teachers and administrators who are able to leave do so. Additional resources without clear strategy and commitment to implementation over time do not have the intended effect. Even when data show gains, the starting point can be so low that the narrative doesn't change. We've heard conversations that sound something like the following:

> Yes, 24 percent of students are proficient in mathematics, up from just 11 percent last year. Is failing with 76 percent of your students something to celebrate?

No, but just maybe it is the beginning of a new story. The story lies not in the numbers but in the explanation about what teachers did to change those numbers and whether they believe those same strategies will work to continue that improvement for other students.

Equity warriors know the narrative about a school is often wrong, particularly the narrative that high-poverty schools are unsafe. Although plenty of data demonstrate that schools are safe, school leaders are often required to convince families that this is true. This is especially the case at the middle level. Families have confidence in elementary schools, and, even if they leave public schools for middle school years, they often return for high school. For sure, some middle schools are chaotic—early adolescence has something to do with that! The reality is that very, very few schools are unsafe and that, even in the most troubled neighborhoods, schools provide a safe haven and nurturing environment.

Equity warriors learn from others—particularly charter schools whose existence depends on convincing families that they offer a better option—that they need to market their school. The starting point is proactive outreach to families to invite them to be inspired. Data on families are available. More often than not, districts can predict which students will be attending which schools. Therefore, school leaders know the families who are their target audience. Equity warriors hire family liaisons/coordinators who know the community to reach out and maintain contacts with families. They encourage families whose children attend feeder schools in the attendance zone to visit their school. When they do, families see that administrators and teachers are vigilant and students trust them. They see that students are valued and administrators, teachers, and staff believe that all students in their care will be successful. They see the benefits of being a member of the school community for their children and themselves. In the best examples, families come to understand that schools are complex social systems that work most of the time for students and their families, and to trust the school with their children's education.

School leaders are most likely to be able to enlist community support in shaping the school's story when students and families feel more invested in the outcome. School leaders can face unique challenges when a specialized program—such as a STEAM theme school—has been thrust upon a community, perhaps because funding was available, perhaps because a small group of community members lobbied for the program. Equity warriors are mindful about including students and families in exploratory conversations about changes in schools and enlisting students in setting and selling the direction. Anything that hints of a "do to" approach rather than a "do with" approach will jeopardize the support of those we are intended to serve. Not including parents and community members in a school's future plans is quite simply asking for trouble.

Equity warriors are mindful about including students and families in exploratory conversations about changes in schools and enlisting students in setting and selling the direction.

YOUR MOVE: ARTICULATE THE PLAN TO DELIVER ON THE VISION AND METRICS.

Equity warriors use metrics important to the community and tell the student success story to communicate a compelling vision for the future. The vision does not have credibility unless it includes a plan to deliver on the vision.

Equity warriors use their analysis of achievement gap data to tell part of the story. The most important part of the story is what they—and their school—will do about it. That is where opportunity gap analysis is important. Closing opportunity gaps can mean providing after-school programming, tutoring, and homework support specifically tailored to the community. We have worked with high schools where subtle pressure by administrators and teachers makes it clear that attending after-school tutoring or advising programs is not optional. At one middle school, the administration required students who were not meeting expectations to attend an after-school program every day—without exception. When parents came to the school to personally release their child from the after-school program, the principal would ask to talk with them in her office. The conversation lasted about 45 minutes, which was the length of the after-school session. Word traveled in the community that the principal was serious!

Equity warriors use their analysis of achievement gap data to tell part of the story.

One of the challenges, particularly for schools with large numbers of students who are not meeting expectations, is the reliability of the data they receive about students. For example, teachers receive students at the start of the year who seem to be performing well below grade level. Experienced teachers know that they need to review concepts and ideas from the previous years so that students have a foundation for new learning. Assessing students' prior knowledge is difficult. Some students experience learning loss during the summer. Some students prefer to "pretend" they don't understand, that they can't remember being taught content and skills that are foundational. There are multiple reasons for the pretending, including lack of engagement, lack of motivation, "testing" the teacher's resolve and determination, or legitimate misunderstandings when content is presented in ways unfamiliar to them. Some students actually have not been exposed to important content in prior grades for reasons beyond their control, or they needed more time to comprehend the material. Any of these reasons can lead to misdiagnosing students, which can stifle growth and/or frustrate teachers' instruction.

Equity warriors help teachers recognize that nobody expects them to be superheroes. Few teachers have the right skills and the right conditions to help students increase multiple grade levels in a single year. Those who are able to do so will tell you they are not successful every year with every student. Students depend on the dedication and devotion of their teachers if they are to achieve more than one year's growth. Nevertheless, individual teachers cannot do it alone. To convince teachers that their dedication and devotion will be recognized and effective, equity warriors engage teachers and school staff in developing an action plan that articulates the journey to the vision.

Equity warriors help teachers recognize that nobody expects them to be superheroes.

We are not suggesting another version of the school improvement plan or compliance documents. Schools have too many of those already. Equity warriors focus on student success by reaching for consensus on student outcomes: What should students know and be able to do as they exit key points in their school careers: end of 5th grade, end of 8th grade, high school graduation? A high-performing middle school we know posted exemplary writing samples for 6th, 7th, and 8th graders in the hallway among the school's English language arts (ELA) classrooms. Teachers selected the samples after they had reached consensus about what student demonstrations of exemplary grade-level work would look like. The work did not follow a formula. Posting the work was intended to send clear messages about teaching and learning for students and teachers: ELA teachers saw learning as an iterative process and that proficient writing was valued as a demonstration of student knowledge—not state test scores. By reaching consensus on the samples, teachers demonstrated that they needed to work together across grade levels, to do their part. By being public about the expectations, teachers were clear about their responsibility for helping students meet high standards of performance.

Another aspect to the equity warriors' vision is to direct attention to the future. This is also done by bringing people together, using data, and establishing a system of mutual accountability. The following example illustrates one way of doing so.

We facilitated a group of schools from across the country—most from the Midwest—committed to learning from each other's experiences over a decade about how to improve student achievement. At one point in the multiyear journey, they began using student data to put a face on students who they did not yet know. High schools examined performance data of 8th graders within their district, middle schools selected data of 5th graders, and elementary schools looked at the work of kindergarten students. They drew upon datasets of students in performance cohorts. For example, they could predict the number of students reading below grade level, students reading on grade level, and students reading above grade level who would enter their schools the next year. To make it personal, they had the actual names of students in the performance band that would be arriving at their schools.

Their essential questions were something like this: José is a 5th grader who is reading just below grade level. His state ELA assessment results are below proficient in mathematics. What systems will we put into place to have José leave 8th grade ready for success in high school? They used the data to reflect on the current opportunities and supports for students. Would these be adequate for the incoming group of students? Was there something else we could do?

Principals began to plan the narrative to welcome students and families to their schools. Anticipating the needs of students, they used the budget process to consider changes in programs and staffing—not waiting until the budget was set and implemented in the fall. They planned communications that would send the message that students and families are welcome, that we know who you are, and we have a plan to help you be successful. Internally, teachers would learn that the administration had a plan for supporting students and teachers and that it was a process to address the needs of students over several years.

Equity warriors draw on district and external resources to establish metrics and analyze data. District planners often have the information schools need to create multiyear strategies. In our experience, schools rarely ask them for information. Communicating a vision internally and externally is critical to establishing believers and easing tension. Communicating is a key tool in leadership. So is using diplomacy to prepare teachers to realize the vision.

Equity warriors draw on district and external resources to establish metrics and analyze data.

REFLECTION: *What assumptions does your school community hold about your school? What metrics will you claim to create a new narrative about your school?*

_____

_____

_____

_____

_____

_____

_____

_____

_____

_____

 # DIPLOMACY: RALLY STAKEHOLDERS TO YOUR SCHOOL'S EQUITY AGENDA

The three ways that diplomacy plays out traditionally—through rewards, consequences, and moral persuasion—are arrows in the school equity warrior's quiver. Teachers and school staff seek approval and recognition that only the school's leader can provide. Teachers rarely watch other teachers apply their craft, and it is rarer still that they use the opportunity to recognize the skills of colleagues. When we first conducted walk-throughs 20 years ago, teachers were so eager for feedback that they would follow us to their classroom door hoping to overhear our conversations. Teachers are still hungry for feedback.

School leaders reward teachers in different ways—teaching assignments, classroom locations, supply money, access, visiting their classrooms more or less than others, release time, salary supplements for special projects, leaving the teacher in charge when the administrative team is offsite—to name a few. These are transactional, meaning that school leaders and teachers give and receive something through their relationship. If you help cover a classroom, you will not be questioned when you need to leave school before the end of the school day. Transactions make the organization run smoothly—they are oil for gears.

Equity warriors use transactions with effect. They rely on teachers, staff, and families to gather and share information about what people are thinking and to check the climate of the school. Transactions are often helpful in building momentum while designing an equity agenda, a strategy, and a plan of action. Transactions, however, move the equity agenda only slightly. The equity agenda relies on a vision framed in moral persuasion. Equity warriors take the story and convince students, families, staff, and teachers to believe that it is the right thing to do for each and every student. Diplomacy lives in the plan to achieve the right thing in ways that are sensitive and effective.

YOUR MOVE: BE EMPATHIC AND USE THE "RIGHT" DATA TO BUILD TEACHER EFFICACY.

Sensitivity and effectiveness are often at odds. Whether you are an athlete, a musician, an actor, a reader, a writer, or a tradesperson, you know what good looks like. Even the untrained eye can recognize what great looks like. You study sports, music, acting, and other skills, such as carpentry, by watching, seeing, practicing, and trying to emulate the finished product. When you are trying to demonstrate proficiency in a task, you know whether you have learned the necessary knowledge or skills.

For longer than we wish to admit, we visited classrooms with principals to collect objectives and agendas, to talk with students, to determine the minutes teachers worked with students, to note whether students were collaborating or just present in groups, to read student work or otherwise to judge the learning climate. We used the data collected to determine, for example, who could write an objective that included content, level of rigor, and means for judging student success. Then, we planned professional development for whole schools and departments based on the data we collected. If we observed that most or almost all teachers were able to write and post an objective we deemed good, the principal would talk with those who did not, and we moved on.

Needless to say, the teachers were not pleased with our visits. Those who were responsive wondered whether they had the right words on the wall. When we entered the room, they would move chart paper stands and other objects so that the agenda was not blocked from view; or they would walk near the agenda so that if we were looking at them, we would see the agenda; or they would repeatedly turn the PowerPoint presentation back to the lesson objective slide. We were unsympathetic when they complained that they didn't see the point. After all, if you cannot clearly express your purpose, students cannot learn.

After a time, we realized that focusing on what the teacher was doing—per se—was not making a difference. It didn't really matter whether the words on the wall were right. What mattered is that students demonstrated what they knew or could do based on the task of the day. So we shifted our attention away from teacher actions to what students were doing. By focusing on students rather than the teacher, we also found that we were able to build trust with teachers by clarifying their purpose and helping them analyze and develop better tasks and assessments of rigorous student learning. This was real work. Teachers know the difference.

Of course, focusing on what students were doing did not mean we were ignoring what the teacher was doing. The difference is that we were not reporting on the teacher's actions; we were reporting on students. For example, a 7th-grade math teacher was pleased to invite us to watch an interactive lesson that had students create a city map where the infrastructure was proportional and used geometric shapes. We wondered, having seen a similar lesson in a 4th-grade math class in another school, whether the lesson was advanced for 4th graders or way below the standards for 7th graders.

Observations and questions like these launch very different conversations with teachers than do observations about whether the objective is stated correctly. The conversation causes teachers to articulate their thinking about the activity and whether the student product is grade-level work. Was the

7th-grade teacher seeking much more in complexity than what was expected by the 4th graders? In any case, focusing on the product helps the teacher and the administrator understand the expectations for student learning through the eyes and actions of students rather than objectives on the wall.

Collecting student products regularly as data on student progress helps equity warriors build teacher efficacy. Another recent learning for us is how many teachers do not believe their daily instruction makes a difference in student learning. For example, we know teachers who believe that some students are good at mathematics and others are not. These teachers believe they can help students learn mathematics, but students will be truly proficient only if they have the disposition to learn mathematics.

Equity warriors go deeper. Working with teachers to set measurable learning targets and collect data on how students do on performance tasks regularly provides evidence of student learning that can change beliefs. For example, in one classroom, a pretest of 15 learning target questions showed five students could answer seven or more questions correctly. By the end of the week, with specific instruction on the learning targets, 10 students could answer 10 or more questions correctly. By the end of the two-week period, 13 students could answer all 15 questions correctly. The results are powerful for students as well as teachers.

When teachers begin to see daily progress from students who they did not believe in, their attitude about their teaching changes. To be honest, it is hard to believe that teachers do not have efficacy. We did not consider that one could teach every day and not believe that students learned something from the instruction. We didn't look for it. However, when we explored beliefs about teaching and student learning and listened to teachers, the lack of efficacy was pervasive. We should not have been surprised. Teaching is a human endeavor, and effective teaching requires an emotional connection between teacher and students. As a teacher, it can be incredibly disheartening to not see growth day-to-day and year-to-year with students who are school dependent. Pouring emotions as well as energy into teaching is demanding. The demand on teachers was evident when I interviewed teachers who had taught for a decade or more at three of the most underperforming middle schools in Jefferson County, Kentucky, before transferring to schools serving more affluent, less school-dependent students. They told emotion-laden stories of poring their heart and soul into teaching at the underperforming schools and seeing little in the way of student progress. This is not because they were not good teachers. They were committing less of themselves in their new schools and seeing greater results. They blamed their lack of experience and lack of skill for not reaching students at the underperforming schools. Had they known then what they know now, they said, those students would have been better served.

These teachers were self-reflective and honest. To survive, some teachers do not allow themselves the freedom to be self-reflective and honest. They are resigned to the way it is.

We will say more about efficacy and daily instruction in later chapters. Collecting student performance data regularly on daily tasks is a best practice to improve student achievement and build teacher efficacy. Equity warriors use this practice because it is sensitive and effective.

YOUR MOVE: JUDGE READINESS AND PREPAREDNESS FOR EQUITY.

For equity warriors, the success of using data to execute an equity vision is tied to readiness—readiness of the district/supervisors, of teachers/staff, of parents/community, of students, and, most important, of the principal and her leadership team. As we consider each, the principal's readiness is the driver. At the end of the day, and there will be some tough days, the principal's commitment to persevere is the determining factor.

Readiness of the district staff and the principal's supervisors is the necessary starting point. Districts vary in the degree of autonomy provided to school leaders. Often, a principal's experience, relationships, success, and powerbase contribute to the amount of autonomy granted or taken. Some districts have constant turnover or changes in reporting structures so that principal supervision is inconsistent. We have worked in districts where principals reported having seven different supervisors in seven years. Just as a supervisor becomes familiar with the school and the principal, the assignment changes. Trust, necessary to advance an equity agenda, does not have a chance to develop. As a result, principals interpret the signs as an indication of the district's intention to support equity and how much support they will receive when teachers, unions, and families push back.

School leaders who are equity warriors need answers to three questions to determine the district's readiness to support the school's equity agenda:

- Does the principal trust the sincerity of her supervisor's announced intention to support and push the equity agenda? (For example, is the supervisor encouraging action in response to a particular political or short-term problem? Is this a multiyear effort?)

- How do district leaders provide cover for the principal in executing an equity agenda? (For example, has the board made policy or voted on resolutions? Have district leaders pushed an equity agenda publicly?)

- Are all schools receiving the same push to execute an equity agenda, and have some acted on it?

Without affirmation on all three questions, equity warriors should be cautious about stepping out on a limb for fear of having it cut off beneath them.

Equity warriors know that being ready is different from being prepared. Being prepared takes foresight to have the people and structures in place for a successful launch, and to anticipate possible resistance. Teacher and staff preparedness depends on leadership. Just as it is important for teachers to understand that it takes teachers working together, equity warriors create a team to distribute leadership across departments and grade levels. In the previous chapter, we described how district leaders might develop a guiding coalition to push on change from the outside. In the same way, school-level equity warriors can create a team of influencers and work with them to shape, guide, and execute the vision. However, the team's success depends on the principal having a clear vision of the achievable outcomes. The size of the school allows for and depends on the principal's leadership in setting directions.

> *Equity warriors create a team to distribute leadership across departments and grade levels.*

Principals use transactions to invite teachers and staff on the team—to get the right people on the bus at the right time. We advise that teams mirror the school's organizational structure so that every adult in the school is touched by at least one member of the team. To keep the team size manageable, schools may need to modify other structures. For example, instead of having a team member from every grade level, team members are responsible for multiple grade levels—kindergarten–grade 2, grades 3–5, and so on.

Team members have dual responsibilities—two-way communication, and informing and leading. Meetings are structured so that team members report back on interactions with others and use the interactions as data in adjusting the plans. This means team members accept responsibility for working on their own time and are comfortable leading other adults. Many teachers are not willing or comfortable. This is where transactions are necessary. Having a full-day release time for team meetings rather than meeting after school demonstrates the school leader's commitment to the importance of the agenda and appreciates team members' time. Team members are more likely to give of their time for follow-up activities. Additionally, team members need to feel comfortable leading. We have used team meetings to design and practice an agenda for follow-up meetings. Doing so allows team members to have a plan of action and a shared experience to critique the meeting and plan the next one.

Reaching consensus on the vision and plan has happened faster at the school level than at the district level, depending on the size of the school and the time of year the work is launched. School life has its seasons! We have seen the pattern repeated continuously. The time to launch new initiatives is in the spring, preferably after state testing. This period has a parallel to spring training for baseball teams. It is a time to prepare, experiment, and practice for learning about the best approach going forward. Summer is for individual development and preparation. The opening of schools is game time. Trying to launch in the fall of the school year is contrary to a school's cycle. Budgets are committed, annual objectives are set. The fall is the time for execution and learning.

Equity warriors understand the patterns of school life and judge the preparedness of the staff.

The implementation cycle for school-level initiatives also has a predictable, three-year pattern. The first year is chiefly awareness. In the second year, the initiative becomes real. If the equity warrior is consistent, the school community begins to realize that the equity agenda is serious. Pushback, deeper learning, and staff transitions are predictable in the second year. It is during the third year that the initiative begins to become rooted in the school's culture.

Equity warriors understand the patterns of school life and judge the preparedness of the staff. Here are three sets of questions equity warriors consider to determine teacher and staff preparedness:

- Do I have a leadership team structure in place that reaches all adults in the school? Are the leadership team members the right people? Can my colleagues and I trust that team members are willing to take on responsibility and are comfortable with leading?

- What equity-focused initiatives are in place? Where are they in the implementation cycle (e.g., just starting, year 1)?

- Is part of the vision ready to be enacted at my direction? Is there a symbolic action that the leadership team will help me plan for implementation immediately?

In partnering with family members, the principal's vision, communication, and confidence are key factors in judging readiness. School leaders have transactional relationships with family and community members. Those are the people the principal calls on for help in organizing recognition events, representing the school on district-required advisory groups, and school fundraising, to name a few. In return, family and community members feel satisfaction in contributing to the school, are privy to information, and know the principal will look after their children.

The principal's go-to people are not always the best at determining preparedness. They may not have the pulse of the community or may have alienated other families because they are seen as having power and/or excluding others from their circle. The go-to people may go along with an idea that is doomed to failure and find they have been placed in an untenable situation. In these situations, the principal may turn against the partner, and/or the person may be ostracized from other families and community members.

Equity warriors build coalitions of family and community members. Principals also need to understand the coalitions that individual teachers and staff members have developed. We know of schools where the teachers and staff members have activated their networks in opposition to the principal's agenda or for their own advantage. When the principal does not have supportive data and other community members to advance his position, it becomes difficult for district leaders to advocate on his behalf.

Equity warriors build coalitions of family and community members.

When equity leaders can speak with confidence about the vision and the effect decisions will have on their children, families and community members follow. However, other preparedness considerations need to be addressed. We have seen families and community members follow equity warriors when their vision makes sense, they are willing to lead, and a coalition of different voices supports the effort. For family members who are fundamentally concerned with their child's experience, the message needs to be communicated clearly and explain what will be different for each student.

We didn't mention the need to evaluate students' readiness and preparedness for equity. Trust us. They are ready! But don't forget that they need to be prepared.

REFLECTION: *What data do teachers consider relevant to improving student learning? How ready and prepared is your school to embrace your equity vision? What tools of diplomacy—rewards, consequences, and moral persuasion—are available to you?*

_____

_____

_____

_____

_____

_____

_____

_____

WARFARE: KNOW YOUR STUDENTS

Assessment data equal accountability. No matter how assessment data are positioned, particularly when assessments are intended to inform teaching practices, teachers feel the data are used to evaluate. We know a district that arranged for twice-a-year district-developed interim assessments as a way for teachers to know if students were making progress toward state standards. The district invested an incredible sum to prepare and administer interim assessments aligned with the state tests. The results from the interim assessments were much higher than the subsequent state test results. District administrators questioned the reliability of the assessments. After a little investigation, we found the problem. Test administrators distributed the assessments to teachers a few days before the date for administration. Unlike state assessment protocols, teachers were not restricted from reviewing the interim assessment questions. Teachers used the intervening days to prep students to memorize and reproduce the answers when the assessment was given. The result was that a well-intended, low-risk tool to provide planning data to teachers was rendered useless.

To be honest, there is no way around it: Assessment data are used to judge teachers, students, and school leaders. Assessment data are only low stakes in schools where students are high performing or when teachers are too tired or frustrated to care. Another exception is teachers new to the profession who have lived through and were educated in the era of high-stakes testing. To the overwhelming number of teachers, a focus on assessment data often feels like an act of war.

Equity warriors anticipate the reciprocal actions of defensiveness, resignation, and/or counterattacks that exposing data is likely to unleash. They know that accurate, authentic, and objective data that truly represent the experiences of students are the best levers to pressure teachers who wish to fight or flee rather than engage.

Equity warriors anticipate the reciprocal actions of defensiveness, resignation, and/or counterattacks that exposing data is likely to unleash.

YOUR MOVE: IDENTIFY MEANINGFUL DATA. ESTABLISH INTENTIONALITY.

Equity warriors set the conditions to use data for teachers to monitor student progress and learn from each other. Meaningfulness of the data and intentionality of the processes are among the conditions that need to be met. Data walls that track progress of individual students on periodic assessments can be an effective way to help teachers see success. But because data walls take time to update, teachers frequently abandon them when the cost in time exceeds the benefit. Similarly, we have seen grade-level or classroom data posted on wall charts in teachers' lounges and principal's offices. Initially, the charts lead to informal conversations. Then, not much else. We have seen student grades posted in classrooms—including classes where 75 percent of the students have a D or F average. Teachers, administrators, and students walk by paying little notice.

Using data to publicly blame or shame teachers is not helpful. We know a principal, a passionate equity warrior, who spent three years of strong instructional leadership and investment in professional learning, only to become frustrated with the lack of student progress. At the start of the fourth school year, he brought teachers together and showed student data by teacher.

Although he did not name teachers, the grade-level teams knew which teacher had students who performed at the high level and who had students who performed 30 percent lower. Instead of motivating teachers to learn from each other, teachers became more defensive and the school's culture divisive. Most other teachers we have shared this story with concur: Shaming is not an effective approach to improving practice.

One of the theories supporting high-stakes testing is that if teachers have the information about what students know and are able to do, then they will make data-based decisions to guide their teaching. This theory makes two assumptions about high-stakes testing: Teachers value the assessment, and the data are helpful in making teaching decisions. Neither assumption is accurate. Yet, schools tend to post data from assessments that teachers do not value or grades from assessments that students do not value. Doing so is inauthentic. Teachers like to see data on their own students. However, like the student who receives a failing grade on a test measuring something they didn't know, data about other students have little effect. It is just an exercise in posting data for the sake of posting data.

Equity warriors know that linking data collection to their vision for how the school should be perceived is important to establish its relevance for teachers and students. The ways that state assessments are positioned—and some would argue the state assessment system itself—undermines not only the importance of the test but also the school's purpose in educating students. Students who do not see, understand, or benefit from the results comply with taking the test only because they are told it is somehow important. It is certainly not important to them. On the contrary, if the school's vision is helping each and every student be prepared for success in the next grade or school level, then students and teachers must be able to see the connections among collecting data and their success. If they do understand the connections, teachers and students are more likely to respect the data and agree that they provide a way to measure their progress toward preparation for the next step.

Equity warriors also know that the processes to collect and analyze data must be intentional about when assessments are *for their learning*, meaning the assessment and results are intended to enable teachers to reflect on their practices and learn, and when assessments are *of student learning*, meaning the results are intended to hold teachers accountable for their effectiveness as measured by student progress. If the vision is to help teachers know their students and be learners themselves, then data that will be used to evaluate teachers must be clearly articulated and

Equity warriors set the conditions to use data for teachers to monitor student progress and learn from each other.

separated from the learning process. There is a parallel to how teachers assess students. Teachers assess students in multiple ways. For example, the daily tasks provide teachers with information about whether students are understanding and learning. At some point, students must demonstrate that they have mastered our expectations for their learning. The same should apply to teachers.

YOUR MOVE: ASK STUDENTS.

We can't achieve equitable outcomes for students if we don't know them as learners. The question is how to gather quantitative data from students that are valid. Multiple methods are frequently used—surveys, questionnaires, polls, and focus groups. They all have a purpose, and given time, the results provide insights into what students feel about their school experience. These methods, by design, are objective and impersonal. We propose *three methods* that lead adults to deeper understanding about their students. These methods also have the benefit of building adult-student trust and relationships that provide advantages to equity warriors beyond the initial purpose.

THREE STRATEGIES FOR ASKING STUDENTS

Students hold answers to the challenges facing them. What tools can equity warriors use to know students as learners?

Student watching: Equity warriors observe students during a class or a few classes and use the data to inform the ways they know students.

Focus students: Equity warriors select focus students who are representative of students in their classrooms and monitor their performance as a way to understand more about all students.

Student interviews: Equity warriors identify a concern in the school, collect data to learn more about its root cause, and then select 10–12 students for one-on-one interviews.

Student watching. The idea is simple. Educators watch students during a class or a few classes and use the observations to inform the ways they know students. The key and the difficult part is to really, really watch students. There are several models of this practice, including a focus on multilingual learners experienced with specific instructional approaches (Soto, 2021). Depending on the purpose, the observer sits in proximity to a selected student or students. The observer notes what students are doing at regular intervals during the lesson. How many minutes are focused on the teacher? How does the student react to the teacher's instruction or direction? Is the student given a task? How difficult is the task? Is it a new task? Is the student part of a group? Are students in the group interacting? Are students engaged? When are they engaged? Where does the student struggle? And so on.

The point here is that watching can tell a lot about teaching. For example, if teachers know that students lose concentration after 15 minutes, then a 30-minute explanation of a mathematical problem is not good teaching. More is definitely not better. If students are in cooperative groups and talk with each other about anything other than the assignment, teachers need to understand the reason. If the assignment is too easy, or too difficult, teachers need to know how to increase the rigor or provide a better scaffold.

As much as the data are important, how data are gathered may be more important. An elementary school principal taught me her version of student watching.

The principal picked the same students every time she entered a classroom and interacted with them for extended periods. She would ask the students to read, ask questions to determine their comprehension and understanding, and otherwise determine how they were doing. She selected students for specific reasons. If she thought the teacher was not rigorous enough, she would follow an average or advanced student. If the teacher was having classroom management issues, she would select students who were the most likely to be disruptive. If the teacher had several students with disabilities, she would select one of them.

Her observations were the subject of her conversations with teachers. The principal had four purposes. The first was to build partnership with teachers around students whose learning was a concern. The conversations were collegial and professional, complimenting the teacher on progress, and brainstorming next steps. The second was to impress teachers with her instructional knowledge by focusing on students who she knew teachers were having difficulty reaching. Teachers at this school preferred for the principal to stay in her office doing whatever it is that principals do. She intended to let teachers know she saw them and knew good from poor instruction. Third, she recognized that teachers cannot notice student actions and reactions to everything that happens in a classroom of 30 students. Another pair of eyes, supportive and constructive, might provide insights that could make a difference in instruction. And fourth, she ensured that teachers attended to students whom they had difficulty reaching. When they realized that the principal would work with the same students each time she visited their classroom, they knew to attend to those students as well.

Student watching helps students as well as teachers. Student watching reinforces the notion that learning about learners is everyone's responsibility. Students gain a personal relationship with school leaders and with teachers who participate in student watching. We know secondary schools where teachers watch their students in other teacher's classrooms and how they engage in learning in other content areas.

Focus students. Equity warriors develop systems to monitor student progress. Monitoring progress of representative groups of students is a way to use sampling data to inform teaching practices.

Equity warriors develop systems to monitor student progress.

Our work with data-based decision-making systems has evolved over time. In the early days of NCLB, several of our partner schools devised data-monitoring systems to track student progress based on state assessment scores. Teachers prepared data binders containing lists of each student in every class ranked from the highest to the lowest performers on state assessments. Lines would be drawn to differentiate groups of students—high, middle, and low. Principals held quarterly data conferences with teachers where teachers presented data on assessments (e.g., teacher-made tests, reading comprehension running records) and district or informal school assessments as a way to monitor student progress.

Principals reviewed performance data from all students. Typically, particular attention was given to the students in the middle—the bubble students—whose performance had the most effect on a school's scores on the state assessments. By moving students who were just below the line to the next level— for example, basic to proficient—the overall school annual progress performance would increase. It was important to ensure that the top performers did not slip, and there was always hope that, with help, lower performers would make progress. Improving the test performance of bubble students was considered a strategic investment that would pay dividends. Some districts employed support teams that visited schools to work with bubble students, often pulling them from class for test preparation activities. State assessment scores increased. Targeted test preparation worked in the NCLB environment.

In addition to raising test scores, school leaders took information from the data binders and targeted students of special interest to them. Some principals had teachers prepare seating charts with the names of students so that they could observe and talk with the targeted students during a classroom visit. Some principals focused on students with learning disabilities, others selected students they knew for some reason—for example, a student who had behavior problems or a student whose family had expressed concern about their child's teacher. In addition to checking on students during walk-throughs, principals observed the teachers' attention to the focus students during observations.

Building on these earlier efforts, equity warriors help teachers select focus students who are representative of groups of students in their classrooms. At the start of each year, school leaders ask teachers to identify four or five focus students. Teachers describe their rationale for identifying each of the focus students and propose approaches to address the students' learning needs. To help teachers think about sampling, school leaders ask teachers to prepare an interim assessment early in the first marking period. As they score the interim assessment, teachers note students whose performance is similar to that of other students in the class. If most students in the class performed similarly, teachers knew they were able to move on or needed to reteach the content. If focus students performed similarly to other students, teachers knew the teaching strategies selected for use with the focus students might also work with other students.

In addition to using sampling techniques to reduce a teacher's feeling of being overwhelmed, sampling assists teachers as they move into differentiating instruction. Sampling techniques give teachers another source of information, beyond reading comprehension assessment data at the elementary school level, for grouping students. At the secondary level, sampling techniques may uncover gaps in content knowledge, vocabulary, or skills for accessing information.

Sampling and recording data about focus students has become considerably easier with the advent of mobile devices and software programs tailored to these purposes. School leaders can check student data on their mobile phones. They can easily access information on focus students, including their photographs, and take notes on progress, raise questions, and/or share with teachers their noticings or conversations with students. Sometimes, different grade-level teachers identify the same focus students, which allows for team conversation about students. School leaders can also follow focus students who have multiple teachers and note the differences in approaches, and the performance of students across classes. Teachers no longer need to transfer data to binders or create seating maps. Once student data are loaded, access is at their fingertips.

Scheduling time to discuss focus student progress is the challenge. Technology is an asset. However, systems are necessary for educators to examine and use the data. When teachers make the leap to sampling, they realize the benefit, filling the gap between whole class and individual instruction.

Student interviews. There is a myth that high school teachers are resistant to change. Maybe. We believe that high school teachers are skeptical. They need to be shown there is a compelling reason to change, that there is a better way. This is equally true in high schools where students perform well and in schools where students underperform. In high-performing schools, feelings of competence, pride, competition, and/or ease of established patterns are enemies of change. In lower-performing schools, feelings of defensiveness, frustration, and being overwhelmed get in the way.

Interviewing students, as the following example illustrates, yields valuable insights to inform planning.

A large high school had a reputation for good performance on state assessments and a high graduation rate. Still, large numbers of students were not successful. They dropped out or transferred to other schools before graduation. The school's size and performance of the majority hid the true story. Teachers were comfortable, complacent, and resistant to any hard look that called into question the school's practices.

The principal created an instructional leadership team composed of the administrative team, the department head and a lead teacher from each academic department, and representatives from other departments—guidance, special education, and student activities. She presented data to the team about the

(Continued)

(Continued)

dropout and transfer rates of students. She faced much resistance for focusing on the few rather than the success of the many. She persisted as the first marking period rolled on. The most vocal team members finally conceded that there was a group of students—about 25 percent of the freshman class—who were not successful. As we dug deeper into the data, the group was largely Black or Latinx but actually represented all races/ethnicities. We had landed on a focus group.

The instructional leadership team meetings began to explore the root causes for the target group's lack of success. The team believed academic grades provided the most reliable data. The most vocal team members argued that excessive absences and not completing homework explained why students received multiple D and F grades. They believed that students would learn if they attended class and did the work expected of them. In other words, students were responsible for their failure.

In preparation for the next team meeting, we reviewed grades for the first marking period by race/ethnicity. Students with As and Bs were at the top of each list; students with multiple Ds and Fs at the bottom. As one of us called out the name of a student with multiple failures, the other checked the database for absences. Four Fs and a D, no absences. Must be the exception. Three Fs, two Ds, three absences. More exceptions. Certainly, some students on the list had multiple absences. However, there was little correlation between failing grades and absences.

Sharing these data with the team changed the conversation—slightly. Teachers were not convinced. They questioned the data out of frustration. Nevertheless, each teacher agreed to briefly interview 10 students who had multiple Ds and Fs, to tabulate the results, and return in a week.

We also agreed to interview 10 students. No two were alike. A few just cut classes and had a good time with their friends. No one monitored them or made them aware of the consequences. However, the majority were students who were attending classes, taking notes, and completing homework or trying to. One student showed us her notebook full of clear, detailed notes. She was spending two hours a night on her mathematics homework and wasn't getting it.

The tone of the next team meeting was strikingly different from the previous ones. Almost all the teachers had similar results. Students were in their classes, were trying to meet expectations, and were unsuccessful. No one checked on those who were absent until after the marking period, and by then it was too late. Teachers began to offer other reasons for student failure:

- Classes of 35 hindered teachers from knowing their students.

- Teachers were more concerned with moving through the curriculum than checking whether students were understanding. As long as students were quiet and attentive, teachers assumed they were learning.

- Multilingual learners and others who had not experienced academic success were reluctant to ask a question in front of their peers.

- Students did not have the study skills needed for success in an academic environment.

- The district had not facilitated transitions from smaller, personalized middle schools to large high schools.

- Middle schools offered few consequences for students' poor academic performance.

- Students were unaware of the importance of earning credits toward graduation.

- Students' homes did not communicate when students were struggling.

- Guidance counselors, assigned to seniors and freshmen, focused all of their attention on scheduling and helping students prepare college applications. They did not meet with 9th graders during the first semester.

- Administrators attended to campus security and establishing routines rather than trying to get to know students.

As the list continued to grow, the adults realized that the lack of systems and supports—not students—was the cause for failures. So, instead of blaming incoming freshmen, the conversation shifted to doing a better job of preparing incoming 9th graders for success. Teachers, counselors, and administrators were not to blame. The system was built to fail students who were school dependent.

Once again, students hold the answers to the challenges facing them. Knowing students, including students in the process, and engaging them as thought partners results in being able to design systems that meet their needs.

REFLECTION: *What protocols and processes would best help you and your leaders know students as learners and advocates for their learning?*

_____

_____

_____

_____

_____

_____

_____

_____

PART II

Lead With Purpose: Values-Enhanced Leadership

INTRODUCTION

Almost three-quarters of a century of education research has shown that we can successfully teach children when we are focused on clear expectations for their learning and when we have the courage, perseverance, and will to do so.

Equity warriors confront the disappointment of not always reaching their expectations by continuing to live their values no matter what happens. Brené Brown describes living one's values as being "clear about what we believe and hold important, and taking care that our intentions, words, thoughts, and behaviors align with those beliefs" (Brown, 2018, p. 186). Living one's values is challenging when we find ourselves in unfamiliar and complex situations. Yet, equity warriors know that living their values during times of uncertainty is the surest way to set the standard for advancing equity. For equity warriors, living values requires the following:

> *Equity warriors confront the disappointment of not always reaching their expectations by continuing to live their values no matter what happens.*

- Courage to name the problem and confidently stand up for their beliefs.

- Perseverance to stay the course through certain opposition when challenging the status quo.

- The will to act on their beliefs. Equity warriors know that will is different from courage. Will is measured and clear—collecting political capital and using political capital to further one's aims.

(Continued)

(Continued)

Thomas J. Sergiovanni (1992) proposed that educators can achieve success in creating higher-performing schools by emphasizing moral leadership or what we choose to call values-enhanced leadership. He argued that most improvement efforts do not fully recognize the most important difference between education systems and other organizations: Each district and school is more of a community and less an organization. Being a community rather than an organization suggests that individuals are joined together by shared values and that their association is voluntary.

Members of an equity-focused community clamor for values-enhanced leadership—leadership committed to doing the right thing, not just doing things right. In Sergiovanni's words, values-enhanced leadership has two elements: "the hand of leadership," which describes behaviors that seem to make more sense in some situations than others do; and "the heart of leadership," which is what a person believes, values, dreams about, and is committed to as the foundation of her reality.

Values define our communities. As we get to know each other, we recognize that we share values. While on occasion we emphasize the importance of our differences, through familiarity we learn that we are more similar than different.

Values hold communities together, whether they are the communities in which we live or the communities in which we work and learn. Anyone who has moved from one community to another or changed jobs recognizes the subtle differences between communities.

Values also exclude people from communities. There remain examples, too numerous to count, of communities whose values explicitly establish economic, racial, and social barriers to admission. More often, people are just not as comfortable in some communities as they are in others. For example, some prefer urban, suburban, or rural lifestyles and can't imagine being part of a different lifestyle. When barriers are removed, joining a community is still a choice. Defining values helps make the choice.

Equity warriors are selected for a leadership position because their vision and values are believed to be the right fit for the community they are being chosen to lead.

Values-enhanced leadership, therefore, is a high-level force for bringing people together around a shared moral purpose. Leaders help define and make explicit the group's shared values, organize around the values, and call out when the values are violated. As with vision setting, discussed in the previous chapters, establishing a community's values is a process. Equity warriors are selected for a leadership position because their vision and values are believed to be the right fit for the community they are being chosen to lead.

From the start, values-enhanced leadership is a combination of "who I am" and "who I aspire to be." While holding firm on some values, leaders realize individuals must work together to fully enact a shared value. For example, we hold equity as one of our core values. We have accepted opportunities to work in places that did not fully share our equity vision. We did so with the understanding that the district or school was ready to move an equity agenda—or so they said. Sometimes we learned from each other how to successfully move the agenda. Other times, our values were at odds, and we failed.

Sometimes values-enhanced leadership is as easy as calling out values as they are demonstrated by members of the organization. In other instances, the leader must begin by gently expressing expectations. We know one superintendent who would question decisions by cabinet members by telling them, "That is not who we are." These became teachable—and somewhat uncomfortable—moments when real examples brought clarity to values in action.

Of course, in the best situation, values are clearly articulated and understood before any decision is made. Values-enhanced leaders create systems, protocols, and processes that are consistent with the community's values. For example, communities prosper when there is shared leadership—members stepping up, looking out for each other, and assuming responsibilities. If shared decision making is an espoused value, top-down processes that limit or hide decision making give members reason to question the leaders' commitment to the espoused values and diminish the leaders' effectiveness. Even when not espoused, the lack or absence of shared decision making is especially problematic for equity warriors who are expected to be inclusive.

We are reminded that leadership is grounded in conscious choices among real alternatives and there is always competition and conflict among alternatives (Burns, 1978). When leaders are more clear about articulating their values, community members are more able to decide whether they are comfortable staying in the community.

We have seen countless examples of staff voluntarily leaving districts or schools because they are uncomfortable with the leader's direction. Equity warriors benefit by messaging that is not judgmental but firm about "our" values and shared expectations. Traction on the equity agenda comes when a critical mass of like-minded individuals who have values in common bonding them together.

Equity warriors benefit by messaging that is not judgmental but firm about "our" values and shared expectations.

Finally, values-enhanced leaders understand that they get their work done with and through other people. They start with the assumption

(Continued)

(Continued)

that if people are not acting in ways that are consistent with their espoused values, then they need to learn to do so. Values-enhanced leaders reinforce the organizational culture so that everyone in the organization understands their role in leading others to accomplish a shared mission. By definition, a successful equity agenda requires everyone to be committed in order for all students to succeed. People must make a choice. Equity warriors know that the long journey requires that we leave no adults behind so that we leave no students behind. However, leading looks different depending on one's role within the organization.

Equity warriors know that the long journey requires that we leave no adults behind so that we leave no students behind.

Equity warriors use values-enhanced leadership to advance their equity agenda because it is a good fit. One can be a values-enhanced leader without being an equity warrior. However, we believe that successful equity warriors must be values-enhanced leaders in order to succeed.

In the previous chapters, we identified moves and examples that could be made with audiences external and internal to the organization to better understand what is possible in the local context. In the following two chapters, our primary focus is on how values-enhanced equity warriors lead to advance equity.

CHAPTER 3

District leaders identify and engage with shared values

☞ POLITICS: SURFACE AND ARTICULATE VALUES

The politics of values-enhanced leadership is largely about balancing conflicts among competing interests in order to govern effectively. Superintendents and district leaders begin by building trusting relationships with their school boards.

For the past 25 years, we've had the good fortune to engage in board development with dozens of school boards. Board development entails helping board members understand their role, adopt best practices of effective boards, and strengthen relationships between school boards and superintendents and their leadership team. Board membership and board/superintendent relationships change constantly: When even one board member leaves, board dynamics shift.

Not all boards are configured the same. Most communities elect their school boards. But some are appointed by mayors, and a number are a hybrid of mayoral appointees and elected members. Some boards are appointed by city councils, and some boards are in transition from state control.

Equity warriors know that managing the relationship between the board and the district is critical to the success of the equity agenda.

Boards come in different sizes. We have partnered with boards responsible for large districts with five members or as many as 14 members. Each board has strengths; each has its challenges. In every district, staff complain that board members get in the way. Equity warriors know that managing the relationship between the board and the district is critical to the success of the equity agenda.

YOUR MOVE: DO THE HARD PART THAT ONLY YOU CAN DO.

Equity warriors lead up and lead down the organization. A very successful superintendent once said, during a rather difficult discussion about his leadership and support for his leadership team, that his job was to manage and respond to his board. His leadership team, rather than worrying about what they needed from him, should manage and respond to what *he* needed from *them*. At the time, his response seemed very harsh and was not the message his leadership team wanted to hear. Nevertheless, it was a critical lesson. Successful superintendents do not delegate their most important responsibility, which is the care and feeding of their board and the external constituents who influence them. The superintendent's ongoing working relationship with the board and the capacity of the superintendent's leadership team to anticipate and follow through on the superintendent's initiatives are keys to her success.

Effective boards understand the importance of staying above a metaphorical line that divides the realm of boards—policy and governance, which includes finance and accountability to the community—from the administrative and management realm of superintendents (see Figure 3.1). Crossing the line happens frequently and, when it is done without clear understanding of the consequences, can create dysfunctions in the systems unintentionally.

FIGURE 3.1 ● How Does a Highly Effective Governance Board Act?

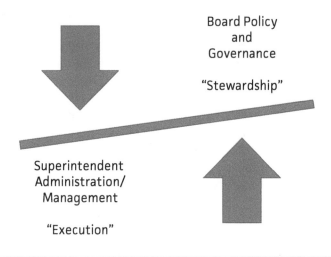

Board Policy
and
Governance

"Stewardship"

Superintendent
Administration/
Management

"Execution"

Board members regularly gather or receive information from staff and community members relating to the administration of the district. Additionally, board members have their own agenda or interests they wish to pursue. Board members often believe pushing their agenda is how they can make a difference. After all, why would they seek to serve on the board, be available constantly to the public, and devote their time and energy sometimes at a personal and financial cost if not to make a contribution and to be helpful? Dysfunctions happen when board members act in ways inconsistent with their roles. For example, we know a board member who accepted a teacher's invitation to evaluate his teaching. The board member didn't understand his actions would undermine the principal's authority and could jeopardize the evaluation process.

Likewise, superintendents, particularly equity warriors, shape and push policy and finance directions around their equity agenda. Board members rely on the administration's expertise and experience in education, as they should. Superintendents and district leaders can overmanage boards by packaging policy recommendations so tightly that board members feel they are just rubber-stamping the administration's wishes. Even when board members may have been consulted and had their questions or concerns addressed before a meeting, the public perception may be that the superintendent is operating unilaterally. Nevertheless, concerns that the public will perceive board members as ineffectual often feed the need for board members to challenge and criticize the superintendent.

Keeping these cautions in mind, effective boards and superintendents do not stay on their sides of the line. Quite the contrary. Effective boards and superintendents build relationships in which they seek to clarify the rules of engagement so as to limit the unintended consequences of crossing the line. Without crossing the line, board members cannot assist superintendents by surfacing issues the community and staff are reluctant to share. They may be reluctant to share for a variety of reasons, such as not having access, fear of how their issue may be received, or not knowing how to ensure that their issue gets attention. Without crossing the line, superintendents cannot be clear about the limits and timing of pushing the equity agenda and the community's appetite for change. Taking the board's pulse is critical to understanding the limits to the board's support and ultimately the ability to sustain the agenda. Effective superintendents find solutions, sometimes tabling issues or moderating expectations when board members are conflicted. Board members who are equity warriors need to remain on the board to be helpful. Their self-interest is consistent with the equity agenda.

Equity warriors know they cannot delegate their responsibility for keeping the board engaged.

Superintendents cannot delegate the care and feeding of the board. Equity warriors know they cannot delegate their responsibility for keeping the board engaged. Communication—continuous and patient—is at the heart of the care and feeding, particularly around the equity agenda. Board members must be educated and sometimes convinced about the wisdom of contemplated moves. They need to be heard—not told—so they are able to contribute to the move. They also need to be armed with talking points and data so they can educate those who influence them. We know superintendents who spend hours on the weekends talking to board members so there are no surprises, so that moves are fully understood and personal concerns are considered.

YOUR MOVE: DETERMINE THE INTERESTS OF THOSE AROUND YOU.

Many board/superintendent relationships are not as productive as they could be. Too many superintendents have learned that counting on the majority members of the board for support and distancing themselves from outliers and those in opposition to their positions are short-term strategies. Those who are outside the tent spend their time trying to attract allies to the board and undermining the administration's ability to push its agenda. Power politics—counting votes—is the only approach to move the agenda forward when the board is split and entrenched. Nevertheless, power politics often results in flipping the majority of the board, removing the superintendent, and reversing progress on advancing equity.

More than almost any other factor, the relationship between the school board president or chair and the superintendent is the key to successful policy governance. The board president controls the meeting agenda, designs and executes communication protocols to keep board members informed of developments, establishes and implements procedures, is the chief spokesperson for the board, and sanctions members. Effective board presidents often act as the first among equals. Still, their power is in controlling access to information and timing.

Equity warriors become adept at the politics behind board members. Just to be clear, we are not recommending that superintendents become involved in school board appointments or elections. That is an unwinnable strategy, and we know only a very few superintendents who have tried to influence elections, often as a last resort. In almost all cases, it *was* the last resort, and superintendents were removed. We are suggesting that equity warriors be aware of shifts in the political winds within the district and clearly articulate their need for support to board members, their allies in the community, and those who support the equity agenda. Equity warriors know the opinion leaders in the community and which ones support their agenda and which ones are opposed. As we said in the introduction to this section, equity warriors understand that the ultimate success of the agenda depends on everyone leading within their roles. School board members who champion the agenda need to fight for and retain their positions for longer than they might like. Community leaders need to run and back candidates who support the agenda. If equity warriors in the community do not provide superintendents the tools necessary to support the agenda, they share the blame for its failure.

Equity warriors understand that the ultimate success of the agenda depends on everyone leading within their roles.

Boards are often in transition. We have been called in to support boards that are highly political. We define highly political as when board members have chosen to serve on the board to promote a particular, sometimes singular, purpose or when board members are not independent. Even on an elected board, some members are instructed how to vote, even by text messages, during meetings. In one of our sessions, a board member turned to her colleagues and said, "I get a call before every meeting about what is expected of me, and I know each of you do, too." In such districts, an equity agenda is rarely a primary concern. Some equity warriors continue to carry on, trying to limit damage and finding opportunities to push equity when they can. It takes incredible political acumen and extraordinary luck for an equity agenda to survive in a highly political board. Many superintendents choose to flee at the first opportunity rather than impugn their reputation. They hope they could do more to advance equity by announcing their reasons for leaving. Sometimes it helps.

YOUR MOVE: EDUCATE THOSE AROUND YOU.

Most school boards are not highly political. They are fertile ground for equity warriors. For these boards, we have applied our own version of Lev Vygotsky's (2002) concept of the zone of proximal development. That is, rather than assume board members will be able to solve complex equity problems on their own, we evaluate board members' experiences, what they feel capable and competent to do, and assist them in solving problems of equity with increasing complexity.

None of us is immediately—or ever—successful at solving the most complex equity problems. Equity warriors must take it step by step. They begin by thinking about who is in the group. Many school board members—even those who had roles within school systems—have little knowledge of schools and equity challenges beyond their personal experience. When board membership changes, moving the group forward is difficult. Equity warriors keep moving everyone forward while recognizing that areas of growth in solving equity problems will be uneven based on the board member's time and experience. Educating takes time and patience.

Equity warriors balance their point of view and others' agendas. Success comes from working and learning together.

Equity warriors balance their point of view and others' agendas. Success comes from working and learning together. The superintendent who is not committed to learning alongside board members about how to solve complex problems misses an opportunity. When board members or district leaders are absent from the learning sessions, they send the message that learning is not important, and learning is rarely sustained.

Learning about equity issues is hard work. It requires vulnerability to put opinions, experiences, and doubts on the table. We often begin our retreats with board members and superintendents with icebreakers that help participants become more comfortable with each other. We're often surprised to learn how little people who work together know about their colleagues. One board president told us he "didn't go in for that touchy and feely stuff." Frankly, neither do we. Yet, board members and district leaders need to know each other, discover that they share much in common, appreciate that each person is at a different point in the journey—and know that nobody has finished the journey.

Let's look at an example of a values-enhanced, equity agenda from the Montgomery County (Maryland) Board of Education. Its 2018–2021 Strategic Plan shows that the board understands its role as equity warriors (Montgomery County Public Schools [MCPS], 2018):

> This Strategic Plan represents our continued commitment to the five core values that define what it means to be an exceptional school system: Learning, Relationships, Respect, Excellence, and Equity.
>
> MCPS is committed to educating our students so that academic success is not predictable by race, ethnicity, gender, socioeconomic status, language proficiency, or disability. We will continue to strive until all gaps have been eliminated for all groups. Our students will graduate with deep academic knowledge and become prepared for tomorrow's complex world and workplace.

The MCPS board continues to articulate its values by defining the skills and traits students are expected to demonstrate by graduation:

> Our students will be able to:
>
> - Display effective communication through reading, writing, and literacy
> - Clearly articulate thoughts and ideas that are purposeful and meaningful
> - Use technology to support learning now and in the future
> - Appreciate the arts as a strength of learning
> - Accept diverse perspectives, cultures, and multilingualism as a part of becoming a global citizen
> - Act responsibly in every situation
> - Engage in diverse thinking that impacts self and others positively

- Display personal characteristics that support problem solving, critical thinking, and inquiry
- Share in the belief of service that benefits others
- Participate as active citizens in the community, nation, and world
- Demonstrate a desire to become reflective as a way to set goals and accomplish tasks
- Display character traits symbolic of good citizenship (MCPS, 2018)

Further, the board defines the mission and states its expectation to close opportunity and achievement gaps for all students and clarifies its role to monitor progress in reaching its expectations:

> The mission of Montgomery County Public Schools is to ensure every student has the academic, creative problem-solving, and social-emotional skills to be successful in college, career, and community, regardless of background.
>
> While many of our students achieve at the highest levels, not all have had the opportunities, support, and resources needed to meet their full potential. MCPS is committed to addressing disparities in student outcomes by closing gaps in opportunity and achievement for all students, in all classrooms, in all of our schools. MCPS has identified the following focus areas of student, school, and system performance to monitor:
>
> - Students ready to learn
> - Reducing and eliminating disparities in student learning
> - Students prepared for college and careers
> - A safe and healthy learning environment
> - Efficient operations
> - Highly effective employees (MCPS, 2018)

The MCPS board posts updated progress on each of its six focus areas on its website.

Through the process of creating an equity-focused vision, mission, and outcomes, equity warrior board members and superintendents demonstrate the characteristics of "Peak Performing Governance Teams." As described by Tim Quinn (2010), such teams have five characteristics:

- Team members are united in their commitment to the service of children.

- The board and superintendent have an interdependent relationship.

- Indicators of success are established for the district.

- Governance team relationships are based upon trust and respect.

- The governance team has developed strong and durable linkages with the community. (pp. 19–25)

Board and superintendent learning is not separate from the processes of creating products that demonstrate their development. The MCPS strategic plan began even before Jerry Weast became superintendent in 1999. It has continued through two successive superintendents. Of the eight current board members, one has been a member for more than 20 years, one for 14 years, and five (including the student member) are serving their first term. The MCPS strategic plan evolved through consistent attention to the values of its community and leadership.

YOUR MOVE: COMMUNICATE YOUR VALUES THROUGH POLICY AND ACTION.

When equity warriors work together, understanding their roles and responsibilities, and follow processes to balance conflicts, they can produce clear expectations for action. Employees, more than the community, watch the board/superintendent deliberations to determine which issues are important, where resources should be devoted, and how much risk to take. District leaders determine by watching the process whether the equity agenda is real or just hyperbole. When the board and superintendent agree on an agenda, those in the organization have guidelines or parameters for execution.

Equity warriors know that making the organization's values transparent aids in overcoming resistance. When equity warriors who are system leaders communicate clearly and consistently and make their agenda equally clear, other equity warriors within the system are enabled to reveal their support for the equity agenda. They will contribute if they trust their leaders. Leaders build trust when they stay the course, communicate clearly and consistently, and act in accordance with their values. They build trust when they are predictable and accountable for their actions and missteps. They build trust when they

Equity warriors know that making the organization's values transparent aids in overcoming resistance.

are reliable, when they anticipate when encouragement is need, and when they support those who are taking appropriate actions in service of an equity agenda.

Equity agendas are contextual. Let's look at an example from Roanoke City (Virginia) Public Schools, nestled in the Roanoke Valley in western Virginia, a district of 14,000 students.

In 2008, with the arrival of its new superintendent, Rita Bishop, the Roanoke City School Board wrestled with two challenges—replacing school infrastructure and adjusting attendance zones due to shifts in student enrollment. Of particular importance to the school board and its chair, David Carson, was building trust in the school board and system by addressing long-standing systemic inequities resulting from demographic shifts.

According to the Virginia Department of Education (n.d.), 13,600 students enrolled in Roanoke City Public Schools (RCPS) in 2003–2004, 46 percent were Black and 3 percent were Latinx. By 2007–2008, student enrollment dropped by 5 percent while the percentage of Black and Latinx students each grew by 2 percent. More affluent and white families settled in a section of Roanoke City or in the Roanoke County school district.

It was time for the board to make its values known. Before launching an infrastructure renewal plan and adjusting attendance zones, the board adopted an Equity Policy in June 2009. RCPS's Equity Policy begins with its purpose:

> The School Board is committed to creating, building, and sustaining a racially, ethnically, culturally, and economically sensitive environment that provides equitable access to a high standard of educational success for all students. The School Board recognizes that equity does not mean equal but rather the establishment of high standards for all students while providing the opportunities, support, settings, and resources so that all students receive a high-quality education in order to achieve the high standards established by the School Board.
>
> The School Board recognizes that a number of critical factors must be considered to ensure that all students achieve at high levels. Some of these factors include, but are not limited to: (1) the quality and stability of

the teachers in a school; (2) the quality and stability of leadership in a school; (3) the allocation of resources, both fiscal, operational and structural necessary to support high levels of student achievement; (4) the goal of high expectations for all students; and (5) the provision of school and classroom settings with students from diverse backgrounds. In recognizing these critical factors, the School Board reaffirms its commitment to the goal of educational excellence and equitable opportunities for all its students. (Roanoke School Board, 2019)

The Equity Policy contains specific measurable goals to "promote the equitable distribution of resources and opportunities" including staffing ratios and facilities. Specific "critical factors" are mentioned and expected to be measured annually. The superintendent is instructed to report on the critical factors at the board's December meeting. Finally, the policy creates an Equity Task Force—including the superintendent and five members appointed by the school board—to "assist . . . in developing strategies for ensuring equitable educational opportunities are being provided to all students who attend Roanoke City Public Schools" (Roanoke School Board, 2019).

Each December, the Equity Task Force and the superintendent present the Equity Scorecard to the school board and community (Roanoke School Board, n.d.). The scorecard contains three-year disaggregated data on staff and student diversity; participation in gifted, advanced, dual enrollment, Advanced Placement, career, and technical education programs; performance on ACT and SAT exams; graduation and dropout rates; and post-secondary education or military plans. All the information is readily accessible to internal and external audiences on two sides of a single page. RCPS lives its values through enacting board policy, monitoring its progress, and reporting progress openly with the public.

Equity warriors understand that people know their values by what they expect and inspect. Leadership politics require boards, superintendents, and district leaders to work in concert to formulate and advance their equity agenda. Boards that name the problem and articulate their values in established policies set the stage for superintendents and district leaders to execute on their directions.

Equity warriors understand that people know their values by what they expect and inspect.

REFLECTION: *Do the board and superintendent work in concert in leading the district? Are the board and superintendent's values articulated clearly in policy? Does your district have policies to assess the actions on the values in place, and are those policies followed?*

_____

_____

_____

_____

_____

_____

_____

_____

_____

 ## DIPLOMACY: LEAD CHANGE FOCUSING ON VALUES

In Part I, we examined data processes that equity warriors use to engage external and internal stakeholders in sensitive and effective ways to achieve the district's equity vision and agenda. We now turn to how values-enhanced equity warriors use the tools of diplomacy—rewards, consequences, and moral persuasion—to lead internal audiences. Fundamentally, leadership diplomacy is about creating change.

Michael Fullan (2001) has been writing about leading change in educational systems for nearly 40 years. He has concluded that "change cannot be managed. It can be understood and perhaps led, but it cannot be controlled" (p. 33). To understand complex change, Fullan suggests leaders develop mindsets and actions such as the following:

- Leaders know that the goal is not innovation but developing the organizational capacity and commitment to solve complex problems.

- Leaders know that having the best ideas is not enough. Others within the organization must also buy into the ideas.

- Leaders will anticipate the inevitable implementation dip, appreciating that others in the organization may be fearful about change and need time to learn before they are ready to move ahead.

- Leaders know that resistance is part of change and will engage and learn from those who disagree with them and/or resist change.

- Leaders know that changing the organizational culture—or reculturing—is key and that that process is broader, deeper, and more complex than structural reorganization.

- Leaders recognize that change is a complex process that is never linear and cannot be measured by a checklist. (pp. 35–46)

Equity warriors understand the importance of values-enhanced leadership that is synonymous with moral purpose and leading, not controlling the change process.

Having a moral purpose binds together these mindsets and actions and helps sustain the process through twists and turns. Equity warriors understand the importance of values-enhanced leadership that is synonymous with moral purpose and leading, not controlling the change process.

YOUR MOVE: MAKE YOUR VALUES REAL.

Equity warriors articulate their values and use values to reflect, refine, explore, and, most of all, learn how values show up in their lives and work. Values are not fixed at a point in time and are open to multiple interpretations. Charging headfirst into a chaotic situation may be some people's idea of demonstrating courage, while quietly and resolutely standing up for an idea in the face of oppression may be another's. To an earlier point, values-enhanced leadership embraces the complexity of dynamic situations and knows that struggling for meaning enables people to make choices about how much they believe in the values. In other words, articulating values provides parameters for self-reflection and accountability that can be examined and tested over time.

Equity warriors articulate their values and use values to reflect, refine, explore, and, most of all, learn how values show up in their lives and work.

Everyone has values that guide their actions. Leaders through history have used values to spur people to action and transform societies—not always for good. Equity warriors identify values that set the expectation that employees throughout the organization will lead the equity agenda from where they are. No one can be exempt if the equity agenda is to be successful. Nevertheless, roles, responsibilities, readiness, and capacities vary across the organization and among the adults holding positions. Articulating the expectation that everyone is a leader and placing a stake in the ground around a few core, shared values sets the stage for adults to find their place.

Since values are preexisting, the context dictates the approach for surfacing values that advance equity. In the MCPS example, the board determined that naming five core values for the entire organization was part of its roles and responsibilities. In other places, leaders of offices, teams, or schools have entered into a process to define expectations for their part of the organization. We found that it is most effective to name no more than five or six core values that are shared, are relevant to advancing equity, and can stand the test of time. Processes for identifying core values should be short. The longer the process, the lower the effect. In other words, if the organization cannot agree on its values quickly, the values are not core. We have witnessed boards, district leaders, and divisions identify core values that were spot on in a matter of hours.

The aim is to name core values that are aspirational and abstract in order to invite others to make meaning and wrestle with the ways that the values can show up in their actions. Interdependence is a good example of a value that is held by highly effective teams because it is aspirational and foundational. We define interdependence as believing that my success in accomplishing my responsibilities depends on the success of my colleagues in accomplishing their responsibilities. Advancing equity is difficult in siloed organizations that avoid conflict or give in to pressure to complete a project for the sake of expediency. An organization does not become a highly effective team just by putting on the same color jersey!

Having the common language of espoused core values begins the process of understanding the implications of acting consistently. While core values can be identified quickly, reflecting and acting on how core values appear in everyone's work is a process. For example, conversations help participants understand that interdependence is a value that informs how people go about teamwork, collaboration, trust, and mutual respect. Dialogue is needed to examine what interdependence would look like in practice, both in ways that could lead to a change in organizational culture to advance equity and in ways in which it would not.

Core values are used to clarify mutual expectations; help guide decision making; shape the organizational culture; and attract and retain talented, dedicated adults who share the values. Understanding the importance of articulating values leads to practical actions aimed at changing organizational culture. The act of having core values and expectations explicit in the job descriptions and hiring processes helps attract and select employees committed to the equity agenda. Professional learning integrates opportunities to reflect on and reinforce core values. Growth and development systems can shift from a focus on compliance (e.g., checking off whether a candidate has been a member of a professional learning community) to evaluating how employees live out the core values in their work.

Core values provide guidance, but not rules, on how adults are expected to think and act wherever they are in the organization. As complexity increases, clarity on shared values provides guidance for decision making aligned with the equity agenda throughout the organization. There is no policy book that can give specific guidance to each person encountering a situation. In complex education systems, adults and students cannot predict the consequences of their decisions based on the past. Yet, if they use values to clarify their intent, they can more easily anticipate and explain their decisions, and have a common basis for learning from their decisions.

Equity warriors sometimes use symbols to jump-start conversations about their values in advancing equity.

Symbolism matters. Equity warriors sometimes use symbols to jump-start conversations about their values in advancing equity. Again, as the following example from Norfolk Public Schools illustrates, the story of students offers a powerful launch to a careful examination of values.

In Norfolk, district administrators and principals traditionally kick off the school year by meeting together. Typically, school board members and superintendents greet administrators, introduce and celebrate administrators new to the district or in new positions, discuss the year's priorities, and plan for the first weeks

(Continued)

(Continued)

of school. The gathering is intended to motivate, reinforce a sense of community, and send key messages that administrators will cascade through the organization as they later meet with their staff.

On this occasion, superintendent John Simpson seized the opportunity of his opening message to make his values real to administrators. After a few celebrations, he introduced a group of 30 rising kindergarteners, all dressed in their very best clothes. As 5-year-olds are, they were cute and full of joy even though they were surrounded by an audience of adults. Simpson introduced them as the incoming kindergarteners to much applause. He told the children they were going to play a little counting game and asked the administrators to watch carefully.

He asked all of the students to take two steps forward. Then, he asked 20 of the children to take one more step forward. After a moment to let the children settle, he asked 15 of those 20 students to take three steps forward and let them settle again. Next, he asked eight students to take three more steps forward. He once again asked the audience to look closely at the children, as he thanked the children for helping him play this game. The children left the room to thunderous applause and smiles.

When it was just the adults in the room, Simpson explained. We could all agree that we wanted all children to start their education journey with so much joy and enthusiasm, with so much hope and promise. But, as they step through the grades, we begin to see difference. The first step represents the attainment of 3rd-grade reading proficiency, and the data at that time showed that about one-third of students fall behind. The next step is passing algebra by the end of 8th grade, and another 25 percent fall behind. Finally, by high school graduation, a little more than 50 percent graduate on time.

Simpson had made his point. Data about the failure of the system to educate all students had faces. Using children to tell the story touched the hearts as well as the heads of administrators. They also began to understand that improving opportunities for all children was a personal challenge for Simpson. When he reviewed numbers, he saw children's faces. His values could not have been more clear.

Motivating adults to confront the real results of the equity agenda underscores the necessity of leading at all levels. None of the adults in the room was directly responsible for the future success of these 5-year-olds. Yet, each of them was responsible for the future success of students represented by these kindergartners. It would have been even more poignant had Simpson made children move or stay back based on their race. Norfolk's achievement gap at the time was similar to other districts. Of course, he was careful not to let the children know the purpose of the game. He hoped they never would!

YOUR MOVE: USE SYSTEMS THINKING TO UNDERSTAND COMPLEX CONTEXTS.

Equity warriors know that while stating values and having a plan for engaging adults in understanding values is an important step, doing so does not change beliefs or actions. We agree with Fullan that buy-in to ideas is essential. The question is how to create buy-in to advance equity in ways that are sensitive to the risk-taking necessary to explore biases and beliefs and also effective in piercing the protective armor that everyone carries.

> *Equity warriors know that while stating values and having a plan for engaging adults in understanding values is an important step, doing so does not change beliefs or actions.*

Often, attempts to create buy-in through professional learning are unsuccessful because inadequate time is spent on addressing resistance to unlearning the values or beliefs that people come with, or learning introduced in one session is not reinforced consistently. Educators know this to be true in student learning. Learning involves transfer of knowledge from previous experiences. Existing knowledge can make it difficult to learn new information (National Research Council, 2002). When activating prior knowledge as a teaching strategy, we are trying to understand not only whether students are familiar with the content we are presenting but also if they are holding misconceptions from their previous learning experiences in or outside school.

Peter Senge (1994) discussed a similar notion in his work about creating learning organizations. New ideas often fail to get into practice "because they conflict with deeply held internal images of how the world works, images that limit us to familiar ways of working" (p. 182). Senge explains that our mental models are powerful in affecting what we do in part because they affect what we see. We develop "defensive routines" that insulate our mental models from examination, including adult learners "who are 'highly skillful at protecting themselves from pain and threat posed by learning situations,' but consequently fail to learn how to produce the results they really want" (p. 182).

Senge proposed that those in learning organizations would develop their skills of reflection and skills of inquiry to make key decisions based on shared understandings of interrelationship and patterns of change. Reflection and inquiry are important tools to make sense of complex situations, such as equity warriors face in the global pandemic, the expansion of remote and blended learning, and challenges to systemic racism. David J. Snowden and Mary E. Boone (2007) describe complex context as having the following characteristics:

- Large numbers of interacting elements are involved.
- Nonlinear and minor changes produce disproportionately major consequences.
- Solutions cannot be imposed. They arise from the circumstances.
- The system's history is integrated into the present.
- Hindsight does not lead to foresight.
- Agents and the system constrain each other.

In complex contexts, Snowden and Boone identify the leaders' job as probing and responding, seeking patterns to emerge, increasing level of interaction and communication, and locating methods that can help identify ideas.

The systems-thinking iceberg analogy helps tie these ideas together (see Figure 3.2). Imagine an iceberg. Only 10–15 percent of an iceberg can be observed above the waterline. Most

FIGURE 3.2 ● The Systems-Thinking Iceberg

Events

Patterns/Trends

Structures/Frameworks

Beliefs/Values

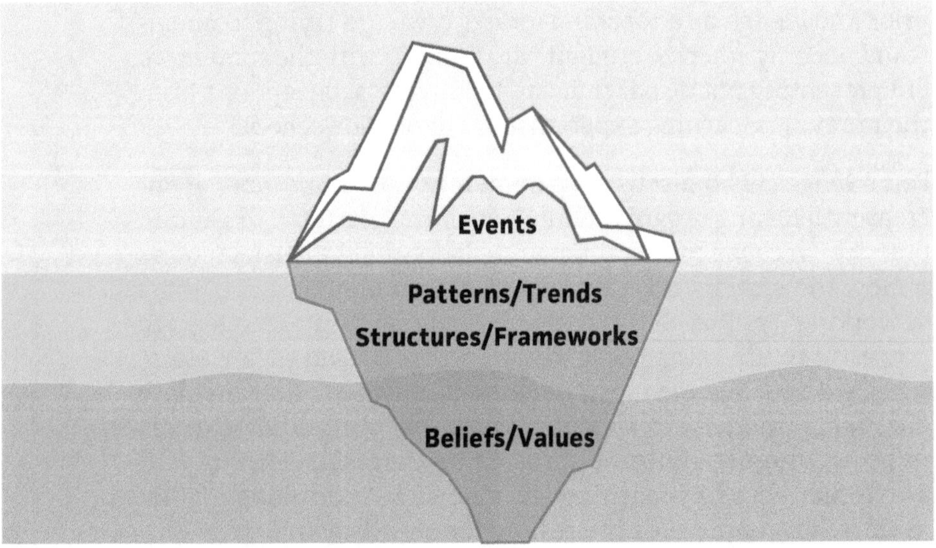

Image Source: https://www.istockphoto.com/portfolio/MicrovOne

of the iceberg is hidden by water. Exploration—going deeper and looking at the iceberg from different angles—is required to describe an iceberg accurately. System thinkers use the iceberg to describe four stages of analysis. Gathering evidence from single events is the stage above the waterline. Hidden below the waterline are three stages: patterns and trends; underlying structures and frameworks; and assumptions, beliefs, and values. Let's apply the analogy to a complex situation facing district leaders.

When something occurs, say a spike in suspensions of Black males, the initial reaction might be to treat the spike as a single event. District leaders might look across schools to determine if the spike has occurred at a single school or a group of schools. If the analysis ends there, district leaders have considered only the tip of the iceberg.

Additional analysis is needed to discern patterns. Looking at suspension data over a period of years could reveal that the spike might be explained by the time of the school year or a change in student population or staffing. The analysis might also reveal that certain schools or administrators are more likely than others to use suspension as punishment. Finding the patterns helps us see the iceberg just below the waterline.

The next level below the waterline involves looking at structures that contribute to the patterns and asking why the patterns are occurring. Structures include policies that allow or encourage high levels of suspension and collective bargaining agreements that have provisions about disciplining students, how schools are organized, and class sizes. However, we have not reached the deepest and most substantial parts of the iceberg.

Mental models, our worldview, our beliefs, and our values undergird the structures that contribute to—intentionally or not—the patterns and events. For example, in thinking back to our discussion of achievement gaps, if we believe external factors contribute to a higher rate of infractions by Black males, then higher suspension rates are not only acceptable but expected. If we believe that suspending students protects teachers from aggressive behavior, then higher suspension rates are acceptable. Structures won't change until the mental models are challenged.

When equity warriors consider how their values influence the structures, patterns, and events in their district, they realize that mandating policy changes, such as eliminating suspensions of Black males, by themselves will not solve the problem.

When equity warriors consider how their values influence the structures, patterns, and events in their district, they realize that mandating policy changes, such as eliminating suspensions of Black males, by themselves will not solve the problem.

We have also experienced that when buy-in is espoused quickly, change is rarely genuine or long-lived. Creating a policy change that is more closely aligned to equity warriors' values can be an important short-term step. In this case, however, discussions about proposed changes should occur regularly and include discussion about other options that build on beliefs—for example, tools to examine implicit biases that are the foundation of the structures. When such discussions are lacking, policy changes will be short-lived or result in unintended consequences.

YOUR MOVE: USE EXISTING PROCESSES TO BRING COHERENCE.

Equity warriors know, for example, that if they expect adults in the system to be accountable for progress on goals in their equity agenda, they too must be accountable.

Leaders communicate their values and expectations in multiple ways. One of the strongest is by publicly walking the talk. Equity warriors know, for example, that if they expect adults in the system to be accountable for progress on goals in their equity agenda, they too must be accountable. The more publicly accountable they are, the stronger is their position both in clarifying expectations and in protecting them from attacks. Public accountability as protection may be counterintuitive, so we will explain.

The Chicago School Reform Act of 1988 ushered in a dramatic experiment in shifting accountability. Until that time, principals reported to the general superintendent and school board through a typical chain of command. Frustrated by low student performance and absence of community trust, the state legislature disrupted the system by making principals responsible to an elected local school council, not a central office supervisor. Each local school council would adopt an improvement plan, determine the school budget from a lump-sum allocation and, most unusually, hire and dismiss the principal. Principals became mini-superintendents with their own boards, a four-year contract, and much more control over budgeting and staffing. They were also required to manage their local school council.

My doctoral work focused on whether the shift in accountability structures changed principal leadership. I found that principals who were successful in leading within the new structure determined early on what they needed to do to survive. They immediately disengaged from the central office structure, built the capacity of their local school councils to develop and monitor plans and budgets, and used their evaluation process to protect themselves from council member attacks. The council's role was to set the plan and approve a budget aligned to the plan. Principals had to find the balance between having the council's trust and confidence, and respecting their role as decision makers. Successful principals tied their evaluations to the plan's objectives, not to the interest of individual board members, which allowed them to set the terms of their evaluation. When principals controlled the evaluation, they controlled their jobs.

Many district superintendent contracts contain a provision that the board and superintendent will agree on the superintendent evaluation. Too often, neither the board nor the superintendent takes this provision as seriously as they should. Superintendents and board members agree to check the box by using a generic evaluation process with general categories such as superintendent/board relationship, educational leadership, operational and fiscal leadership, external relations, and professional growth. State superintendent associations have general evaluation processes and forms that can be refined based on local interests.

Equity warriors understand that the lack of attention on evaluation instruments is a missed opportunity to communicate district leadership consensus on the most important elements of their vision and equity agenda. Evaluations are also a powerful tool to protect equity warriors who face resistance in executing on an agreed-upon direction. We counsel superintendents to aggressively establish an evaluation process that sets clear expectations for the superintendent's implementation of the equity agenda and contains quarterly progress monitoring. Rather than shying away from being held accountable, superintendents and district leaders who are equity warriors insist on accountability for their own protection.

Equity warriors understand that the lack of attention on evaluation instruments is a missed opportunity to communicate district leadership consensus on the most important elements of their vision and equity agenda.

Having a public evaluation document communicates the superintendent's priorities for the year to the community and the district leadership team. Let's look at the example of San Diego Unified School District superintendent Cindy Marten, who used her evaluation to communicate expectations and bring coherence to central office work.

Each July, the San Diego Unified Board of Education, Marten, and Chief of Staff Staci Monreal discussed the superintendent's performance against goals and metrics agreed upon the previous September. Marten's evaluation process brought together three district-level strategic documents created for different purposes and audiences. The three documents were Vision 2020, the California Local Control and Accountability Plan, and the board members' annual priorities:

(Continued)

(Continued)

- *Vision 2020*—In 2009, the Board of Education identified goals to achieve by the 2019–2020 school year, the year when that year's 1st graders would graduate from high school. Subsequently, the board adopted 12 Indicators of a Quality Neighborhood School to define and measure school-based best practices (San Diego Unified School District [SDUSD], n.d.).

- *The Local Control and Accountability Plan (LCAP)* is a three-year, district-level plan required by the state. The district designs and updates the plan annually with community participation. The plan describes specific district actions (with expenditures) to reach the goals and the metrics to measure progress. The LCAP must address California's eight priority areas. San Diego Unified includes its 12 quality school indicators from Vision 2020 (SDUSD, 2019).

- *Board's focus areas and annual priorities*—The evaluation process joins these interests together into a set of focus areas and rating metrics. The evaluation process has three parts:

  o **July:** The board and superintendent determine areas of focus for the upcoming school year: 1. Multilingual learners; 2. Students with disabilities; 3. Integration of academics with social-emotional learning; 4. Improve outcomes for priority schools; 5. Develop a culture of formative assessment, data, and monitoring; 6. Secure funding for early literacy, numeracy, and intervention; 7. Improve allocations for elementary schools; 8. Improve hiring practices; 9. Finalize growth and development process; 10. Improve employee relations; 11. Maintain and service schools; 12. Successfully launch enhanced mathematics and provide measurable outcomes; and 13. Equip every school with a comprehensive marketing plan. This comprehensive list of areas of focus remains constant from year to year with some tweaking.

  o **September:** The board and superintendent agree to specific goals and metrics organized within the six categories of LCAP: 1. Closing the achievement gap with high expectations for all; 2. Access to broad and challenging curriculum; 3. Quality leadership, teaching, and learning; 4. Positive school environment, climate, and culture; 5. Parent and community engagement with highly regarded neighborhood schools; and 6. Districtwide support and communications. Within each of these goals, there are three to nine specific metrics that are rated. For example, three of the nine metrics in goal 1 name specific schools that the board has targeted for improvement.

○ **The following July:** During the evaluation session, the board and superintendent discuss the district's performance metrics. At the end of the discussions, the board and superintendent report key accomplishments and continuing challenges to the community, the board's rating on each of the metrics using a four-point scale (beginning, developing, accomplishing, and extending), and focus areas for the following school year. They also decide whether to extend the superintendent's contract for another year.

The launching of Vision 2020 predates the tenure of Marten, three of the five board members, and California's LCAP. San Diego Unified's honoring of Vision 2020 sends the message of consistency and alignment. Rather than abandon the prior initiatives when a new board, superintendent, or state mandate appears, the district intends to stay the course over time, to communicate expectations, to measure and reflect on progress with community stakeholders, and to align accountability and budget to priorities.

Warren Bennis and Burton Nanus (1985) write, "When the organization has a clear sense of its purpose, direction, and desired state and when this image is widely shared, individuals are able to find their own roles both in the organization and in the larger society of which they are a part" (pp. 90–91). The San Diego Unified example shows how the evaluation process and naming accountability allows individuals within the organization to judge for themselves how they can best contribute to the organization's purpose.

Equity warriors use the evaluation process thoughtfully, particularly in choosing goals and metrics.

Equity warriors use the evaluation process thoughtfully, particularly in choosing goals and metrics. As we saw in the Atlanta example in Chapter 1, using a private-sector approach to set quantitative performance targets and bonuses for reaching targets does not have the desired result in a public-sector context. Having an aligned, coherent evaluation process outweighs the risks and should not be feared. The evaluation process is rarely used to discipline or terminate a district leader. However, it is effective as an early-warning tool when there is a problem.

YOUR MOVE: DEVELOP LEADERS.

Equity warriors know that education is a people business and that the adults in the system are our greatest assets.

Equity warriors know that education is a people business and that the adults in the system are our greatest assets. We say equity warriors and not educators because too often throughout the history of public education the people—teachers, staff, and administrators—have been treated as cogs in a machine. Teacher-proof or scripted curriculum, models built on high turnover of inexperienced teachers and staff, computer-based instructional programs, and policy designers whose only prior experiences with education were as students are examples of devaluing the individual contributions made by the education profession. Treating adults as interchangeable parts wastes our greatest assets.

Equity warriors know the importance of having a values-enhanced leadership development system in place. The purpose of the system is to attract, select, develop, and sustain high-quality leaders who share and live core values. To be effective, six components of a leadership development system operate in concert. Districts generally do not have leadership systems in place. The following is one attempt to build such a system in a high-need district.

East Baton Rouge Parish Public Schools (EBRPPS), with 41,000 students, is Louisiana's second-largest district. In 2006–2007, the district received 4.4 applicants for each principal vacancy. The number of applicants was lower for schools that had the most underserved populations. At the time, 77 percent of the principals were eligible to retire, and half of those eligible had more than 30 years of experience (Perry, 2007).

A committee of district, school, and community leaders met over four months to frame a leadership development system for district, school, and teacher leaders. The purpose of the system is to "provide a clear, comprehensive, and strategic structure for identifying and preparing future leaders and sustaining the continuous improvement of current leaders. The system's purpose is to enhance the efforts of EBRPPS leaders at all levels to improve student achievement" (Perry, 2007, p. 10).

The proposed system clarified expectations and proposed strategic directions to support leaders at three levels of the organization: teacher, school, and district leaders.

Framework of the EBRPPS Leadership Development System

The six components of the leadership development system are as follows:

- **Recruiting and onboarding:** Leaders are actively recruited and prepared to assume leadership. Expanding the pool of leaders includes identifying potential candidates for leadership positions, encouraging potential candidates to meet the requirements for positions, preparing or orienting candidates for the demands of leadership, and providing new leaders with the knowledge and support to adjust to positions of leadership.

- **Training and education:** Learning does not stop once leaders are selected. Opportunities for learning are continuous. Best practices suggest that the most effective learning is embedded into the daily activities of leaders. Opportunities for intensive learning consider the need of leaders to perform their responsibilities. Further, training for leaders does not focus exclusively on short-term needs.

- **Evaluation and development:** Staff evaluation systems add the most benefit when they measure what is most important. Leaders know the difference between real staff evaluations and "going through the motions." Effective evaluation systems clarify expectations, identify areas of growth that are attainable and important, include clear measures of progress, recognize leaders who meet expectations, and are aligned to district goals and rewards systems. Also, evaluation clarifies to supervisors and leaders which leaders are effective and which are not.

- **Supporting policies:** Organizations have policies and practices that stand in the way of meeting changing expectations. Careful, periodic study of policies and practices is necessary to remove obstacles to new expectations. Also, policies and practices require revision to recognize the knowledge, skills, and attitudes of a new generation of leaders.

(Continued)

(Continued)

- **Staffing and position planning:** As is the case with policies and practices, the amount and types of positions available may provide obstacles to achieving changes in expectations. Equity is not allocating equal resources to schools or departments. Increasing expectations without the careful review of capacity to deliver on expectations may result in unrealistic demands on school and department leaders.

- **Compensation and benefits:** A leadership development system addresses whether the compensation and rewards for leaders are sufficient to attract and keep high-quality leaders. Money alone is not the determining factor. How leaders are recognized and valued in the broadest sense is part of their compensation. (Perry, 2007, pp. 10–11)

Leadership development is a system of codependent parts. We have partnered with districts that tried to tackle just one part of the system—such as professional learning—without the others and had limited success recruiting a pool of highly qualified candidates for leadership positions. Even within the six system components in the EBRPPS example, experience has revealed gaps. School districts committed to increasing the diversity of their leadership team will often invest in attracting candidates but fail to provide compensation or onboarding supports to ensure new employees are successful. We have observed recently that more superintendents include a budget for mentoring or coaching as part of their contracts. But few districts afford the same opportunities to other district leaders.

Equity warriors know there is no better way to further develop leaders than to place them in real situations.

Equity warriors commit to developing leaders. They cascade expectations that begin with the superintendent's leadership team sharing values and learning from each other's experiences and perspectives. Through continuous, regular professional learning, leaders grow together and build trust through respect for differences and deepening understanding. By modeling these experiences, leaders are expected to replicate learning opportunities that develop their leadership teams and make clear the organization's expectations for its leaders.

Equity warriors know there is no better way to further develop leaders than to place them in real situations. As learning and development cascade through the organization, problems of practice surface challenges and gaps. They respond by tackling the challenges within their own spheres of influence. When they recognize that similar challenges exist in other vertical teams within the organization, district leaders collaborate on systemic policy and financial solutions. When this happens, learning and development are reciprocal throughout the organization. Most important, equity warriors emerge as they seize opportunities to own and address the challenges within their reach and recognize and advance systemic responses to broad challenges.

As we bring the diplomacy section to a close, the words of corporate CEO Robert Knowling echo disappointments that equity warriors often feel. His words ring true for us:

> The most painful thing that I've ever gone through as a leader is leaving an organization and seeing the good work, the results of a lot of hard effort on the part of brave and dedicated team members who worked with me, get erased because we didn't get the needed mind-sets and values encoded deeply enough in the DNA of the organization. (quoted in Tichy & Cardwell, 2002, p. xviii)

Noel Tichy writes that to change an organization's DNA, everyone in the organization teaches and learns, and makes contributions to the knowledge of others (Tichy & Cardwell, 2002). In other words, deep systemic change requires using processes and practices that are sensitive to the situations equity warriors confront and effective in bringing about results. Change of this magnitude does not occur overnight. Simpson was Norfolk's superintendent for six years, and it was his third superintendency. Marten served as San Diego Unified's superintendent for nine years. Equity warriors know that longevity and a consistent focus on core values that bind the organization are prerequisites to success.

Equity warriors know that longevity and a consistent focus on core values that bind the organization are prerequisites to success.

REFLECTION: *How do you know your organization's values are clear, articulated, and understood? What are the change processes and systems that bring coherence and reinforce your values?*

_____

_____

_____

_____

_____

_____

_____

_____

_____

 ## WARFARE: ACT WITH PURPOSE, UNDERSTANDING, AND RESOLVE

Equity warriors use pressure as a last resort in pursuit of their equity agenda. There are several reasons for hesitating to use pressure. Among them are the following:

- Pressure cannot be applied as a half measure. Once engaged, the objective must be taken and held.

- The use of pressure can be at odds with our stated values.

- Pressure may not work.

Equity warriors have the courage to use politics and diplomacy to build coalitions and legitimize their power to lead. They use persuasion and inspiration to target values, ideals, and aspirations. They identify and trumpet real change that the organization can rally around. They then march into situations as prepared as they can be to make change happen. They continue to execute and expand their political and diplomatic moves as they pressure possible obstructionists. They use their leadership wisely.

Superintendents and district leaders struggle to find just the right balance in applying pressure to force change. Some hesitate and wait for the conditions to be right. If luck is on their side, conditions will be right. Some do not hesitate at all—it is my way or the highway! Operating in the extremes breeds frustration.

Equity warriors find the just-right balance for applying pressure. They also seek to find the balance to be the change they wish to see. The balance is in the space where people are treated with respect and understanding at the same time they understand the consequences for being obstructionists or just not the leader who is needed at the time.

Equity warriors use warfare as a means to reach their objective and act in ways consistent with their values.

YOUR MOVE: SHOW THE SYSTEM'S INTERDEPENDENCE.

Sometimes necessity is the mother of invention. Overnight in March 2020, the global coronavirus pandemic forced district leaders to drastically alter how teachers teach and students learn. Educators had been talking about distance, blended, and asynchronous instruction for decades, yet distance learning had not taken root at scale. Overnight it became THE way instruction was delivered. Not every teacher, student, or family embraced online learning. Nevertheless, many school districts in the United States had no other option.

The pandemic taught that change can happen abruptly when the whole organization is impacted. In Chapter 1, we shared an example from Long Beach Unified School District about high school Key Results Walk-Throughs. The walk-throughs became effective tools and part of the culture, in part, because all high schools were expected to participate. Walk-throughs were not something done to underperforming schools or to celebrate higher-performing schools. All schools were expected to use the walk-throughs for their improvement.

In the preceding section, we showed how San Diego Unified superintendent Cindy Marten's evaluation pulled together the board's Vision 2020, California's LCAP, and the priorities of individual board members into a single goal-setting process. The following example from San Diego Unified shows an early attempt to align expectations and accountability from the boardroom to the schoolroom.

Soon after Marten assumed the superintendency, she and Chief of Staff Staci Monreal wrestled with how to create a learning cycle for schools and the area superintendents who supervised them. They started with the premise that all schools needed to improve in four areas: learning environment, engagement, differentiation, and student voice and agency. All area superintendents and principals needed to grow in their knowledge and understanding in the same four areas. By naming the areas as learning cycles and dividing the school year into four sections, everyone across the district would be learning together.

(Continued)

(Continued)

Each of the four sections had a guiding question:

- **September–November:** How do we develop an academic, social, and physical environment worthy of our children?
- **December–February:** How do we create classrooms that are alive with collaborative conversations?
- **March–April:** How do we create the learning conditions that maximize the potential that lies within the variability of all learners?
- **May–July:** How do we develop students who take an active stance in their own learning and the learning of others?

Of course, directing area superintendents and principals to learn and plan to address the focus areas was not welcomed immediately. Having a teaching and learning focus was new after several years of fiscal belt-tightening. As expected, Marten and Monreal discovered that principals and area superintendents had much to learn in each of the areas and that applying the professional learning across the grade levels and contexts would take more than a few months. Principals complained that just as they were gaining comfort with one area, they were forced onto the next. So, year one was declared a learning year. The four areas were repeated in the second year, and the following years as well.

Building an accountability system around the 12 indicators of a quality school and in following years around the LCAP goals remained a board priority. In prior years, data reports were presented to the board based on the data's availability. Marten and Monreal established a work group to create protocols and a sequence of board reports aligned to the learning cycles, arranged as closely as possible to annual reporting cycles. Once a month, the board received a data report. The following are examples:

- **September:** Suspension, expulsion, and attendance data
- **October–November:** Enrollment in rigorous courses, tracking on-time graduation
- **December–February:** Professional development, teacher credentialing, and diversity
- **March–April:** Early learning, multilingual learner reclassification, attendance, Ds and Fs, chronic absentee rates
- **May–June:** High school student performance, reading, and elementary performance

To build trust with the community and better use the districtwide advisory councils, district leaders scheduled advisory council meetings to preview and discuss preliminary data before board meetings. Advisory boards were helpful in raising questions about the data in advance so that presenters would be prepared for questions and would have time to make necessary adjustments to their reports.

Fullan (2001) reminds us that "change arouses emotions, and, when emotions intensify, leadership is key" (p. 1). The changes to autonomy of schools and central office practices about sharing data were not always well received. Nevertheless, the leadership decisions to maintain consistency of the learning cycles over years and to align regular data reporting to the LCAP goals created more openness with the public and clarity of direction for central office leaders and principals.

YOUR MOVE: GET THE RIGHT PEOPLE INTO THE RIGHT SEATS.

Jim Collins (2001) discovered that *Good to Great* leaders "*first* got the right people on the bus, the wrong people off the bus, and the right people in the right seats—and *then* they figured out where to drive it" (p. 41). We have witnessed very few major reorganizations in districts that resulted in bus *passengers* changing. Typically, we have seen the following:

- Leadership team vacancies due to retirements timed to coincide with changes in administration
- A few negotiated positions created so that the superintendent will have trusted allies accompany her into a new district
- A strategic termination by the superintendent of someone generally known to be ineffective
- A negotiated "opportunity" for a politically connected but ineffective leader to move into an organization that partners with the district
- Changing leadership team members or direct reports— someone who was in is now out, someone who was out is now in

We know of one politically adept superintendent who was able to change the entire inherited leadership team over a few years through a series of maneuvers, such as navigating soft landings into positions in other districts and organizations. This is a rare talent.

Superintendents weigh whether it is best to bring in a leadership team from the outside or to promote from within. The decisions are situational and depend on the role. We have observed that operational roles are best suited for internal candidates who have local history, know the political context, and have relationships. The exceptions for central candidates—or poor choices—are those who have their own agenda or whose loyalty to district leaders is suspect. External candidates can bring expertise and fresh approaches, although their learning curve about the organization may be steep and their experience may not transfer well to the new situation. We know a superintendent who filled vacancies with external candidates on consulting contracts as interim appointments. The candidates had a few months to prove they were a fit before they were offered the permanent position.

When he served as Long Beach Unified's superintendent, Carl Cohn believed principals needed a broader view of the district, rather than simply a school-focused view. He managed this through strategic assignment of principals. Principals had about three years to show progress at their assigned schools. At the end of the third year, if the expected progress had not occurred, Cohn reassigned the principal to another school, hoping for a better fit with the principal's skill set, and the cycle began again. If the next school did not experience progress by the end of three years, Cohn assigned the principal to a temporary position in a central office unit.

But three years of success in a school did not mean a lifetime assignment in that school. If a principal was meeting expectations and was in her fifth year, she could expect a reassignment to another school. Cohn believed the principalship became routine after five years and that the school and the principal would benefit from a new opportunity. Cohn's approach also fit Long Beach Unified's culture. The district culture encouraged principals to cooperate and not build animosity by trying to lure teachers and staff from other schools since they might find themselves at one of those schools next.

Cohn's example highlights the greatest personnel challenge we have experienced with districts. It is not moving people on or off the bus. It is putting leaders in the right seats on the bus with the authority and support to exercise the right amount of power in a given situation.

Superintendents and district leaders have different sources of power. Superintendents' sources of power are external to the organization—state and local laws and regulations, the school board, and the larger community. Their sources of power cannot be transferred to others in the organization because they are ultimately responsible to authority outside the organization. Their power is checked by the extent to which they can operate freely without political or organizational pushback. Superintendents can anticipate reciprocal actions when they operate within and beyond defined parameters. The parameters are situational and often have nothing to do with an equity agenda. For example, our experience in districts of all sizes taught us that removing a "connected" staff member or popular high school basketball coach or principal could result in a superintendent's departure.

District leaders' power is thought to be largely positional—they have authority over a defined sphere of influence given to them by the superintendent or by her direct reports. The superintendent's leadership style and relationship with district leaders are key factors in determining how district leaders exercise their power. District leaders, particularly those who leave the safety of a successful principalship, are serving at the pleasure of someone for the first time since they earned tenure as a teacher. They enter an arena in which their responsibility is spread across a geographic area or multiple programs. They rely on the judgment of supervisees who they do not see every day to do the right thing. They are learning the nuances of their positions continuously.

Equity warriors operate with trust and confidence to achieve their equity agenda. District leaders must be able to anticipate how principals or parents will respond to any decision and plan accordingly. Too often, leaders fail to anticipate that there will be any response, leaving them unprepared to react, especially when the response is negative. But we also have known too many high-level district leaders who fear the consequences of their actions and believe they are powerless to effect change. They are more comfortable exercising leadership with their staff or the principals they supervise than problem solving with peers across the central offices. They compensate for their fear by keeping silent until they are confident about the right thing to say.

Equity warriors establish the conditions so that other leaders can be successful:

- Regular conversations—in groups and one-on-one—are essential to develop the safe space needed for learning.

- Clarifying the expectations and the authority to meet the expectations builds confidence.

- Reacting to setbacks as learning opportunities demonstrates commitment and leads to deeper understanding about the supports leaders need to provide to each other.

Equity warriors establish the conditions so that other leaders can be successful.

- Expecting and reinforcing a culture that recognizes the interdependence of each other's success on our individual success—my success depends on you being successful in accomplishing your work—is essential to moving the equity agenda across the organization.

Equity warriors know that cooperation and coordination around a shared objective has a better chance of success than dividing and pitting sides against one another.

YOUR MOVE: ALIGN YOUR DISTRICT BUDGET TO YOUR EQUITY AGENDA.

Equity warriors know that if you want to understand an organization's priorities, look at how it allocates and spends its money.

Equity warriors know that if you want to understand an organization's priorities, look at how it allocates and spends its money. Even when a community supports equity as a concept, the bottom line is . . . the bottom line. Once stakeholders understand the budget, they attend to how spending affects their interests, their families, and their students. When that happens, people's true colors emerge.

School district budgets are resilient. People, history, and outcomes are among the reasons that budgets are able to withstand radical changes:

- **People:** In most school districts, 80 to 90 percent of district budgets fund people. Many of these people are providing services that directly affect students and families. In most districts, a high percentage of central office positions perform operations, human resource, compliance, or accountability functions. Typically, state and federal dollars fund a good number of positions. Collective bargaining and working conditions agreements determine changes in positions and salaries. This is all to suggest that, even if school boards were inclined to change budgets, most changes can be made only at the fringes.

- **History:** Each dollar in the budget has a reason for being where it is. Some states legislate how dollars are allocated with different degrees of specificity. Schools, programs, and positions are often created because of interest or pressure from the community or board members, or in response to a particular situation. During times of budget tightening, the programs and initiatives that are the most recent additions—the ones that have the least history and were most likely created with discretionary dollars—are likely to be the first to be cut.

- **Outcomes:** Reflecting back on earlier chapters, there are few objective measures for determining optimal funding levels. We know more affluent communities support public education when they entrust their children to the schools. Federal and state funding are available for students with disabilities, students whose families qualify for reduced-price meals, and multilingual learners because the data tell us they need more support to close opportunity gaps. Yet, there are little data suggesting that we can predict outcomes based on investment.

Equity warriors know broad community support is the best pathway for either increasing or protecting funding for the equity agenda. Community support is personal—equity warriors are convinced it is the right thing to do for their community, and it is the right thing to do for themselves. The strategies mentioned in Chapter 1—universal preK, promises to hold harmless—are examples of how broad support is gained when budgets are not being threatened. Convincing external audiences requires the strong narrative, compelling data about effect, and a critical mass of people able to influence their opinions. It means making moves necessary to set the stage for reasoned confrontation.

Equity warriors know broad community support is the best pathway for either increasing or protecting funding for the equity agenda.

Equity warriors strive to have their budget reflect their values and highlight areas of the budget that do so. One example of a values-enhanced budget comes from Boston Public Schools, which, like at least 27 other U.S. districts (Levin et al., 2019), has instituted a weighted student funding formula (Boston Public Schools, 2020, slides 7–31).

Boston Public Schools, the largest district in Massachusetts, serves 54,000 students, of whom 43 percent are Latinx, 33 percent are Black, 14 percent are white, 9 percent are Asian, and 32 percent are multilingual learners. After years of discussion, the school district was successful in introducing its weighted student funding formula in 2011–2012. The formula is intended to provide equitable funding based on the needs of each school's student population and increased transparency and flexibility across the district. Weights are assigned to the following categories: grade level, three levels of disability severity (low, medium, and high), multilingual learners, students whose education was limited or interrupted, high risk, economic disadvantage,

(Continued)

(Continued)

and program supports. The weights are calculated to generate per-pupil funding for each school based on the needs of its student population. The higher the weighted number, the more money the school receives.

In addition, the formula enables the superintendent to supplement allocations to stabilize schools based on school size or changing enrollment patterns. Each school receives foundation dollars to fund the principal, school secretary, a nurse, and basic supplies. Funding for some direct services to schools, such as special education coordinators, are in the central office budget. Schools receive a "sustainability allocation" to ensure they meet all compliance requirements. Schools might qualify for additional foundation funds based on concentrations of students in weighted factors such as poverty and homelessness.

In addition to tying funding to students and more transparency to the budget process, principals have more autonomy and flexibility to allocate funds to address student needs. Principals do not have complete flexibility as they are constrained by certain nonnegotiable staff positions, collective bargaining agreements, and resource limitations. Yet, they have the authority to allocate percentages of the operational funds to meet the needs of their student population. The central office monitors expenditures. Schools that overspend their budgets in one year will see their allocation reduced in the next (Boston Public Schools, 2020, slides 7–31).

Using weighted student funding formulas is one way districts show their values. Weighted student funding formulas produce winners and losers. One of the intended outcomes of the formula is to encourage schools to attract and retain students who are weighted more heavily. Doing so increases funding but may not result in better services for students. It will be interesting to learn whether increasing competition across schools for students who are weighted more heavily results in more of these students attending higher-performing schools and whether higher-performing schools are adequately prepared to serve students well.

Equity warriors know direct warfare happens when individuals with position authority stand in the way.

Equity warriors know direct warfare happens when individuals with position authority stand in the way. Those who hold position authority include school board members representing more affluent communities and stakeholders within the district, elected officials having direct control or budget approval, media influencers, opinion makers, and other power brokers. It can also mean coalitions or individuals able to exert influence over those who have position authority. All politics are local. In some communities, power brokers change over time. In others, they remain the same.

Successful equity warriors know who might stand in the way or attempt to divert funding to a different agenda. Equity warriors make judgments about the appetite for the changes, timing, and seriousness of the opposition. Being strategic is knowing how far to push, when to push, and who to push. Some equity warriors prefer to sacrifice themselves for the cause by reaching well beyond the limits of acceptance and refusing to compromise. It might seem heroic to do so—be bold or go home. Most often, it means the end of their effectiveness and/or their position. Equity warriors know that a failed attack can undermine future efforts.

YOUR MOVE: MAKE NO EXCUSES.

Organizational culture—which we define as the way we do things—is anchored in relationships among individuals and between individuals and the organization. District leaders know relationships are vitally important for moving any agenda. Without relationships, ideas and plans stall, information is not shared, credibility is undermined, power is lost, and personal effectiveness is questioned. Position authority rarely compensates for the inability to create relationships.

District leaders build relationships over time. Often, relationships are transactional—creating bonds with people who will have your back as you have their backs. Sometimes district leaders purposefully mentor others to extend their influence across the organization or into the future. The number of people bonding together in a circle of trust is typically few. Yet, relationships among like-minded people can be powerful, especially when a convergence of values transcends gaining personal power or future advancement. We have observed this when a leader has arrived in a position that has been her goal—a head of a department or in a particular role—and does not aspire to any other position. Her purpose is solely to advance a particular mission—for example, arts education—and she builds relationships within and external to the organization with like-minded individuals.

A district leader's relationship with the organization also changes over time. Traditional pathways through which one moves up the ladder to positions of increasing responsibility require years of experience and maturing. The experiences temper and reshape one's attitudes toward the organization and influence one's perspective on what is and what is not possible. Weighing risk versus reward, effort against competing interests, and future opportunity versus current expectations are on the minds of district leaders who we have coached and counseled over the years. Where they are in their lives—age, family, financially—contribute to an individual's relationship to the organization. The default is to exercise caution and not rock the boat in ways that would disturb existing relationships.

Equity warriors know that rocking the boat is essential if you want to address systemic racism and advance an equity agenda. Equilibrium and comfort are the enemies of change strategies. Yet, one cannot lead if no one is following. The challenge is how to create disequilibrium in order to redirect the culture without destroying relationships. Equity warriors have at least three tools at their disposal: providing cover, strategically placing disruptors, and confronting opposition.

> *Equity warriors know that rocking the boat is essential if you want to address systemic racism and advance an equity agenda.*

Providing cover. District leaders set expectations and advance an equity agenda through their words, actions, and directives. We offer an example from New York City.

In New York City, as it is in other places, school leaders join in professional learning programs to sharpen their leadership skills. As a best practice, principals commit to using their learning and experiences to design and implement a project, which is presented to a public audience in a showcase event.

One New York City principal's project was to detrack her middle school. She was a veteran principal and had been the school's leader for nearly a decade. The school had a reputation as high performing, it served a large and diverse population, and the principal had support and strong relationships with staff and families. In her presentation, the principal spoke about the history of grouping students by abilities at her school and said students of color were overrepresented in lower tracks. Believing tracking was a form of implicit bias, she committed to changing the schedules so that all students would be heterogeneously grouped.

Yet, scheduling in a large school was difficult, so she and her staff developed algorithms to detrack students. She was successful in leading the school staff, students, and families through the technical and adaptive challenges to face assumptions about students' abilities and prepare for a new beginning. They trusted her and her judgment, and she was able to exert her will in the face of opposition.

While admiring the equity stance and leadership of the principal, the audience wondered why it had taken so long for a leader who believed in equity and could expend ample political capital to act on her equity agenda. The answer was that New York City Chancellor Richard Carranza had begun a citywide conversation about systemic bias and racism. He had created the conditions for school leaders to act on their beliefs. The time was right, and the principal acted.

We have witnessed similar situations in other districts when school leaders have lived with inequitable practices that were not consistent with their values and beliefs about sound instructional practices. Sometimes prodding change is as easy as giving permission and watching equity warriors show up. It can be most effective when a superintendent directs change by working with the school board to create policy or by sending directives outlining expectations and having district leaders follow up to support implementation. We supported one school that was slow to detrack. Teachers whose children attended the school opposed heterogeneous grouping, apparently because their own children might no longer be included in high-ability groups. Yet, other schools had complied with the superintendent's directive, and the message was clear across the district. Because the superintendent had made clear his desires and because other principals were moving ahead, this school's principal eventually maneuvered the scheduling change with little opposition. But she believed she had to wait for various signals to be in place before it was safe for her to act.

Strategically placing disruptors. Strategically placed disruptors who have an equity agenda and know how to play the game can create the disequilibrium necessary to effect change. We turn to another example from San Diego Unified.

California school boards have options in setting graduation requirements. In 2009, the San Diego Unified board, in an effort to raise rigor and prepare students for college and careers, decided to require students intending to graduate in 2016 to complete courses that fulfilled what is known as the California university system "A-G" graduation requirements. Completing courses approved by the university system with a grade of 2.0 or better

(Continued)

(Continued)

and a GPA of 3.0 would qualify students to enter the University of California and California State University systems. Only one other large California district had done the same. The board faced critics who thought more rigorous graduation requirements were unfair to students who had been traditionally underserved and that the expectations were set too high for students to reach in a few years.

In fall 2014, a year after Cindy Marten assumed the San Diego Unified superintendency, the board had a sense of urgency about knowing whether students were on track to graduate on time, particularly for multilingual learners and students of color. Chief of Staff Staci Monreal created the position of high school resource officer, and for the position she tapped Cheryl Hibbeln, a high school principal who demonstrated success in raising the achievement of all students, including multilingual learners. Monreal and Hibbeln began the 2014–2015 year by engaging board members and the instructional cabinet, which included all area superintendents, in reviewing data and analyzing barriers to students graduating on time. Area superintendents developed action plans to have high school principals keep track of student progress toward graduation.

Marten, Monreal, and Hibbeln were courageous in sharing the projections that surfaced doubts about raising the graduation rates. Doing so heightened the attention on high schools to delve deeply into problem solving. The high school resource office reviewed the transcripts of every student in the class of 2016. What they discovered was unsettling. Incoming 9th graders who were multilingual learners were placed in courses that did not grant A-G credit. Further, while some students were newcomers, many had been in the district for several years and either had not qualified for reclassification or had not been tested. Students did not have the opportunity to graduate on time because the course offerings were a barrier for them to do so.

The district employed a combination of strategies to help students recover credits, have better counseling supports, and take courses for A–G credit. As a result, 91 percent of San Diego Unified's class of 2016 graduated, the highest graduation rate among large urban districts in the state. Although only 60 percent of students met the university entrance requirements, the percentage was 13 points higher than in 2012 (Koran, 2017).

Efforts did not end there. In spite of area superintendents' supervision of principals, some principals did not change schedules as needed and did not provide supports to all students. In some cases, principals were deferring to teachers or delegating responsibility for creating the master schedule to others. Through several day-long institutes, the high school resource office helped all principals learn how to design a master schedule that would best serve student needs.

San Diego Unified continues to have the highest high school graduation rate of California's large urban districts. More important, for the class of 2017, there was only a 3 percent gap between the overall graduation rate and the graduation rate of Black students and a 5 percent gap for the graduation rate of Latinx students.

Helping principals change their master schedules was not popular and was met with strong resistance. One element that the New York City and San Diego Unified examples have in common is that the tools to address bias and improve student achievement are known to those within the system. Disruptors who know the levers to pull, who are supported, who are willing to take risks, and who *will not make excuses* get results!

Confronting opposition. There are times when there is no alternative but to take a stand. Equity warriors know the extent that they can be pushed and when stepping back places them in an unsustainable situation. Standing up for the right thing is the right thing to do. Let us be clear: Standing up for the right thing does not mean taking an extreme position. In warfare, the purpose is to obtain the objective, not eliminate the opposition. Opposing forces need to be able to adjust when beaten; otherwise, their resolve is strengthened.

When equity warriors place a line in the sand, opponents can shift their strategy to attacking the equity warrior rather than addressing the issue. The problem becomes the person, not the issue. After all, letting someone resign over a principle is easier than addressing complex problems. Transparency and directness are effective tactics that result in either wins or compromises that allow the progress.

Equity warriors use values-enhanced leadership in warfare to pressure those who oppose their equity agenda.

Equity warriors use values-enhanced leadership in warfare to pressure those who oppose their equity agenda. We conclude this section by suggesting that the moves and examples point out that no one can advance an equity agenda alone. There is no superhero able to vanquish the opposition. No one can be left out of responsibility to address bias and systemic racism.

Equity warriors align and connect systems to values and seek and create teams of like-minded individuals who use transparency and directness to question the current reality. They make no excuses for advancing their equity agenda.

REFLECTION: *Where are the inconsistencies between your values and current systems? Which colleagues exhibit values that are closest to yours? Which colleagues are your allies? Do they share and act in ways that demonstrate your values?*

_____

_____

_____

_____

_____

_____

_____

_____

School leaders communicate and live their values, and expect the same from others

☞ POLITICS: HELP OTHERS STAND WITH YOU

Equity warriors imbue their values in their every action—especially in how they show leadership and balance conflicts among competing interests. At the school level, they make their values explicit and encourage those closest to the problems to take responsibility and make decisions.

Equity warriors lead by working through and with other people. While school leaders share responsibility for the success of all students enrolled in their schools, their primary responsibility is to lead the school community. We have worked with several principals who devote hours to nurturing students one-on-one. While we admire their intent, committing time to the growth and development of one student can come at a cost to the majority of students and staff. In one case, we were unsuccessful at breaking the principal of her practice of spending a few hours every day with the same student who was acting out. The school was in chaos due to her lack of leadership, teachers transferred because they felt unsupported, and student enrollment declined.

School leaders cannot delegate responsibility for leading the school and pointing to the North Star. As they work with and through people, they realize their control is limited to their decision making and their motivation for making their decisions. Even in the smallest school, they cannot control how others respond to their decisions, particularly facing complex situations when consensus on the best path is difficult to reach.

Equity warriors know that being explicit about their values can provide clear direction for how to lead.

Equity warriors know that being explicit about their values can provide clear direction for how to lead. They recognize the interdependency of every member within the community. They live their values by setting the expectation that everyone is a leader and by creating a vision, a framework, and systems for building or resetting the organizational culture necessary to achieve an equity agenda.

YOUR MOVE: BE A VISIONARY VALUES-ENHANCED LEADER FROM THE START.

Why are we here? In the day-to-day of fulfilling operational responsibilities, supporting adults, and caring for students, school leaders have difficulty finding time to reflect on their vision for the school. District leaders do not help often enough. Too often, when we ask a newly appointed principal about the goals identified for them by their supervisor, they reply, "I don't know" or "Nothing really." We are no longer surprised by that response. When we began coaching principals 25 years ago, district leaders typically gave principals the keys to the school and very little guidance. The message was that principals should take the first year to learn their school, master operations, figure out what they needed to know, and try not to bother district leaders with questions others could answer. Principals could expect district leaders to check in with them the following summer. Principals frequently described their first year as learning to swim by being tossed into the deep end of the pool.

Most often, principals learn about their schools informally. In some instances, incoming and outgoing principals have a few days or weeks to compare notes when a leadership transition has been planned. There are better ways. Long Beach Unified School District provides an example of a formal process that enables principals to exchange information about a school.

The Change of Principal Workshop has been part of the Long Beach Way for decades. Within the first few weeks after a new principal enters her school, she is invited to a four-hour workshop where she will learn from the school staff about what is working and what needs to change. A district-appointed facilitator, typically a retired principal, leads the conversation among teachers, administrators, guidance counselors, office staff, and custodians who have been selected to represent their colleagues. Representatives often have checked in with colleagues before the workshop or check in with them during breaks to ensure they are presenting a fair view of their colleagues' observations.

The new principal joins the workshop at the beginning and participates in icebreaker activities but steps away during the bulk of the conversation to allow the staff to speak more freely. She returns to hear the results of the deliberations.

Participants respond to three questions beginning in small groups: What is working? What can be improved? What does your new principal need to know that will help her be an effective leader?

(Continued)

(Continued)

The deliberations are taken seriously. Participants are selected to report the summary of their conversations, particularly the strengths of the school. The summary includes three recommendations for long-term change and three recommendations for immediate attention by the principal.

Although the principal is invited back to hear the summary comments, she is not allowed to respond to reports in the moment. After the session, the facilitator prepares notes from the chart paper, anonymous individual responses to the questions, and anonymous responses to open-ended evaluations that prompted participants to share messages they did not feel comfortable surfacing during the workshop. The notes are provided to the principal, the principal's supervisor, and the district coordinator.

Over time, Long Beach has adapted its process, recounts Cynthia Terry, a highly respected member of Long Beach Unified and one who participated in the process as a new principal three times and as a facilitator of a few dozen sessions (Terry, personal interview, Aug. 9, 2020).

In the beginning, only the principal saw the notes, and she had discretion to respond. More recently, principals meet with their supervisor to review the recommendations, develop a response, and determine expectations for the principal's leadership. This step increases transparency and accountability for all involved.

Understanding the context of the school quickly enables equity warriors to be on solid ground as they communicate their purpose. Clarity of purpose is a theme that runs throughout each chapter of this book. It cannot be overstated. Equity warriors begin by clarifying their purpose from the beginning. One way of doing so is to develop and announce an entry plan.

Superintendents often have an entry plan. Sometimes they develop their plan after participating in a listening-and-learning tour. Other times, a committee is formed from a cross-section of stakeholders to gather information and provide recommendations about the district's assets and challenges. Sometimes districts hire an external firm to conduct a program or financial audit to provide guidance for an incoming superintendent. Although they are not common, each of these practices deserves consideration by leaders new to the school.

The few school-based entry plans we have seen include the following:

- **Goals:** What is to be accomplished through the entry process?
- **Sequenced focus areas:** What is the focus of the principal's first 30, 60, and 90 days? What are the deliverables or outcomes for each focus area?
- **District due dates:** What are the district's required deliverables calendared throughout the year (e.g., budgets, evaluations, annual reporting, state reporting requirements) that principals can anticipate?
- **Off-campus meetings:** What are the calendared district professional learning and/or operational meetings?
- **Schedule of activities:** Month-by-month activities and meetings.

Not everything that is urgent can be done at once. Having a plan enables school leaders to pace their work by anticipating due dates and finding times in their schedules for meetings and tasks. Making the entry plan public to the school community allows the school leader to invite input into how she will gather and share information, and it helps her manage her time. It also helps teachers, staff, families, and community members know when they will be involved.

Entry plans are better when they are simple. Districts can preload information about district priorities, expectations, and due dates, as well as links to agendas, forms, and documents. We have helped school supervisors and principals set entry plan goals to clarify expectations for each party. Having agreement on a few goals establishes what is most important, what is reasonable to accomplish, what is acceptable evidence to measure progress, the support available from the supervisor, and the timeline. Principals and their supervisors can reach agreements quickly and with less formality and more effectiveness than in typical evaluation processes.

Entry plans rarely include explicit values statements, particularly those specific to the equity agenda. This is a missed opportunity. By stating values upfront, equity warriors can frame conversations as well as their information gathering. Interviewees can get to the point because they know what is most important to the new school leader. Transparency about the questions helps eliminate surprises when the principal shares his conclusions.

Whether an entry plan is used or not, veteran school leaders tell us that they wished they had started with values when creating a vision, framework, and/or systems aimed at achieving an equity agenda. School leaders communicate their values in multiple ways as the following two examples illustrate.

Valerie Jurado was appointed principal of Bethune K–8 School in San Diego Unified School District in the middle of the 2015–2016 school year. She was the school's fourth principal in five years. In her first principalship and facing a veteran staff, she met resistance and passive-aggressive behavior from staff who—based on her predecessors—were uncertain of her commitment to remaining at the school. Further, the Bethune neighborhood was in transition. Black and Latinx students were replacing the Filipino-majority students. An uncertain economy created pressures on families. Teachers were struggling with students who came from families less able to support them academically. The absence of consistent leadership also created a culture of isolation. Teachers resisted coaching from the principal or anyone outside the school. Instruction was poor, and test scores and enrollment were dropping. It was a school stuck in time.

During the summer following her first full year, Jurado determined to develop systems and structures around her values and began the process to alter the Bethune culture to align with her vision. She had articulated her beliefs frequently but realized she had to do more. Jurado began by crystalizing her values in language that described outcomes for students. She worked with her leadership team to revise and clarify the following vision statement before sharing it with teachers and staff at the opening of her second school year:

> It is our commitment that all students are college and career ready and demonstrate proficiency in literacy and numeracy at all grade levels. Students develop scholarly behaviors and social/emotional coping strategies to support them in reaching long-term academic goals. (Valerie Jurado, personal communication, Aug. 23, 2017)

The vision statement includes specific examples of student behaviors that define proficiency, behaviors, and coping strategies. The statement was accompanied by a set of expectations for teachers, including teaching practices expected in every classroom. The expectations were accompanied by a description of the systems that would be in place to support teachers in meeting expectations. The systems included a schedule of professional learning and resources that teachers would be encouraged or required to use.

Equity warriors know that just announcing values is not enough to change organizational culture and overcome resistance. Bethune teachers did not argue with the vision. Many believed they were performing at the levels articulated in the vision. Only a few were.

Another example focuses on systems and structures, rather than articulating beliefs, to achieve an access and equity vision.

Equity warriors know that just announcing values is not enough to change organizational culture and overcome resistance.

> Christina Casillas, principal of Roosevelt International Middle School in San Diego Unified, built a systems-based approach to articulate her values-enhanced vision. Casillas had two years of experience as principal of a small high school before being asked to lead the 1,000-student middle school. Casillas began by building trusting relationships with the staff, understanding the strengths and growth areas for each of her teachers, taking principled leadership stands on improving rigor, and developing systems of support.
>
> As the systems emerged over time, Casillas was careful to show connections between the work of the previous year as she added in the next year. Her theory of action—a number of systems and supports that if fully implemented would result in desired outcomes—was anchored in fostering equity and access so that all students would reach proficiency (see Figure 4.1). Creating and maintaining a positive school culture and climate for students and staff was a priority at the large middle school.
>
> Casillas frequently referenced her theory of action when she spoke at staff meetings, professional learning sessions, and start-of-school and end-of-the-year retreats as a way to remind educators about her goals for the year (Casillas, 2018). By providing constant reminders and ways of connecting initiatives and supports, teachers and staff could see the school's direction and progress and know they were part of a systemic response to achieve the school's equity agenda.

Each of these vision statements keeps students at the center. Pithy slogans, such as "Students First," are helpful reminders but have little meaning. Equity warriors may begin with a slogan to attract attention. However, unless the slogan is accompanied by a full vision that clarifies the direction and speaks to the path to achieving the vision—the what *and* the how—teachers and staff are unable to judge the seriousness of the effort, including what is asked of them.

FIGURE 4.1 ● Roosevelt International Middle School Theory of Action

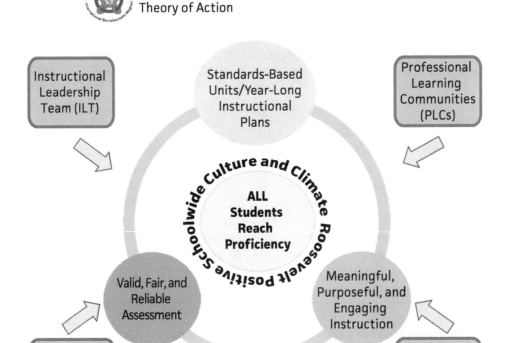

Source: Roosevelt International Middle School.

Equity warriors know teachers and staff focus on their teaching, their relationships with their close colleagues, the progress of their students, and their responsibilities. Therefore, flashing the vision statement at staff retreats, while important, is not enough to build understanding and support. Principals build understanding by inviting teachers and staff into the systems and frameworks and asking them to take on a leadership role. The more defined the role and task, the more likely the buy-in. Also, recognizing and celebrating the legitimate contributions of individuals and accomplishments of the school as a whole provides affirmation and a sense of progress. Being reminded of the vision allows teachers and staff to connect their specific contributions to the schoolwide effort.

We have been guilty of leaving students out of values-enhanced leadership. That is both a shortcoming and a missed opportunity. Not defining our work in terms that students can understand and connect to their daily learning prevents them from being active participants in improving a school's culture. When we intentionally teach values in our curriculum, the values often remain abstract and disconnected. We often fail to recognize the contributions students make in developing a school community and miss opportunities to build their skills. For example, instruction such as having students plant and maintain the school's garden as a biology or ecology lesson can be extended to learning about the school as a community. Many schools give students—even at a young age—a role in tending the garden to teach responsibility. Learning could be extended to help students see their school as a community and to enlist them as contributors, not just consumers, in building the school community.

Equity warriors make the leap from keeping students at the center of their leadership to engaging students as partners in leadership. Just as we know that leaders do their work through and with others, success comes by leading with students. We miss opportunities, especially with students who are school dependent, when we do not trust them with responsibility for shaping their school community starting at a young age. Equity warriors need students as allies and engage them as leaders.

Equity warriors make the leap from keeping students at the center of their leadership to engaging students as partners in leadership.

YOUR MOVE: CAREFULLY CHOOSE STIMULI TO FORGE COMMUNITY.

Competition—us versus them—is a familiar tool available to all leaders. Educators are not immune to attempts to use competition to motivate school leaders, teachers, and students. There are overt attempts to create competition such as comparing schools in external measures, establishing public charter schools, or tracking enrollment patterns to assess family preferences. In addition, there are more subtle ways to create competition such as by establishing programs that distinguish schools or parts of schools from others, or by comparing or promoting teachers, grade levels, departments, or groups of students over others. But using competition to motivate school leaders, teachers, and students is inconsistent with an equity agenda.

We raised some of the problems of pitting groups against one another in our discussion of the achievement gap in Chapter 1. An equity agenda cannot be successful if some students win and some lose. In addition to the overall mismatch of using competition to advance equity, competition does not fit with teachers' mindsets, and it does not promote student learning. Teachers primarily focus on their classrooms and their students. Frankly, we find most teachers are not very interested in what other teachers are doing. Suggesting that competition among teachers is motivational is misguided. Furthermore, students need a safe learning environment in which to learn. More important, students learn as much from other students as they do from their teachers, if not more than. For example, we studied student and teacher interactions in high school mathematics classes. We were interested in cracking the code about why some students were successful while others were not. In classrooms where students were successful, students frequently reached out to other students to augment the teacher's description of solving a problem. Sometimes students would walk across the classroom to ask another student for help while the teacher was explaining his approach.

School leaders can struggle with the unintended consequences of instituting programs that help students find their academic courses to be more relevant to their lives. For example, many large high schools created small learning communities to better engage students by increasing student personalization and relevance of the course of studies. High school campuses were divided into small schools, each with a professional theme (e.g., health services, public safety), course of studies, and administrative and teaching staff largely independent of the other schools on campus. Although the intention was to better connect students with their teachers and academic program, the schools—sometimes subtly and sometimes overtly—competed for the "best students" and "best teachers" on campus. Some small schools were deemed successful when their achievement levels and student population grew while others struggled from shifts in student enrollment and teacher transfers. More than once, when competition resulted in unhealthy tensions among schools, we were asked to help high schools recombine small schools into a single campus.

School leaders also use external pressures to motivate teachers and students, such as through state testing or school designation, district directives or initiatives, community pressures, declining enrollments, or colocation of a charter school. These create challenges to an equity agenda akin to competition but with a difference. Relying on external pressures for motivation represents a "transfer of responsibility" where the implicit message is that something that they do not agree to is being forced upon them. The transfer of responsibility allows school leaders, teachers, staff, and students to blame someone other than themselves for their problems and the situations they face. Hearing phrases such as "the district says we must . . . ," "the state says we must . . . ," or "a charter school has opened in a space we can no longer utilize because of declining enrollment . . ." are some

Equity warriors know that using competition could ignite rather than balance conflicts.

of the ways external pressures are described. In some cases, the pressures are outside the school's control. Nevertheless, the transfer of responsibility results in temporary fixes applied to a school's problems. If the fix fails, fault lies with the external initiator. It is also temporary because schools know the external pressure will be short term. This, too, shall pass.

Equity warriors know that using competition could ignite rather than balance conflicts. They know that unless managed, competition is harmful to their equity agenda. They also know that blaming others for the current situation shows that they have not assumed responsibility and that their analysis of the situation is limited. In other words, blaming is not leadership. It looks back rather than moves people forward.

Equity warriors lead with their values. They know having integrity means that each of us is personally accountable for those things within our sphere of influence. Finding who to blame does little good to advancing equity. There is too much blame to affix.

Equity warriors do not rely on stimuli external to the school to motivate teachers, staff, and students. Nevertheless, as discussed in Chapter 2, they don't ignore the external perceptions of their school and the conditions. They just don't dwell on the external. For example, administrators and teachers from a charter school colocated with one of our partner schools greeted its students and parents at the front gate every morning. Before long, the partner school principal and a few of her teachers were doing the same. Fortunately, the partner school principal was open to learning a practice that would deepen family confidence in the school.

Equity warriors apply systems-thinking tools, such as naming the current conditions as well as the desired state, to map out their plan for closing gaps between where they are and where they want to be. They use an asset-based approach to find and build on internal strengths. For example, rather than pit teachers against one another, equity warriors identify which teachers are having success with their students and replicate what they are doing that contributes to that success.

Equity warriors identify which teachers are having success with their students and replicate what they are doing that contributes to that success.

Equity warriors look inward first for stimuli rather than looking out. They know that people learn best when they discover things for themselves. They also know that changes in practice that are self-initiated are more likely to be sustained than those introduced from the outside. They look for ideas within the school that stimulate interest and build a community of learners. In finding the ideas, they also find allies who can influence others through their actions.

YOUR MOVE: FORM ALLIANCES WITH FAMILIES AND PARTNERS WHO SHARE YOUR AGENDA.

In the preceding chapters, we examined some of the opportunities, benefits, and challenges associated with engaging community members and families in school partnerships. School leaders and teachers recognize the importance of family support for student learning. While schools alone cannot address the societal and economic inequities and challenges facing neighborhoods and families, there is little consensus on the school's role. In addition, school leaders are often not consulted in planning economic, housing, community, and social development initiatives, though such decisions affect them.

Leaders struggle with determining how to engage community partners. They are eager to ensure that students receive supports and resources that will contribute to their success. School leaders risk damaging their relationships with the community when they refuse assistance and support from community partners. The word spreads quickly that the leaders were not receptive to much-needed help. Nevertheless, school leaders need to be vigilant in protecting schools and students. In addition to the added work and security risks, community partners have their own agendas.

Equity warriors are able to reinforce the role schools play in advancing equity to the future benefit of students, families, and their neighborhoods while keeping community partners supportive and contributing in ways that do not interfere with the school's operations.

Equity warriors can reduce conflicts by sharing information about current conditions and future expectations while also listening to concerns from the community. Unfortunately, as families exercise choice in selecting schools, defining the community served by the school becomes more difficult. In addition, demographic trends and mobility disconnect school populations from social institutions in the community. For example, we partnered with a high school in a historically Black community that had social institutions created for the benefit of its community. Because of changing demographics, Latinx students came to be the overwhelming majority of the school's population. The changing demographics created a dilemma for the community's social institutions that were reluctant to embrace and include diverse populations.

Speaking at churches and meetings of civic, athletic, and social groups regularly helps create relationships and understanding that builds trust. Social media can play a role in this as well, but social media is more effective after relationships are established. Equity warriors must be seen. The politically savvy equity warrior is able to reinforce the role schools play in advancing equity to the future benefit of students, families, and their neighborhoods while keeping community partners supportive and contributing in ways that do not interfere with the school's operations. Internships, mentoring, counseling, employment, and athletic opportunities can exist beyond school time and under the supervision of the community.

Trust is key to building family and community confidence in schools. Families are more likely to trust schools and school leaders when schools demonstrate effectiveness in student learning, have a stable student population, and have no racial and ethnic tensions (Bryk & Schneider, 2002). Even in schools that have the confidence of families, relationship building continues to be critical to advancing equity.

Equity warriors use a variety of cutting-edge and traditional methods and structures to build confidence in schools, depending on their context. They use these methods and structures to continually reinforce their espoused values. For example, schools can organize community conversations about race. They can do so directly by providing a forum for discussions or information sharing through Zoom meetings and webinars. They can also do so indirectly by providing guidance on how to have conversations. Obviously, care needs to be taken to not be preachy. Still, equity warriors can fill a need among students and families of all racial, ethnic, and economic backgrounds by showing how to talk about race and values that students hold.

Equity warriors also use traditional practices and structures available to them. School-based advisory boards, family and social organizations, athletic boosters, and family outreach coordinators can contribute to furthering the equity agenda. Sometimes participants in these organizations need to learn to lead and communicate within their organization. Often, they just need to be asked to be part of the equity agenda. As with community organizations, the purposes are to build relationships, espouse values, develop confidence in the school, and activate social networks. School leaders who have families on their side have strong allies and advocates.

Trust and confidence are difficult to build without contact. Families of all backgrounds make the effort to be present for student performances and recognition ceremonies. As the following example illustrates, equity warriors find creative ways to recognize students, including showcasing their academic performance.

In 2007–2008, Flint Community Schools in Michigan's Lower Peninsula served more than 14,000 students. Under the leadership of Superintendent Linda Thompson and Chief Academic Officer Eugene Rutledge, the school district began implementing a readers/writers workshop approach to teaching English language arts from kindergarten through grade 12. Six units of study, one for each genre with the state standards, guided instruction for a daily two-hour literacy block. The school's academic schedules built in time for publishing parties that would celebrate students as authors.

Over three weeks, students worked through the unit of study as they brainstormed ideas, prepared drafts, critiqued each other's drafts, and rewrote their papers until they had a piece ready to "publish." Principals invited families to attend grade-level publishing parties that were scheduled for different times so that families could attend multiple parties if they had more than one child in the school.

At the parties, adults and students sat in circles on the classroom floor while students took turns sitting in the centrally located author's chair, reading their papers aloud. Much to the surprise of district and school staff, the publishing parties were well attended by families even in high-poverty neighborhoods where adults took time off from their jobs to be present. Not only did families see their children blossom as authors, but they were able to see the iterations of drafts and feedback stapled to the final paper. The combination of seeing students perform with pride in their accomplishment, having evidence of the teaching process and products, and participating in an authentic celebration of academic success was a powerful confidence builder for all involved.

Equity warriors seize opportunities to engage families in celebrating learning for the benefit of everyone.

Equity warriors seize opportunities to engage families in celebrating learning for the benefit of everyone. Technology—and increasing access to devices for all students—opens opportunities for families to appreciate and gain confidence in their schools by seeing student work. Just to be clear, we are not advocating for daily school events to be broadcast, nor is it necessary to do so. Communicating via technology is not an adequate substitute for personal contact. Nevertheless, organizing and sharing performances of student work is so much more powerful for all involved than sending home student projects crumpled in the backpack. Especially as we rush from assignment to assignment to address all the necessary content, pausing to celebrate learning is important.

Equity warriors realize that schools are social institutions that are vital to their communities. School leaders must involve others as they work to build public confidence in their schools by espousing values, building trust, and engaging with families and communities. Schools cannot achieve their equity agenda alone.

YOUR MOVE: COMMUNICATE YOUR VALUES THROUGH WORD AND DEED.

To state the obvious, school leaders are part of their school's community. Unlike district leaders, they have the opportunity to continuously reinforce their values through proximity to teachers, staff, and students. Their actions are also closely scrutinized because of proximity. Equity warriors walk the talk. They act in ways that demonstrate that they know schools are less of an organization than a community.

Equity warriors are not alone in recognizing that they are community leaders. In *Turn the Ship Around! A True Story of Turning Followers into Leaders* (Marquet, 2012), a U.S. Navy captain recounts the steps taken over two years to turn the crew of the submarine *USS Santa Fe* from having poor morale, poor performance, and the worst retention rate in the fleet into a top-performing crew. The transformation was accomplished, as the title suggests, by valuing the leadership potential in everyone working in the submarine.

There are surprising similarities between schools and naval submarines. Both are communities with their own culture, often isolated, and able to operate independently of direct supervision for periods of time. There is something about operating underwater that underscores the critical nature of interdependence and having a strong, positive culture.

Also, like any complex organization, schools and submarines have staffs with technical expertise and deep knowledge of their job functions. Of course, educators and sailors are working toward different outcomes, and leaders measure efficiency and effectiveness differently. Nevertheless, protocols and procedures in schools and submarines rely on human judgment and competence, particularly when situations are nuanced as they often are when dealing with complexity. As in schools, the effect of frequent changes among naval leaders and personnel places a priority on continuity, communication, and culture.

I should not have been surprised that a submarine captain would lead with his values as he tried to improve effectiveness and morale. The captain valued the leadership potential in everyone. Therefore, he ensured that those closest to the action had the authority to act. In schools, teachers would ideally have full authority for educating students because they are the ones closest to the action. But, since the standards era, teachers have seen their authority to make decisions diminish. Instructional leadership teams, grade-level teams, and department teams rarely are clear about the parameters of their authority. As a result, they often are unwilling to accept responsibility for their actions and often are reluctant to test new approaches, lest they make an error.

There are some structural and organizational barriers to devolving authority and responsibility. Frankly, if school leaders are not intentional and present in leading teachers to act and take responsibility, only some teachers would do so on their own. Most of the barriers are personal and depend on the willingness to act or take responsibility for the overall conditions in our community. Sometimes, luck enters into a situation, as the following example from my experience illustrates.

Early in my career, I was fortunate to have assembled a team of talented, smart, and hard-working individuals. They were very good at their jobs and shared the same values. Though they all "wore the same team jersey," they were not a team. They were organized as a bicycle wheel—I was in the center, and they were on the rim, familiar with each other but really connected only by the center. This structure was somewhat effective, comfortable, and definitely flattering for the leader. Nevertheless, I had made a decision to move on from my role and was struggling with how to sustain the work and the team during transition.

After a few attempts at succession planning, something unexpected happened. We had the opportunity to take on a new initiative, which required us to rethink how we were organized. We scheduled a half-day planning session, designed an agenda with clear objectives, and the team prepared for the discussion. Now, I had been one of those people fortunate to not miss many days of work because of illness. However, on the day of the planning session, I awoke violently ill—unable to move from bed. I called to inform one of my colleagues. Her immediate reply was that she would contact the group and postpone the meeting until I could join them. I urged them to meet as planned and for her to report back on progress at the end of the day.

She reported that they had made progress, met longer than scheduled, and decided to reconvene the next day with the hope that I would join them. Hiding that I was no longer feeling ill, I asked that they meet without me the next day. The deadline for our redesign was a few days away, and they should continue to make progress. I added that I was looking for them to agree on a recommendation and would concur with their decision if they were agreed.

The report after the second planning meeting was encouraging. They continued to make progress, but there were several heated disagreements about a few sticking points. They had agreed to meet again the next day and hoped I would be well enough to join them. I gave a few words of encouragement and appreciation, reiterated my support for their decision, and said that it was unlikely I would be well enough to join them before the deadline.

The report from the next day's planning session was less encouraging. There was no further progress, and the sticking points remained unresolved. My colleague's update outlined the points in contention and asked for my decision so that they could move the planning forward. My response was that I was not making this decision. I had every confidence in them. So, they needed to reach agreement before the due date.

No surprise, they did reach agreement, and they presented it the following week when I returned to the office. Their decision included compromises that were reasonable though not ideal. However, each person on the team concurred with the decision, and I held to my part of the agreement. To seal the deal, I asked the team to present the decision, their rationale, and the process to the final decision makers later in the day. They did so as a team. Mission accomplished!

Values-enhanced equity warriors design systems so that everyone can lead. We will provide several examples of how it is done in the next sections. We advise school leaders to begin with defining the purpose for bringing any group together or for holding any meeting. When establishing or expanding an instructional leadership team, we ask school leaders what they think teachers will want to know about the team before deciding to accept the invitation to join. Typical questions are, "How often will it meet?" "How much time will it take?" and "What do you want me to do?" While the practical considerations cannot be minimized, teachers are more likely to join if they know the purpose from the start. A small group of equity-focused teachers and staff who understand their purpose and are willing to assume and learn how to use authority to act are more effective than a larger, representative group who ask only, "What would you like me to do?"

Equity warriors realize that command and control are not effective in governing and resolving conflicts in schools.

Equity warriors realize that command and control are not effective in governing and resolving conflicts in schools. An equity agenda is best achieved when everyone in the school—teachers, staff, and students—is a leader for equity. They become leaders by having the opportunity to try and learn in a trusting setting, their decision-making authority is nurtured and recognized, they share a commitment to learning from each other, and they devote time for discussion and debate that deepens understanding. In short, equity warriors run their school as a leadership development program.

REFLECTION: *How do you know your equity vision and values are clearly articulated and understood by the school community? How are you engaging teachers, staff, students, families, and community members as partners in advancing the equity agenda?*

_____

_____

_____

_____

_____

_____

_____

_____

_____

_____

DIPLOMACY: LINK VALUES TO INTENDED OUTCOMES

Coaching new teachers is always refreshing work. They help us remember what it was like to learn to swim by jumping into the deep end of the pool! When we ask them why they entered the teaching profession, almost to a person, they talk about wanting to make a difference and to give students the opportunities to learn and grow that their teachers gave to them. They are inspiring and exciting.

But, sadly, few imagine themselves to be teachers in 5 to 10 years. We might be able to dismiss some of their anticipated departures as wanderlust since they really don't have any specific future in mind. However, they share their disappointment in teaching and schools without hesitation. Many would not enroll their children—when they have them—in the schools where they teach. They describe the behavioral problems and lack of discipline—often attributed to dysfunctional parenting—that disrupt teaching and learning. Most of all, they are tired and overwhelmed by the enormous task of educating students and preparing them for success, and the lack of support and appreciation they receive from school leaders, families, and students themselves.

Equity warriors know they can do better to create school communities that are sensitive and effective in meeting the needs of teachers, staff, and students. They use the tools of diplomacy—rewards, consequences, and moral persuasion—to lead. They know that articulating and acting consistent with their values is essential but inadequate to reach their equity agenda. Thomas J. Sergiovanni's (1992) review of research on effective schools and school culture shows that effective school leaders operate on two dimensions: goodwill (what we call values) and success (that is, effectiveness in getting things done).

Equity warriors strive to stay true to their values and get things done by judicious use of tools of diplomacy in service to an equity agenda. In that way, they can build on the aspirations articulated by new teachers to be members of a values-enhanced community and address the concerns new teachers have voiced about system effectiveness.

Equity warriors strive to stay true to their values and get things done by judicious use of tools of diplomacy in service to an equity agenda.

YOUR MOVE: CREATE A PURPOSEFUL COMMUNITY.

Robert Marzano and colleagues (2005) describe a purposeful community as "one with collective efficacy and capability to develop and use assets to accomplish goals that matter to all community members through agreed-upon processes" (p. 99).

They define collective efficacy as a shared "belief that they can dramatically enhance the effectiveness of an organization" (p. 99). Teacher self-efficacy was discussed in Chapter 2. The idea that one's actions do make a difference is of critical importance to leadership and one that is often overlooked. The equity agenda is lost if educators do not believe that their daily efforts matter in the lives of the students they serve, and collectively with their colleagues, that their actions matter for all students in their community.

Marzano et al. (2005) used meta-analysis to identify 21 responsibilities or specific school leadership behaviors that have well-documented effects on student achievement (p. 99). Of these 21, they point to nine responsibilities that are foundational to creating purposeful communities. We have mentioned six of the responsibilities previously, including the following:

- Fostering shared beliefs and a sense of community and cooperation
- Communicating and operating strong ideals and beliefs about schooling
- Recognizing and celebrating accomplishments and acknowledging failures
- Inspiring and learning new and challenging innovations
- Having quality contacts and interactions with teachers and students
- Demonstrating awareness of the personal aspects of teachers and staff (p. 99)

We will consider the remaining three responsibilities in more detail:

- Establishing strong lines of communication with and among teachers and students
- Involving teachers in the design and implementation of important decisions and policies
- Knowing the undercurrents in the school's functioning and using the information to address current and anticipated problems (p. 99)

Equity warriors develop organizational structures that are purposeful and that work.

Equity warriors develop organizational structures that are purposeful and that work. The structures can be formal and regular, such as instructional leadership teams, department teams, and grade-level teams. They are most effective when clear lines of communication connect the structures and when members have the information necessary to make decisions. In the following example, Oakland High School demonstrates

FIGURE 4.2 ● Oakland High School PLCs

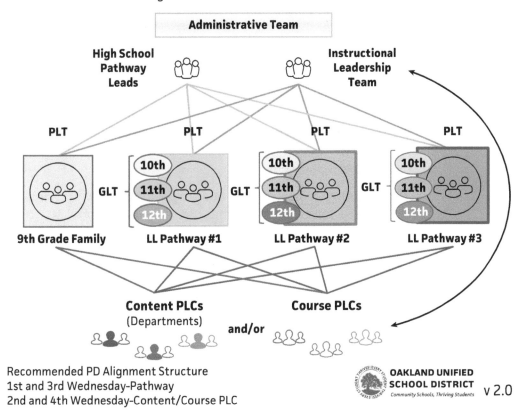

Recommended PD Alignment Structure
1st and 3rd Wednesday-Pathway
2nd and 4th Wednesday-Content/Course PLC

OAKLAND UNIFIED
SCHOOL DISTRICT
Community Schools, Thriving Students v 2.0

Source: Oakland Unified School District.

how it plans to improve communications and decision making (see Figure 4.2). Students entering 10th grade would choose one of three theme-based courses of study called pathways.

The instructional leadership team members were school administrators, department leads, and the leads of the three theme-based pathways. Each pathway had a pathway leadership Team that included the pathway lead and the lead of each grade-level team. The intent of this part of the structure was to ensure that there was a two-way vertical flow of information and decision making about pathway operations, student enrollment and programming, and resource distribution. In addition, Content Professional Learning Communities (PLCs) used common planning time and release days for department-focused professional learning and course design. Course PLCs served the same purpose for courses specific to a pathway but not affiliated with a department—typically when one or a few teachers were responsible for a specialty course within a pathway.

The Oakland High School example is typical of theme-based high schools where teachers have two roles. One role is a member of a pathway community. In this role, teachers support each other in making decisions about how their pathways are structured and operated. The other role is as a subject-matter colleague. In this other role, teachers work with colleagues who are outside of their pathway area and teach courses in the same subject area. In this way, for example, algebra teachers can plan lessons and improve their mathematics instructional strategies with other teachers who are part of another program and not in proximity to them. Through a system of PLCs, school leaders can ensure that all students across the programs are receiving similar, rigorous content.

Equity warriors communicate purpose and expectations for outcomes for elementary, middle, and high school teachers who are organized into grade-level or course-alike teams. The most purposeful communities use time for effective planning and collaboration and have accountability to their colleagues to communicate their outcomes. We advise school leaders to create simple templates for sharing outcomes from team meetings electronically. We suggest that the template contain no more than three or four questions, such as the following:

- What was the purpose of today's meeting?
- What are a few key accomplishments from today's meeting?
- What challenges or questions remain after today's meeting?
- What specific work should we plan to do before the next meeting?

Equity warriors build purposeful communities by following the maxim of form follows function, meaning to be clear about the work to accomplish before deciding how to accomplish it.

Collective efficacy is furthered when teams periodically communicate the outcomes of their meetings and their learning.

Equity warriors build purposeful communities by following the maxim of *form follows function*, meaning to be clear about the work to accomplish before deciding how to accomplish it. Scheduling a meeting and then preparing the agenda is backward. Work expands to fill the time available for it. We have also observed that smaller teams are more likely than larger teams to accomplish objectives. Putting the right people together for a common purpose can produce a powerful result, as the following example suggests.

The assistant principal, guidance counselor, social worker, nurse, custodian, other members of a San Diego Unified middle school administrative team, and a few teachers were determined to better support students considered at risk of failure or destined to fail. Under the assistant principal's leadership, they came together to brainstorm a list of 50 students whose attendance, discipline, academics, family situation, and/or mental health were of concern to them. The list was compiled quickly, and many of the adults around the table knew the students. Most of the team had come in contact with the students at one time or another.

They quickly agreed on 10 students who were most at risk. They discussed what they knew about the students, why they were at risk, and the support these students needed. Then, each adult at the table agreed to be the case manager for one student. The selected case managers were the ones who best knew the students or had knowledge or resources to support them.

The group met weekly and more frequently at their request at first. They relied on each other for support, advice, and encouragement. Case managers checked on their student daily and sometimes multiple times during the day and intervened as needed with the student's teachers and other service providers.

After about two weeks, the group saw enough progress with most of the initial 10 students to identify a few more students from their list and assign new case managers. The group's weekly meetings became check-ins to compare notes on students, acknowledge progress, move students off the list, and assign more students to case managers. The group learned that students responded to the attention from the case managers and the rest of the adults in the school. When students understood that the adults cared, the students cared more about their behaviors.

The list of students grew shorter. There were fewer meetings as the adults began to identify and case manage students outside the list. Case management became part of the school's culture.

The example is noteworthy for several reasons. Adults came together when there was agreement on a clear problem and a willingness to do something about it. The right people—those with the skills and desire to work on the problem—were at the table. They set manageable targets, problem solved, acknowledged success, and moved on when they were ready. Further, they used their situational awareness to identify problems and create solutions, the last of the nine responsibilities of school leaders who want to build a purposeful community.

Situational awareness requires time and openness to listen to the pulse of a purposeful community, to know when to push, when to go slow, when to be hard, and when to be compassionate. Equity warriors rely on others to be honest and willing to share information about what is really happening or what people are really feeling or thinking. Situational awareness is essential to advancing equity. Without it, the community fails to understand why situations exist or is unable to anticipate roadblocks.

Equity warriors rely on others to be honest and willing to share information about what is really happening or what people are really feeling or thinking.

YOUR MOVE: CREATE A CLIMATE OF TRUST.

The importance of trust is woven throughout all the dimensions up to this point. It will continue to show up in the remaining dimensions. Advancing an equity agenda is about creating the conditions for change. Trust is a critical factor in setting the stage for change, particularly in complex organizations. Values-enhanced leadership provides the best chance to create the conditions needed to support changes that advance equity.

Trust is something you know when you see it. We have advised school leaders that they build trust over time by acting in trustworthy ways. But that short answer is inadequate. There is no easy way to describe the variability of trust building. There is no universal formula for building trust. Fundamentally, trust is built from a person's ability and the receptivity of others to establish relationships. Simple, right? Try unpacking receptivity in the context of advancing equity. We have struggled to build relationships between and among people of different racial and ethnic backgrounds. The obstacles to building relationships between people of different backgrounds are easier to recognize. Deeply held beliefs about others are supported by real, lived experiences that cannot be fully comprehended by someone who has not shared them. Even when individuals make sincere efforts to suspend disbelief and try to create relationships, the parties are often hesitant to trust, as if they are waiting for the one incident that proves what they knew to be true. Unpacking relationships among people within the same racial and ethnic heritages is even more complicated. Racial and ethnic groups are not monolithic, and the nuances are not easily understood. Nuances require deep understanding of history and culture that few "outsiders" have.

Some leaders insist on bringing trusted associates with them when they assume positions of authority. Unfortunately, school leaders rarely do this. Left to strike out on their own, new leaders often make the mistake of seeking teachers and staff who seem receptive to having a relationship rather than finding those who share their values. Other new leaders are cautious to avoid showing favoritism to the wrong people and keep their distance or isolate themselves for a time. Keeping a distance does not build trust. As we suggested previously, having an entry plan that schedules time with each teacher and staff member helps the principal understand who shares her values.

Equity warriors are intentional about establishing the conditions for creating trust. It starts by having a better definition than "acting in trustful ways"! Megan Tschannen-Moran (2014) defines trust as "one's willingness to be vulnerable to another enhanced on the confidence that the other is benevolent, honest, open, reliable, and competent" (pp. 19–20). She further describes the five facets of trust as follows:

Equity warriors are intentional about establishing the conditions for creating trust.

- **Benevolence:** Caring, extending goodwill, demonstrating positive intentions, supporting teachers, expressing appreciation for faculty and staff efforts, being fair, and guarding confidential information

- **Honesty:** Showing integrity, telling the truth, keeping promises, honoring agreements, being authentic, accepting responsibility, avoiding manipulation, being real, and being true to oneself

- **Openness:** Maintaining open communication, sharing important information, delegating, sharing decision making, and sharing power

- **Reliability:** Being consistent, being dependable, showing commitment, expressing dedication, and exercising diligence

- **Competence:** Buffering teachers from outside disruptions, handling difficult situations, setting standards, pressing for results, working hard, setting an example, problem solving, resolving conflict, and being flexible (p. 39)

These facets and ways of acting may seem overwhelming at first. The following example from Jefferson County (Kentucky) Public Schools shows how many of the facets fit together to establish the conditions for change.

Jefferson County is home to the Kentucky Derby and the nation's 29th-largest school district, serving more than 98,000 students, of which 62 percent qualify for free or reduced-price meals. At the time of my visit, it was also home to one of the lowest-performing middle schools in Kentucky. Let's call it Dexter Middle School (DMS). DMS served a Louisville neighborhood overwhelmed by poverty, by high rates of cancer due to environmental conditions, and

(Continued)

(Continued)

by violence. After a decade of attention and resources focused on improving instruction, the school remained the lowest performing.

There were multiple reasons for poor student performance. However, digging into the data revealed that there had been three years in that decade when student academic performance nearly doubled. The difference was the community's trust in the leader's values and the consistency of his actions.

Ron Brown's (not his real name) journey to DMS was unpredicted. He was a senior district administrator known for turning a poor-performing school into a school that earned a Flag of Excellence for improvements in student achievement. An economic downturn caused the school district to restructure its central office team, and Brown's position was scheduled to be eliminated. With just a few years before retirement, he volunteered to be DMS's principal.

Brown welcomed the challenge. DMS had been neglected in many ways. The building was in poor physical condition, and violence from the neighborhood found its way into the school. Brown breathed life into the school. He used foundation funding to provide professional learning opportunities for teachers. He believed that progress on so-called soft indicators preceded progress on hard indicators, and he was transparent about his high expectations for students and teachers. He tightened operations to provide a safe learning environment. Brown pushed teachers with his charismatic style and decisive comments, which let teachers know he expected more from them than they had shown. One teacher explained his approach as when a teacher had compassion and worked for the kids, Brown found resources . . . but he made life difficult for those who did not respect and believe in students. By the start of the next school year, 20 percent of the teachers were new to the school.

Brown used his standing and relationships in the district to launch a $4 million renovation for DMS during the summer between his first and second years. Improving the physical structure signaled to teachers and students that DMS was not forgotten and, just maybe, his vision was attainable. Brown knew the transition would take time and that inexperienced teachers who were filling vacancies might be intimidated or feel unsafe when realities from the neighborhood spilled over to the school. After explaining his vision and expectations, he asked new hires to promise to stay at DMS for three years to provide continuity for students. Teachers said remembering their promise to him carried them through discouraging moments.

Brown's expectations came with social and emotional supports for adults. He initiated incentive awards, student recognition programs, and programs that recognized teachers and caretakers of students. Students wrote about adults they admired and read their stories in celebration events. Brown sent a daily newsletter containing announcements, recognitions, and resources. He visited classrooms, observed teaching, and talked with students. Brown expected teachers to use the professional learning resources, and he made his expectations known. He reorganized counselors so that they could know students better.

By the time Brown retired after three years, student performance on state testing had increased significantly—from 28 to 37 percent in reading, 9 to 12 percent in science, 17 to 32 percent in mathematics, and 18 to 31 percent in social studies. An important beginning.

Brown's example touches many but not all five facets. His teachers, students, and staff trusted him. However, he did not stay at the school long enough to develop internal leadership and shared decision making. He relied on his charismatic style and competence to carry the day. Unfortunately, his successors did not have his charisma, confidence, or energy and—sadly—they struggled to sustain the upward trajectory.

Equity warriors can use values-enhanced leadership to build trust, even when their every move is under scrutiny, by staying true to two ideas that operate in unison:

- Keep certain of the values and be less rigid about the steps taken.
- Focus on progress and not on mistakes along the way.

Equity warriors continue to hold up their values and their equity agenda like the North Star to guide their way. However, in times of complexity and in advancing equity, prior experiences and/or solutions to problems may not apply. In fact, those prior experiences and solutions may be the target of change. So, it is desirable and necessary to encourage the exploration of alternative approaches that are consistent with shared values.

Equity warriors continue to hold up their values and their equity agenda like the North Star to guide their way.

When building trust, leaders also embrace a learning stance. Trusting relationships depend on knowing what happens when someone violates the relationship. Mistakes, inconsistencies, and errors in judgment will happen. Getting past the errors and learning from them will determine the future of the relationship. Making snap judgments, dismissing ideas, and criticizing people destroy relationships and signal the absence of trust.

YOUR MOVE: KNOW YOUR TEACHERS AS YOU EXPECT YOUR TEACHERS TO KNOW THEIR STUDENTS.

Equity warriors have a clear vision of instructional practice and the strengths and areas of improvement for each teacher. They design systems of support based on their understanding of teachers as learners. They deploy resources to maximize the benefits. This is easy to say and incredibly difficult to realize.

Let's begin with a clear vision of instructional practice. Advancing equity requires leaders to take a fresh look at the underlying assumptions about what happens in each classroom. Martin Haberman may be best known as an education researcher who developed interviewing protocols to determine whether teacher and principal candidates would be successful at working with students who live in poverty. He said good teaching occurs when students are

- involved with issues they regard as vital concerns;
- involved with explanations of human differences;
- being helped to see major concepts, big ideas, and general principles;
- involved in planning what they are doing;
- involved with applying ideals such as fairness, equity, or justice to their world;
- actively involved;
- directly involved in a real-life experience;
- actively involved in heterogeneous groups;
- asked to think about an idea in a way that questions common sense or a widely accepted assumption, that relates new ideas to ones learned previously, or that applies an idea to the problems of living;
- involved in redoing, polishing, or perfecting their work;
- involved with the technology of information access; and
- involved in reflecting on their own lives and how they have come to believe and feel as they do (Haberman, 2010, pp. 81–87).

In our coaching of school leaders, we have been in schools and classrooms where, over time, many or all of these descriptions of good teaching are in evidence. Our visits begin by asking school leaders which part of their vision is their focus at that moment. A school leader may have a comprehensive vision that includes many of the examples of good teaching described above. The school leader may be trying to strengthen a particular instructional approach across the school or may have several areas of emphasis simultaneously. Nevertheless, having the school leader clarify the areas of emphasis at the beginning allows us to focus our inquiry and feedback on the school leader's work, not our impressions of what should be happening.

Equity warriors realize that a teacher's practices reflect the support and supervision provided by school leaders.

The next part of the visit is to gather evidence by asking three questions of the school leader: What classroom are we entering (e.g., grade, subject area/course)? What are the strengths of the teacher? What are growth areas in which the teacher is being supported? We make regular visits to our partner schools, and we keep track of the responses to the questions and the evidence gathered in a simple tool (see Figure 4.3).

We refer to this tool as a professional development survey so that we don't confuse its purpose with an evaluation instrument. The provided data allow school leaders to plan professional learning by strategically matching teachers who may need growth in a particular area with colleagues who have strengths in that area. School leaders can also use data to group teachers who may have an area of growth in common.

Of course, the final part of the visit is to design systems of support. Equity warriors realize that a teacher's practices reflect the support and supervision provided by school leaders. As coaches, we wonder if the school leader's assessment of the teacher's strengths and growth areas matches our assessment. Is she not being honest in her assessment? If not, are we missing something? Is he not clear on good teaching? Are the recommended supports the right ones?

FIGURE 4.3 ● Professional Development Survey

TEACHER NAME	STRENGTHS	AREA IN NEED OF GROWTH	SUPPORT TO BE PROVIDED	EXPECTED RESULTS

Equity warriors know their teachers' reasons for becoming a teacher and why they remain in teaching. They know who among their colleagues influence their thinking. They know whether teachers are open to visiting other teachers to learn or whether they are more interested in working through the ideas on their own. They understand and respect teachers' fears that may be barriers to risk-taking. They use their knowledge to design differentiated supports for teachers.

Equity warriors take responsibility for teacher learning.

Equity warriors take responsibility for teacher learning. They start with the assumption that if teachers are not demonstrating good teaching, it is because they do not know how to do so. We partnered with a middle school principal who was determined to help a teacher overcome her fear of having students work in groups. For two class periods a day for two weeks, the principal cotaught the class arranged in groups with the teacher. By the end of the two weeks, the teacher had enough confidence to arrange her classes in groups. The principal visited the teacher's classes regularly to give encouragement, praise, and support. An area in need of growth became an emerging strength, and the expected results could be observed.

YOUR MOVE: HAVE A PROFESSIONAL LEARNING AND LEADERSHIP DEVELOPMENT PLAN.

Equity warriors know that effective professional learning is like good teaching, a sequence of ideas that build upon each other in a continuous improvement cycle. They also know that, as Haberman reminds us, learning comes from connecting new ideas to ones learned previously. As we have considered in the previous section, having expectations and knowing what you expect is the first step in the cycle.

Almost all of our partner schools were familiar with a version of continuous improvement cycles, such as the plan-do-study-act (PDSA) cycle. Initially, we found that few schools have experience *applying* a similar cycle to professional learning. There are notable exceptions, such as teachers who use action research as part of their professional learning in a degree program or when action research is used as a substitute for traditional teacher evaluations. Nevertheless, we found that the exceptions are rarely applied schoolwide even in schools that have an academic coach or administrator whose primary responsibility is organizing systems of professional learning.

It is rarer still that the cycles spiral. Spiraling means repeating a cycle that includes setting a learning expectation, participating in professional learning, practicing the new learning in classrooms, and reflecting on its implementation. Ideally, results from the first cycle inform the second cycle and the school differentiates professional learning to meet teachers' needs during the second and subsequent cycles.

Differentiation by knowledge and ability is important to learning. Some teachers will have prior experiences or knowledge that will let them apply a teaching strategy with success faster than other teachers. Some teachers will need the basic version more than once. For various reasons, professional learning often provides little differentiation or the cycle is not extended and teachers move on.

Effective leadership development closes the knowing-doing gap, which simply refers to the differences between what we know and what we do (Pfeffer & Sutton, 2000). The solution to the knowing-doing gap is to do and then learn from your actions. Almost to a person, school leaders tell us that the most valuable part of their leadership development was having the chance to lead as an intern, being given responsibility with close supervision, and/or being dropped into the job. Yet, these same school leaders do not replicate the experience for their teachers and staff.

So, what would it be like to run a school as if it was a leadership development program? Such a school would have at least three components: clearly articulated values, cycles of learning, and opportunities to lead. We have the following example from our four-year partnership with the San Diego High School campus (SDHS).

The SDHS serves 2,600 students, of whom 70 percent are Latinx. The campus houses three schools—International Studies, Science and Technology, and Business and Leadership—which are the last remnants of a small school experiment that began with seven schools. In the summer of 2015, Carmen Garcia, principal of International Studies, was appointed principal of all three schools. Each school was administered by a vice principal and an administrative team. Garcia was charged to work with stakeholders to do the following:

- Build a culture that is welcoming, open, accepting, responsive, collaborative, and committed to the success of every student

- Establish a vision for a unified campus

- Provide opportunities and access to rigorous courses for all students

(Continued)

(Continued)

- Create a climate of trust, respect, and caring

- Improve communication and collaboration among adults including families, and between students and adults (Recommendations for the San Diego High School Campus, 2015)

Garcia formed a 25-member SDHS Instructional Leadership Team (SDHS ILT) with representatives of teachers, administrators, and guidance staff. The teachers and staff from the three schools did not know each other and, due to the competitive environment fostered by the small schools being colocated on one campus, in some cases didn't like each other.

The leadership development program was designed to advance a simple theory of action.

If the SDHS ILT members:

- developed processes, protocols, and products,

- engaged in professional learning with their colleagues across the campus, and

- were supported in exercising leadership,

then they would own responsibilities for the work and lead their colleagues in building a campuswide culture and systems to improve teaching, learning, and student success.

The intent was to build relationships and learn to lead by doing the work. Along the way, the SDHS ILT learned and developed several processes and protocols for working together. As these processes and protocols were introduced, the members interpreted them, determined their appropriateness to their objectives and their experiences, and led others in learning and using the protocols.

The members created the SDHS teaching wheel to connect and communicate curriculum design processes to their colleagues (Presentation to the San Diego High School Instructional Leadership Team, 2017). The teaching wheel begins by adding the curriculum design to the PDSA cycle (see Figure 4.4). Then, it frames the cycle's "plan" phase as collaboration that links to the protocols they established for collaborative planning sessions. The instructional strategies they selected to reinforce across the campus are the content of the "do" phase. Finally, the wheel separates the "study" phase of the cycle into two parts—assess and reflect—as placeholders for the data collection and data analysis protocols they developed.

FIGURE 4.4 ● SDHS Teaching Wheel

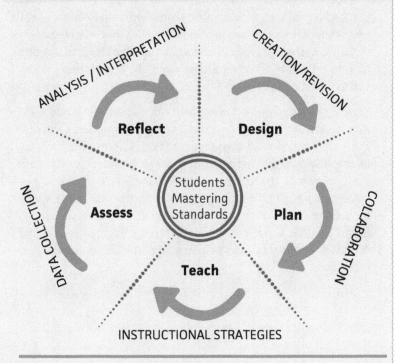

ANALYSIS / INTERPRETATION

CREATION/REVISION

Reflect

Design

Students
Mastering
Standards

Assess

Plan

DATA COLLECTION

COLLABORATION

Teach

INSTRUCTIONAL STRATEGIES

Source: San Diego Unified School District.

The teaching wheel was a useful learning tool. The SDHS ILT members knew teachers were familiar with the PDSA process, even though there was no evidence of its use. In this way, the SDHS ILT members could make connections among their prior knowledge, their curriculum design, and their objectives. When they showed what they knew, their presentation of the teaching wheel helped to better identify the problem. Teacher leaders knew the cycles and what needed to be done to accomplish the objective of students mastering standards. But they were not applying what they knew.

By using evidence to better frame the problem, we could see that leadership development needed to focus less on the content

(Continued)

(Continued)

and more on how to help teachers do what they knew how to do. To do so, after SDHS ILT members had agreed on a process or product, we asked them to present it to their colleagues and lead them in its use. They hesitated. They voiced two concerns: inclusion and consistency. First, they wanted assurances that all SDHS ILT members would participate in presenting a new idea. After they reached agreement, it was to be shared with every department and school across the campus. The SDHS ILT asked administrators to create a schedule, and members created a professional learning plan to articulate when new ideas would be introduced and the cycles would begin.

The second concern was consistency of expectations and messages. So, SDHS ILT members designed an agenda and presentations that would send consistent messages across the campus. In the beginning, the protocols, processes, and products were uniform across the campus, and the members delivered the collectively planned presentations. As time passed, the departments and course-alike teams differentiated their presentations based on their situations. Administrators provided support and feedback on progress and helped when SDHS ILT members met resistance.

Equity warriors know that advancing equity and learning happen through action.

Equity warriors understand that professional learning is a continuous, spiraling process. They learn what people know, build on prior knowledge to make connections, and look for evidence of understanding in planning next steps. Most important, equity warriors know that advancing equity and learning happen through action. They recognize they cannot lead learning alone and create systems for leadership development throughout the school. Again, this is easier said than done. For example, we were surprised to learn that some of the SDHS ILT members who had the most knowledge and strongest voices could not lead or were reluctant to do so. Team members were replaced with others who were willing. Yet, the original team members were still expected to have a role and make contributions—which they did.

REFLECTION: *What expectations, opportunities, systems, and supports are in place to develop leaders? What is the right balance of leading with values and leading to get things done for the current situation in your school?*

_____

_____

_____

_____

_____

_____

_____

WARFARE: ACT DELIBERATELY

Never give in. Never give in. Never, never, never, never—in nothing, great or small, large or petty—never give in, except to convictions of honour and good sense.

Winston Churchill, 1941

The first part of Winston Churchill's "never give in" speech is widely quoted, but the second part is often overlooked. Churchill, with the voice of a great leader, admonishes his listeners to always act in accord with one's values and with good sense and judgment. Values, he says, should always take precedence over stubborn perseverance.

Values-enhanced equity warriors know there are multiple ways to engage in warfare, However, warfare is intended to gain an objective, which for us is advancing equity. Equity warriors never lose sight of that objective or confuse that objective with other goals. We know leaders who, in the name of advancing equity, have attacked people and forcefully eliminated opposition. Sometimes vanquishing opposition is unavoidable, but crushing opposition is not the primary objective and should be attempted only as a last resort to achieve the objective. More

Equity warriors never lose sight of that objective or confuse that objective with other goals.

enduring success comes when equity warriors stay true to their values and use pressure to reduce the opponent's ability to fight.

Equity warriors have tools at their disposal. Among these are the cultivation of a critical mass to anchor change in the culture, supervision systems, control over schedule and budgets, and the will to act on their moral imperative. Equity warriors know there is a very thin line between gaining support for the equity agenda and erring too much on the side of expediency, particularly out of frustration.

YOUR MOVE: SHOW GRADE-LEVEL INTERDEPENDENCE.

Equity warriors help teachers recognize that nobody expects them to be superheroes. Few teachers have the right skills and the right conditions to help students increase multiple grade levels in a single year. The few who are able to do so will tell you they are not successful every year with every student. In all cases, teachers need to be dedicated and devoted, and to have the right supports in place to accelerate student learning. Teachers cannot do it alone.

One of the most remarkable teachers we had the opportunity to know taught in a school in a barrio in the south side of San Diego. The school, located in an industrial area and isolated by gang territory, served new arrivals, homeless families, and others who moved out of the neighborhood as soon as they were able. Each year, this teacher helped her kindergarteners read and write with proficiency, often at the 2nd-grade level. Her teaching and the success of her students inspired us as well as the many visitors to the school and the student teachers she supported.

Unfortunately, there was little evidence that students who had been successful in her classroom continued to do exceptional work in other grades. Student mobility in and out of the school was high, so cohorts of students did not advance grade levels together. Nevertheless, the 1st- and 2nd-grade teachers were unable and ultimately unwilling to teach in ways that built on the solid foundation that students had at the end of kindergarten. Collective efficacy, even when an example of student success due to individual efficacy was present on the campus, was not built into the school's culture. Students regressed academically.

Changing organizational culture is difficult. Peter Drucker is credited with saying that "culture eats strategy for breakfast." Equity warriors know that a change in culture can be their greatest ally, as the following example from one of our partner schools in Texas illustrates.

This elementary school enrolled just under 600 students, of whom 68 percent qualified for free or reduced-price meals. While most students performed well on state assessments, many students, particularly entering kindergarteners and 1st graders, were not ready for academic success and struggled. The school's culture had been shaped by two principals—each spent four or five years as the school's assistant principal before being appointed as principal.

The principal invested resources in teaming to build staff capacity, particularly among experienced teachers whom the principals believed did not want to do the work. Grade-level teams met two or three times a week, and vertical teams met once a week with a structured agenda developed by the principal with lead teachers. Slowly, teachers became more comfortable with open conversations. They developed weekly pacing plans and engaged in close review of student work. The principal provided close supervision and regular feedback.

The most remarkable process was the use of vertical team time for planning. Teachers visited other teachers' classrooms periodically. With about a month remaining in the school year, grade-level teams conducted an extended visit to the grade level immediately before their grade (for example, 3rd-grade teachers visited 2nd-grade classrooms). The visits were intended to help teachers determine the readiness of students who would be entering their classrooms the following year and to advise current teachers on the content and skills they needed to reinforce during the last month of the school year. The visiting teachers observed student interactions with their teacher and other students and reviewed student work and student data. The visiting teachers and the visited teachers later gave and received feedback from each other. The principals did not participate in the visits or in the feedback sessions.

The district had a strong teachers union presence, and the principals complained about struggling with union representatives when they evaluated teachers. Yet, the school's culture allowed these nonevaluative collegial visits. Teachers gained from giving and receiving feedback that would help them better prepare students for success. They valued their colleagues' feedback more than the feedback from their principals or others.

The powerful example from this school stayed with us. Building an organizational culture that sustains collective efficacy takes time, stable leadership, attention, and the right conditions. We have seen other examples of teachers and staff embracing strategies to move the organizational culture.

In Flint Community Schools, referenced earlier, we saw culture changes in schools following the introduction of a district-required, fully aligned, standards-based literacy and mathematics curriculum at each grade level. The first step was preparing teachers in using the curriculum, including the daily lesson plans available in the units. While teachers were not required to follow the script provided in the units, they were expected to follow the scope and sequence of the yearlong curriculum and use the research-based instructional strategies. Flint's leadership had decided that uniformity in curriculum and instructional strategies across schools was critical to the success of students whose families were highly mobile.

Extensive investment in professional learning, including support from school-based coaches, helped convince teachers to try the district's curriculum. Many did so reluctantly. However, when students began to respond positively and teachers realized that students were learning and demonstrating their learning, they embraced the units and lessons in significant numbers. As teachers and students deepened their knowledge and use of the curriculum, student academic achievement increased for the first time in recent memory.

Part of Flint's professional learning was intended to help teachers understand that the curriculum was aligned vertically and horizontally. There were two explicit messages—keep the pace required by the scope and sequence as students will have multiple opportunities to master concepts each year and over time, and teachers could make a difference in student learning by working together. In the next few years, teachers could identify gaps in student knowledge and understanding of key concepts over time. In some schools, they also noticed that students who spent the previous year with one teacher were further behind than students taught by other teachers. Teachers understood, as did the teachers in the previous example, that when students come to them unprepared because their colleagues were not doing their part, there are consequences: Teachers have to work harder.

Equity warriors create opportunities for teachers and staff to take responsibility for building collective efficacy. Teachers first need evidence that their efficacy comes from a culture that supports collaboration on student learning. Once they are reminded, then looking beyond their classroom helps them realize their interdependence. Savvy equity warriors persuade teachers that working together and bringing more alignment to curriculum, instructional practices, protocols, and processes builds their capacity to learn from each other and reinforces student learning. The cycle becomes complete when collective efforts result in measurable gains in student learning.

Equity warriors create opportunities for teachers and staff to take responsibility for building collective efficacy.

YOUR MOVE: USE SUPERVISION AS AN EXTENSION OF YOUR VALUES.

Teacher evaluation—removing teachers whose practice is at best ineffective and at worst harmful to students—most often comes to mind when thinking about confrontation. Kim Marshall (2009) suggests there are 12 ways that teacher evaluation breaks down:

- The principal sees only a tiny fraction of teaching time.
- Teachers often put on a dog-and-pony show.
- The principal's presence changes classroom dynamics.
- Doing good lesson write-ups requires lots of skill and training.
- Even high-quality lesson write-ups can miss the bigger picture.
- Many evaluation instruments are cumbersome and legalistic, making it difficult to give helpful feedback.
- Checklists and numerical ratings lack bite and don't guide improvement.
- Critical evaluations can shut down adult learning or be shrugged off.
- The whole process can feed isolation and jealousy.
- Some principals don't confront bad or mediocre teaching.
- Many principals are too harried to do effective evaluations.
- The focus of the evaluation is on pleasing the principal, not student learning.

In other words, the ways that teacher evaluation systems are structured do not work. They are cumbersome, not focused on teaching and learning, and are most often a waste of time for all involved.

Not having an effective evaluation system poses a dilemma for equity warriors. They know that student success depends on the knowledge, skills, and attitudes of teachers to be able to reach and teach all students. They create systems and structures, processes, protocols, and procedures to support student growth and learning. Yet, some teachers refuse to engage. When that happens, students suffer.

Some teachers know how to beat the evaluation system. We watched as a series of principals over a decade wrestled with a teacher who believed his students could not learn mathematics. Student performance and learning were directly linked to his substandard instruction and attitude. Each principal had used the evaluation process to pressure the teacher to improve or to be dismissed. He continued teaching at the school. The district's evaluation system had failed to achieve its purpose.

We have seen some of the poorest teachers and staff hide out at the lowest-performing schools in districts. In more than one district, the district-sanctioned strategy was to evaluate out teachers. Principals were trained how to use the evaluation system, received resources to help them write observations and feedback letters, and were expected to evaluate as many teachers as possible. An experienced principal assigned to the school for one year was a model. She spent most of her time in classrooms evaluating teachers. She took notes and completed reports on teachers very efficiently using her laptop, which was unusual for the time. She showed us that she was responsible for 14 teachers leaving the district or the profession—"notches in her belt," she said. The school was decimated. No doubt all of the terminations were justified in a school that was neglected and had continuous leadership turnover. But the terminations excused school leaders from their failure to support teachers over time. The consequence was that the school could not attract high-quality staff and only first-year teachers and long-term substitutes would work there.

Strong, fair, and persistent leadership is key to achieving an equity agenda. Rather than blaming the evaluation system or professional associations, equity warriors look to themselves for not adequately evaluating teachers. For example, in most districts, the evaluation process is designed to deny tenure to teachers who do not improve their teaching in their first two or three years. However, too many of our partner principals do not use evaluation to dismiss or postpone tenure for teachers who they feel are unfit. Some principals express guilt for not providing the support teachers needed and want to give them another chance. Others are honest that they do not have the time to follow the evaluation process or to search for and hire a replacement. In most cases, they regret granting tenure to unfit teachers.

At the end of the day, supervision systems reflect the values of those who design and execute them. Equity warriors understand that building trust is necessary to enable learning and risk-taking. Using evaluation to punish, intimidate, or remove teachers does not create trust. On the other hand, ignoring teachers who are harmful to student learning conflicts with espoused values. Effective supervision systems balance moral imperative with effectiveness.

Equity warriors differentiate supports and supervision based on the individual. As they know their teachers, they recognize their strengths and areas of growth and devise their responses. Sometimes families are effective allies. When families approach school leaders with well-founded complaints about a teacher, principals are better able to challenge resistance from the teacher, union representatives, and their supervisors who may question the principal's motive or the validity of his assessment.

Equity warriors differentiate supports and supervision based on the individual.

Constant supervision and feedback may be effective in helping a teacher improve his practice or change behavior. Site-based staff developers or instructional coaches can help when there is clear communication about expectations among all parties, and roles and responsibilities are clear. When peer support is available, the principal maintains responsibility to clarify the expected outcomes of any professional learning or supports the teacher receives. The site-based coach provides confidential support so that the teacher can take risks as she changes her practice without fear of constant evaluation. Ultimately, improvement is the responsibility of the individual. Change can be stimulated and supported, but not forced.

Equity warriors are transparent about supervising and supporting teachers and staff. It is often assumed that teachers would not learn about a principal's intensive supervision of a teacher. Word travels in a closed community. Depending on the size and structure of the school, teachers tend to know who among their colleagues are successful with students, even tracking their students' performance data to prior teachers. When a leader avoids taking action with a teacher who is harmful to student learning, that lowers the bar for all teachers and undermines the equity warrior's effectiveness.

We have partnered with equity warriors who have used various approaches with teachers and staff who they thought unfit. A few used evaluations effectively and are committed to not passing the problem along to another school leader. Most of the time, principals have used administrative tricks of the trade to push or release unwanted teachers and staff from their school. We have watched experienced principals use many administrative maneuvers after exhausting other options. When done well, the school community responds well to the result. Of course, the problem is not solved, just passed along.

An equity warrior's ability to use supervision, evaluation, and administrative options depends on experience, timing, and context. Nevertheless, avoidance is not an option for equity warriors focused on advancing equity. Students, teachers, staff, and school leaders all suffer immediately and in the long term when students do not receive high-quality instruction. Postponing confrontation is never a viable solution.

YOUR MOVE: ALIGN YOUR SCHOOL BUDGET TO YOUR EQUITY AGENDA.

Equity warriors view their budgets as a tool to accomplish their objectives.

Equity warriors view their budgets as a tool to accomplish their objectives. Ideally, dollars should be aligned with the equity agenda and spent on strategic priorities intended to advance equity. Yet, no matter the context (strong economic times or recessionary periods) or the locus of decision making (centralized or school-based), the budget process is seldom ideal. A major structural factor is that budget decision making in the public sector is about the interests of adults and the exercise of power. Almost all of a school's budget is spent on adults. Each person has a vested interest in how dollars are allocated and how they will spend their time. Maintaining the status quo, protecting their interests, and staving off attacks that threaten their interests are the undercurrents of budget battles.

Given the strong pull to maintain existing structures and interests, it is little wonder that budgets and adults are considered fixed. Districts allocate funding to schools from two sources primarily—the general fund (from local and state tax revenue) and the district's portion of state and federal supplemental or formula funding. School leaders have little control over the total dollar amount of their budgets, which is determined by a district's formula and decision making. School leaders typically have two options if they're not satisfied with the allocated funding: They can advocate for additional funding from district leaders, or they can be entrepreneurial and seek additional funds from sources outside the district. Districts typically have funds set aside, as in the example from Boston Public Schools in Chapter 3, to support schools with exceptional situations. Since these decisions are discretionary, district leaders consider the effect on existing structures and district interest in decisions about allocating additional funding. District leaders tread carefully when they make an exception to the formula or when political pressures intervene to force them to make a particular choice.

Structures and interests also govern entrepreneurial efforts. District leaders seek grant funding and philanthropic support and determine which schools or school leaders are best positioned to participate in an externally funded initiative. We have been in the room often enough to know that school leaders rarely have the option to refuse additional supports or funding, even when the conditions are not right or the opportunity does not fit within their current priorities. In other cases, school leaders who take the initiative to seek external funding may be denied the opportunity to apply for grants or programs that require district approval when doing so will conflict with district interests. In both situations, school leaders invest considerable time for questionable returns.

Many districts allow schools to create separate foundations to raise funding to augment the school's budget. Fundraising by school leaders raises equity issues. Schools that serve more affluent families and neighbors may be able to raise funds more easily because of families' ability to contribute and the availability of experienced volunteers. In many cases, school leaders have no control over who runs the foundations or their values and beliefs, which can be in opposition to the equity agenda. Realizing equity issues, some districts limit fundraising or how such funds can be spent. For example, Portland (Oregon) Public Schools allows school foundations to raise funds to support teaching and staffing; however, one-third of all funds raised by a foundation after the initial $10,000 is diverted into a districtwide Fund for Portland Public Schools. Schools that qualify based on student need can apply for grants from the fund. Nevertheless, certain Portland school foundations are able to raise significant funding for their schools beyond the amount most others can, even after contributing to the districtwide fund.

In spite of limitations in accessing funding, equity warriors are able to make decisions that align interests to the equity agenda. In practice, school leaders have real power over using resources to advance equity. There are four components to exercising power successfully: clear vision, courage, knowledge, and relationships.

Equity warriors continue to ask questions about how the deployment of their resources, including every staff position, contributes to advancing the school's equity agenda.

We have referred multiple times to the importance of a clear vision. Here we add that having consensus on a clear vision is a vital lever to accomplish the equity agenda. When stakeholders agree on the ultimate aims of the equity agenda, agreements provide criteria for funding and staffing decisions. We have seen equity warriors use agreements as criteria in excessing staff whose functions or contributions are not aligned to the school's purpose. These are not easy decisions because they pit adult interests against the interests of students. This is when the time and effort taken to create a vision based on meaningful student data are rewarded. Equity warriors continue to ask questions about how the deployment of their resources, including every staff position, contributes to advancing the school's equity agenda.

Knowing and doing are not the same thing. Equity warriors act courageously, which in all cases means taking risk. When a decision is well reasoned, consistent with one's espoused values, and aligned with the school's equity agenda, announcing the decision does not come as a surprise. A teacher or staff member whose position is to be eliminated and the funding reallocated is not often surprised—they have been waiting. Staff are not surprised when decisions have been made to replace or reorganize guidance and student support systems to better know and serve students. Often, they wonder why the decision was not made sooner. Nevertheless, since these decisions affect adults and their lives, school leaders agonize over situations. Courage to act comes from putting the equity agenda first.

Equity warriors have knowledge of the budget, protocols, and contracts before acting. School leaders learn the technical limits of their decision-making authority from their colleagues, their experiences, and their supervisors. School leaders who do not know and respect district policies, protocols, and collective bargaining agreements are often unsuccessful at making change. Union leaders have repeatedly told us that school leaders have the tools to manage their schools effectively and for all students. When they do, everyone—including the unions—benefits.

Equity warriors know that anything is possible if they have trusting relationships with students, teachers, staff, and families.

Equity warriors know that anything is possible if they have trusting relationships with students, teachers, staff, and families. Using inclusive approaches to site-based budgeting decisions enables stakeholders to wrestle with finding the possibilities in reaching agreements. Equity warriors continue to stay in the conversations either by asking questions or by reminding participants of the charge. School leaders cannot abdicate final decision-making authority and are the ones to have the tough conversations with teachers and staff whose positions will change. Nevertheless, teacher leaders often discover and own decisions after exploring options about reallocating funds to create time for curriculum planning. Trusting in the equity warrior and her vision allows families to accept the expansion of heterogeneous grouping and larger class sizes so that more supports can be provided to all students.

Equity warriors do not back away from using their budgets to advance their equity agenda. Budgets are where the rubber meets the road, where interests clash, and where the stakes are highest for individuals within a community. Budget decisions are not made to vanquish opposition but, rather, to strengthen the community as it advances equity.

Equity warriors do not back away from using their budgets to advance their equity agenda.

YOUR MOVE: MAKE NO EXCUSES.

Equity warriors have the will to act on their values. We define will as being measured and clear, and collecting and using political capital to advance equity. Equity warriors continually assess their political capital—resources and power built through relationships, trust, and influence—so they can determine how much they can spend. They determine the conditions around them to know the right time to act. They collaborate with allies so they are not facing opposition alone. They find the opportunity and charge forward.

Equity warriors have the will to act on their values.

Karin Chenoweth (2007) studied 15 schools that had a significant population of students living in poverty, students of color, and high rates of achievement. In *"It's Being Done": Academic Success in Unexpected Schools*, she described what the educators in these schools do differently from those in schools that do not have high rates of achievement:

- Think deeply about what their students need to learn and how to make sure they learn it
- Don't teach to the state tests
- Have high expectations for their students
- Recognize that without a good education, students face the probability of a lifetime of poverty and dependence
- Embrace and use data and focus on individual students
- Constantly reexamine what they do
- Embrace accountability
- Make decisions on what is best for students, not adults
- Use school time wisely
- Leverage community resources
- Expand the time struggling students have in schools
- Do not spend a lot of time punishing students
- Establish an atmosphere of respect
- Like students
- Ensure that students who struggle the most have the best instruction

- Distribute leadership
- Pay careful attention to the quality of the teaching staff
- Provide teachers with time to plan, work collaboratively, and observe each other
- Think seriously about professional development, particularly for new teachers
- Acculturate new teachers
- Ensure that high-quality, dedicated, and competent office and building staff feel part of the education mission
- Create nice places to work (Chenoweth, 2007, pp. 216–225)

As equity warriors collect political capital by making the moves described in these chapters, they assess where their school is on each of the above or similar attributes that research and experiences tell us make a difference in student achievement. As part of their assessment, they think about the strategic levers—what will advance our equity agenda—and the cost of using the levers. They make no excuses—utmost to themselves—as they consider how and when best to use their political capital.

District leaders' support for their equity agenda and the readiness of the staff are among the considerations for deciding which levers to pull. School leaders are caught in the middle. During complexity and change, ambiguity and uncertainty at district levels hamper school leaders' ability to lead their school community. A school leader who moves forward without checking with his supervisor regularly to explain his plans and progress and to ensure he has support may find himself in a precarious situation. In Chapter 2, we introduced some of the questions that equity warriors ask to determine the level of support and readiness in place to move their equity agenda. Risks are measured by the support available to face the challenge of the moment. If no political capital has been built with their supervisor, equity warriors make safer choices among the various options available to them in order to survive.

We have seen equity warriors find themselves in situations in which they have district support to act boldly or are expected to clean up a mess. Though less than ideal, they have acted unilaterally. Starting with the basics, they have held teachers accountable for being present and for being prepared to teach and deliver standards-based instruction. It is not an exaggeration to say that some school leaders have had to stand in or close the gates to school parking lots to ensure that teachers and staff stay on campus during working hours or call teachers who are absent on Mondays and Fridays to confirm they are too ill to be in school. They limit approvals for teachers to be off campus for professional development that is not aligned with the school's equity agenda.

They are in classrooms and in halls and confront teachers when their behaviors and attitudes toward students are inconsistent with creating a safe, secure, and nurturing learning environment. They monitor discipline referrals, return students who are wandering the halls or have been sent out of their classrooms, and confront teachers whose classroom management is not meeting expectations. They have zero tolerance for student-to-student, student-to-teacher, and teacher-to-student interactions that are harmful, hurtful, or just wrong. They are vigilant in anticipating and responding to bullying or hate crimes. Creating a safe environment requires that all adults model acceptable behaviors for students, so equity warriors are swift in responding to extreme teacher behaviors of yelling or belittling students.

School leaders who face extreme situations operate with expedience. It is fully understandable that they need to put out fires before they can start living in the house. Nevertheless, unless they concurrently build values-enhanced systems, they will not move beyond responding to fires. For example, we partnered with a high school principal who spent her days in her office focused on the school's operations. There was a clear absence of academic instruction that could be called rigorous. Students wandered from class to class without purpose. Yet, she did nothing to create conditions for student success, including showing students that their attendance, participation, and effort would result in learning. For equity warriors, dealing with the daily challenges is not an excuse for delaying the advance of equity.

Most equity warriors do not face extreme situations, or the extreme behaviors are confined to a few adults and students. Equity warriors are able to see challenges, and rather than make excuses, they see opportunities. Sometimes, periods of budget reductions provide opportunities to eliminate programs or revise systems so that they are more closely aligned to the equity agenda. Behaviors by a few staff members or students that violate the community's values can provide opportunities and resources to introduce social and emotional supports that would benefit all students and adults. Equity warriors find the moment to strike and act deliberately.

Equity warriors are able to see challenges, and rather than make excuses, they see opportunities.

Equity warriors often fall into periods of disappointment and isolation. It is in these times that they rely on other school leaders for support, encouragement, and alliances. In several of our partner districts, principals have monthly voluntary, school-level luncheon meetings called informals. The agenda for these meetings tends to focus on sharing concerns and advice on operational issues, but the meetings also enable principals to network so that they can build relationships with like-minded colleagues or colleagues facing similar situations. Collegial gatherings among principals can lend support for coming together and advancing a shared agenda, particularly during difficult periods.

None of the principals in the Chenoweth study had all the attributes in place. They had not achieved their equity agenda . . . yet! Their journeys took place over a period of time. Nevertheless, they made no excuses for their students, teachers, staff, or themselves for where they were in the journey. They did not think of themselves as powerless or that their individual actions did not matter. Their actions mattered!

REFLECTION: *What are your next moves to advance your equity agenda? What is your assessment of your political capital—the resources and power built through relationships, trust, goodwill, and influence? How much capital can you spend?*

_____

_____

_____

_____

_____

_____

_____

_____

_____

_____

PART III

Educate Each and Every Student Well: Teaching and Learning

INTRODUCTION

Education is the most powerful weapon you can use to change the world.

Nelson Mandela (2003)

Educators alone cannot rid America of racism, classism, and the other isms, or poverty, abuse, and the other systemic challenges facing our society. Yet, educators have in their hands the most strategic lever for advancing equity—which is knowing and educating students one at a time so they have the tools that will enable them to think, learn, and act independently and to apply their skills to situations they face now and in the future.

Equity warriors create an equity agenda using student data to address the situation and conditions within which they find themselves. They demonstrate leadership consistent with their espoused values. They achieve equity by building coherence around the gift that educators can offer to students—teaching and learning.

Michael Fullan and Joanne Quinn (2016) define coherence as "a shared depth of understanding about the purpose and nature of the work in the minds and actions individually and especially collectively" (pp. 1–2). They suggest that coherence is the result of leadership that guides districts and

Equity warriors create an equity agenda using student data to address the situation and conditions within which they find themselves. They demonstrate leadership consistent with their espoused values. They achieve equity by building coherence around the gift that educators can offer to students—teaching and learning.

(Continued)

(Continued)

schools through dynamic processes that include four drivers for whole system change:

- **Focusing direction:** integrating what the system is doing

- **Cultivating collaborative cultures:** using relationships and shared expertise to produce strong groups and strong individuals

- **Deepening learning:** clarifying learning goals, building precise pedagogical practices, and building collective capacity

- **Securing accountability:** creating conditions to maximize people's internal accountability that is reinforced by external accountability

Fullan and Quinn's definition of coherence paints a picture of a destination in which the district culture is deeply ingrained into the minds and hearts of everyone in the district. We have partnered with districts—large and small—that have strong, shared cultures. In reality, most districts do have shared cultures, and like all systems, they produce exactly what they are intended to produce. Equity warriors know that districts can have coherence around the wrong idea.

Equity warriors recognize the importance of creating conditions for learning in schools, including fostering the social-emotional development of students and teachers. Social-emotional development is essential in creating the motivation and confidence needed to teach well and to learn. Yet, equity warriors know that social-emotional development is a necessary means to assisting every student to achieve academic success.

Equity warriors know that educators have more knowledge about effective teaching and learning than at any time in history. They know that teaching and learning comprise three dynamic elements: the teacher's instructional and content knowledge, the student's knowledge and engagement, and the content and instructional materials that students and teachers have at their disposal. Equity warriors also know that the key to unlocking and understanding learning is to use processes that look carefully at what "tasks" students are asked to complete and how well they are able to complete them. By tasks, we mean daily assignments, problems of practices, weekly assessments, unit assessments, quarterly assessments, worksheets, homework, standardized tests, state competency tests, and other assessments of learning that students are asked to complete.

The processes are called paying attention to the *instructional core*, and the formula is this:

- Focus on building teacher capacity (knowledge, instructional strategies, planning and designing, and efficacy).

- Have materials and content that are grade appropriate and developmentally appropriate, rigorous, relevant, and culturally responsive.

- Engage students' experience, prior knowledge, and habits of mind as they interpret and respond to materials and teachers.

- Measure whether students are learning by assessing their performance on tasks given to them each day.

While the formula is simple, a lot goes into building each element—and the grade-level and developmentally appropriate and rigorous tasks. The task is the essential, and typically undervalued, part of the instructional core. The task combines all three elements and measures the success of the lesson or unit. For example, the task needs to be rigorous and be right for the grade and it needs to address student strengths and needs. It answers the questions about what we want students to know and be able to do at the end of the class period, and how we will know it. Finally, the task provides clues as to whether the instructional strategies were effective for all or only some students. Designing tasks requires teachers to plan lessons in which the purpose, content, instructional strategies, and student preparation are aligned to the intended outcome. Tasks can be fragile. When changing one side of the instructional core triangle, teachers need to address the changes in the other sides of the triangle as well (City et al., 2009).

> *Equity warriors believe that advancing equity and sustained academic achievement for every student are one and the same. A focus on the instructional core is the only way to improve student learning at scale.*

Regardless of the district context and student population, equity warriors believe that advancing equity and sustained academic achievement for every student are one and the same. A focus on the instructional core is the only way to improve student learning at scale (City et al., 2009, p. 24). It is as simple and as complex as that! In the following chapters, we examine ways to alter the design of education systems to support improvement of the instructional core so that all students can achieve to high levels. Change is necessary when the system is comfortable with not educating all students well.

CHAPTER 5

District leaders focus and maintain attention on teaching and learning

☞ POLITICS: BRING COHERENCE TO SYSTEMS, STRUCTURES, RESOURCES, STAKEHOLDERS, AND CULTURE

There has never been a time in the life of the American public school when we have not known all we needed to in order to teach all those whom we chose to teach.

Ron Edmonds (1979), p. 16

Is Edmonds right? Do educators know all they need to know? We will see that we probably do, but we have been unwilling or unable to act on that knowledge. So what is stopping us from using what we know to improve the education of all children?

The political challenge for equity warriors is focusing the district's attention on teaching and learning and corralling competing interests. Improving instruction is at the heart of advancing equity. Equity warriors have the will and know the way.

Equity warriors do this by adopting *a coherence framework* that drives conversations, balances conflicts, and governs effectively. The framework guides the evolution of an equity-focused organizational culture. The framework is anchored in student experiences—the data that personalize the agenda—and is driven by values-enhanced leaders determined to focus the district on teaching and learning. We have partnered with superintendents who have been completely transparent in launching their framework. We have partnered with others who have rolled out bits of the framework over time, though never losing sight of their North Star. Being successful at achieving an equity agenda depends on operating from a framework.

Building coherence in a complex organization is not about creating the perfect structures and strategies or perfectly aligning the structures to the equity agenda. Building coherence requires analyzing existing structures and strategies; adapting those that can serve the equity agenda; jettisoning or shrinking in importance those that do not serve the purpose; and continuing to analyze, adapt, and jettison as the situation demands. In other words, the goal is the equity agenda, not creating the perfect system or strategy.

Equity warriors know the superintendent and district leaders cannot delegate responsibility for defining the equity agenda and coalescing direction, supports, and resources around a focus on teaching and learning. That is the important, difficult work that no other part of the system can do to advance equity at scale. The politics of teaching and learning demands that superintendents and district leaders elevate and create focus around what all students are expected to know and be able to do, have board members and internal constituencies share their expectations, and design systems so that everyone learns together how best to advance equity by improving the instructional core.

Equity warriors know the superintendent and district leaders cannot delegate responsibility for defining the equity agenda and coalescing direction, supports, and resources around a focus on teaching and learning.

YOUR MOVE: BRING COHERENCE AROUND TEACHING AND LEARNING.

Some district leaders approach student achievement strategies like decorating a tree—the one who has the most ornaments wins! We caution our district partners about introducing new initiatives by using the "rock in the pond" analogy. Throwing a rock into a pond generates rings that extend well beyond the point of impact. So it is with district initiatives. Decisions to start something have a ripple effect throughout the organization. An organization can handle only so many ripples. The more ripples, the more conflict is created over capacity and resources, and the more confusion about priorities. Limiting the ripples to those that are closely aligned to the core mission encourages those within the organization to make connections and improves the odds that the desired effect will be achieved.

Coherence exists when people agree on what needs to be done to achieve strategic goals, what resources support that work, and what systems and structures facilitate it. Coherence is often confused with alignment. Alignment is sewing together systems, structures, and programs, whether or not they serve the strategic goals. Alignment can be helpful but often just hides underlying problems. Alignment relies on the capacity of those within the district to see the connections and act within their best interest as well as the interest of the district as a whole. Those who can see the alignment might act creatively, and their actions may have unintended consequences for the district equity agenda.

Each summer since 2003, the Public Education Leadership Project (PELP) at Harvard University (n.d.) has invited a small number of teams to spend five days wrestling with a systemwide problem of practice of their own choosing. Participating districts use the PELP coherence framework to analyze their systems, structures, and strategies to determine what is getting in the way of improving student achievement.

The PELP coherence framework recognizes that the instructional core is at the center and the focus of all aspects of the school district (see Figure 5.1). Just naming and placing the instructional core at the center is not enough. Even when the term *instructional core* is part of the district lexicon, district leaders rarely share the same understanding of the elements of the core or the importance of the task. For many district leaders, this is new learning. For many, it has been a while since they have been teachers, or teaching may never have been part of their experience. Others have not taken time to deeply understand the implications of the instructional core. Coherence relies on a shared understanding of the instructional core elements.

FIGURE 5.1 ● Public Education Leadership Project (PELP) Coherence Framework

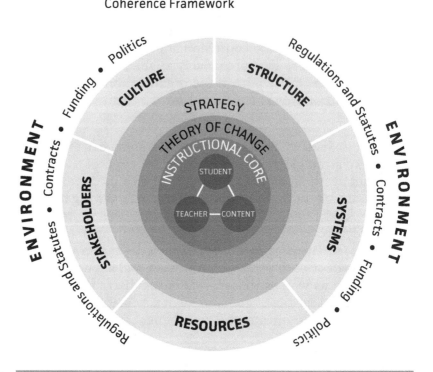

Source: Public Education Leadership Project. Adapted from Tushman and O'Reilly's Congruence Model, 2002. Used with permission. https://pelp.fas.harvard.edu/coherence -framework

The district's theory of action (or its theory of change, as PELP prefers to call it) and instructional improvement strategies surround the instructional core. A theory of action—as discussed in previous chapters—is the district's perspective on actions to be taken and desired outcomes. A theory of action is a set of if-then statements. In the coherence framework, the theory of action connects the district's focus on the instructional core and the district's strategies for improvement.

The theory of action and strategies are informed by and alter the five aspects of a district's organization: stakeholders, culture, structures, systems, and resources. We have discussed these five aspects in detail in previous chapters.

DEFINE THEORY OF ACTION

The theory of action, simply, is a hypothesis about what will happen when a set of strategies is implemented. Theories of action typically take the form of "If . . . , then" statements or "If we do x and y, then z will be the result."

A theory of action serves as

- a statement of the organization's beliefs about what is important to achieve the desired result;
- a tool to communicate the organization's priorities;
- a guide for strategic planning; and
- a framework for accountability.

Many of the theories of action we have seen are organized by

- programs (e.g., use culturally responsive instructional strategies);
- functions (e.g., investing in professional learning to support teachers); or
- responsibilities (e.g., the superintendent does . . . , the principal does . . . , teachers do . . .).

Theories of action propose links between strategies and results. Therefore, the tighter the connection between a few, targeted actions and the results, the better.

When district leaders look at these five aspects through the lens of strengthening the instructional core, they are better able to identify strategic opportunities and obstacles to effective instruction. Equity warriors create a through-line from the instructional core to the five aspects. It is as if each inquiry question ends with "strengthening the instructional core." For example, what assets in our district culture can help us strengthen the instructional core? What formal and informal structures hinder our progress in strengthening the instructional core?

Researcher Susan Moore Johnson and her colleagues used the PELP model in a study of five large urban districts that were selected because of their performance and improvement. The research team wanted to learn whether coherence making improved student achievement. The study focused on how the districts managed relationships between the central office and schools around three strategic priorities: staffing, budgeting, and academic programming. Academic programming was shorthand for curriculum, instruction, and assessment.

The researchers selected these three strategic priorities because they are indicators of a school's autonomy. The priorities provide the opportunity to quantify decision making. In other words, schools in decentralized districts would likely have more decision-making autonomy in staffing, budgeting, and academic programming than schools in centralized districts. Would a decentralized or a centralized approach to managing schools have a greater effect on student achievement? They found that either centralized or decentralized districts could achieve coherence. "The essential ingredient to improvement was whether a district could effectively implement whatever theory of action it chose" (Johnson et al., 2015, p. 20).

Districts were successful because they strived for coherence in decision making and establishing mutually supportive relationships and trust among central offices and schools.

> Without coherence, policies intended to spur creative action instead reward principals for gaming the system and often generate troubling inequities across schools. Those meant to bring order unintentionally lead to stagnation and schools' lack of responsiveness to the unique needs of their students and communities. In such cases, the basic elements of the organization (structures, systems, and resources) work in isolation or at cross-purposes. (Johnson et al., 2015, p. 156)

We know from our partnerships with Long Beach Unified and Montgomery County Public Schools, two centralized districts included in the study, that there was shared understanding and agreement on how decisions were made. There was a sense of pride in the "Long Beach Way" and the "Montgomery County Way." Each had individuals who worked for change, but they operated within the prevailing culture. That is, they integrated new ideas in ways that built on long-standing agreements. When someone new or outside the district attempted to introduce a change judged inconsistent with "the way," the systems and structures ceased to function or went underground until the interference was mitigated.

In Chapter 3, we shared an example from San Diego Unified School District, in which Cindy Marten and Staci Monreal worked to integrate three districtwide strategic planning documents into a school-based expectations and accountability plan. The annual school learning cycles aligned school practices to districtwide accountability. Those same learning cycles also provide an example of coherence-making of strategic goals, resources, and systems.

San Diego Unified school and district leaders did not argue with the four focus areas in the learning cycle: learning environment, engagement, differentiation, and student voice and agency. Discussions between school and district leaders were about the pace of implementation. Concerns about the pace were legitimate since the district was asking schools to rebuild—or in some places build—the necessary systems and structures. Achieving coherence depended on the following:

- Clear expectations for outcomes expressed in the learning cycles' guiding questions

- Flexibility in how schools answered the guiding questions based on their capacity

- District leaders' efforts to be supportive

- District and school leaders establishing relationships of trust

Where trusting relationships existed, district leaders could push and support, and principals could try and provide honest assessments of progress.

Equity warriors know that the politics of teaching and learning requires coherence-making to balance conflicts and govern effectively.

Equity warriors know that the politics of teaching and learning requires coherence-making to balance conflicts and govern effectively. By using the coherence framework as a guide, equity warriors can facilitate the analysis of existing or proposed strategies against the probability that the strategy will build coherence. Rather than dropping a rock in the pond and seeing what happens, district equity warriors can analyze the following:

- Whether and how the proposed strategy, initiative, or action will strengthen the instructional core

- Whether and how it is consistent with or informs the district theory of action

- Whether it is part of or consistent with an existing strategic direction and, if not, what the implications are for existing strategies

- Whether it builds on or alters the district culture, structures, and systems, and the implications for the culture, structure, and systems that are contributing to strengthening the instructional core

- Whether it uses or drains the capacity of stakeholders or other resources

- Whether it is compatible with or contrary to the compelling environmental forces

Leading the school board, district leadership team, and external partners through the process of using the coherence framework to analyze existing and proposed changes is a "muscle memory" building process. It requires baby steps. In some places, alignment may be one of those steps. There are others. Sometimes we begin by asking, "How is the strategy strengthening the instructional core and improving student achievement?" Asking the simple question in Norfolk led to eliminating multiple reading programs that neither deepened the district's capacity to teach reading nor resulted in increases in student reading levels. Sometimes district leaders take the next step and ask if they add this initiative, what will they be unable to do or need to stop doing. The simple pro-and-con analysis can help determine whether the benefit of something new (or more of something) is better than the current strategy.

Equity warriors use coherence frameworks as tools to build the district's capacity to analyze the effect of its systems, structures, and resources on its equity agenda.

Equity warriors use coherence frameworks as tools to build the district's capacity to analyze the effect of its systems, structures, and resources on its equity agenda. They build the analytical muscles of school boards, district leaders, and external partners to understand the importance of a focus on strengthening the instructional core. They use analysis based on the framework to move beyond anecdotal and intuitive initiatives and actions.

YOUR MOVE: IMPLEMENT A GUARANTEED AND VIABLE CURRICULUM FOR ALL STUDENTS MEASURED BY THE TASKS.

Standards-based reform and state testing of student performance changed teaching. Local, state, and common standards replaced textbooks as the baseline for defining what students should know and be able to do. Frankly, the so-called good ol' days before standards-based reform were really not that good for student academic achievement, particularly for students of color and students attending low-performing schools. The standards movement unveiled the systemic inequities in student access to knowledge and learning. It placed high accountability for student performance on teachers.

However, standards-based reform did not initially improve student learning and did not guarantee the availability of systems to support teachers to teach in new ways. In our work with some of the most underperforming schools in districts, we found the following:

- Novice teachers were unprepared in core content and charged with developing curriculum.
- Teachers were unfamiliar with or did not understand grade-level standards.
- Teachers were unable or unwilling to keep pace with curriculum pacing guides because of erratic student attendance and/or engagement in learning.
- Teachers did not believe they could work around or through perceived barriers to learning.
- Administrators were unable to hold teachers accountable for teaching to the standards and/or to support students in learning to the standards.

These schools had been neglected. There was no focused direction, little collaboration and sharing of expertise, great need with little opportunity to deepen learning, and no internal or external accountability. In short, there was no coherence.

In many cases, our partner schools were able to design systems and structures, engage stakeholders, make progress toward a positive organizational culture, and repurpose their resources. They made initial gains in student performance and maintained incremental gains over time. In spite of measurable progress, however, we learned that genuine progress in student learning is not possible without a guaranteed and viable curriculum.

McREL International (2017) describes a guaranteed and viable curriculum as one in which all students have equal time and access to learn rigorous content. A guaranteed and viable curriculum is attained when the following are in place:

- Agreements and common understandings of the essential content that all students need to know, understand, and be able to do
- Performance criteria
- Processes for monitoring implementation
- Structures to provide continuous support to implement with fidelity

Equity warriors assume responsibility for ensuring that there is a guaranteed and viable curriculum for all grade levels and within each school. District leaders are responsible for defining essential content and facilitating agreements and common understandings of the essential content. That responsibility cannot be delegated to school leaders and teachers. Just to be clear, we are not advocating a return to large central curriculum offices that produce curriculum binders and daily lesson plans. We believe that districts are responsible for defining the essential rigorous, standards-based content for each grade level. Here is why.

Equity warriors assume responsibility for ensuring that there is a guaranteed and viable curriculum for all grade levels and within each school.

An equity agenda begins with defining what we want for all of our students. Believing that every student should have access to the same educational opportunities that we want for our own children, curriculum should not vary from teacher to teacher and school to school. All students, particularly school-dependent students and high-mobility students, deserve consistency.

That consistency relies on rigorous standards that prepare students for postsecondary success. District leaders are in the best position to define the standards because of their connection with state and national standards, college and university entrance requirements, and 21st-century skills important to employers. District leaders can be more objective in setting standards, with feedback from school leaders and teachers, because of their distance from the daily teaching and learning process.

Equity warriors know that agreeing on the essential content is an ideal—the theoretical premise about what students should know and be able to do. It is not an absolute. But the ideal is an important starting point to anchor all the other steps. W. Edwards Deming (1994) reminds us about what scientists or researchers know—that knowledge acquisition begins with a theory. Without a theory to test, "there is nothing to revise. Without theory, experience has no meaning. Without theory, one has no question to ask. Hence without theory, there is no learning" (p. 103).

Equity warriors know that identifying the essential content is important work, but they also know that the real work is facilitating common understandings of the essential content. Building understanding and supporting teachers in implementation means facing some uncomfortable truths:

- District leaders rarely learn from teachers how to help them build understanding.
- Teachers and schools cannot learn from each other if they are teaching different curricula.
- In underperforming schools, students do not learn when teachers do not teach the entire curriculum.
- Elementary teachers who do not know mathematics do not teach it consistently, fully, or very well.
- Time and resources are wasted on interventions if the essential content is not being taught.

Flint Community Schools (FCS) provides an example of what can happen when a district introduced coherence by focusing on curriculum. In FCS's case, the district developed K–12 curriculum units in English language arts and mathematics.

Initially, my colleagues, led by Tiffiny Shockley Jackson, were charged with designing a system of instructional leadership coaching for district leaders and principals with a focus on walk-throughs as a data-gathering and analysis process. Later, we realized district leaders and our coaches could not provide meaningful coaching because there was no uniformity in curriculum expectations. In some schools, the same grade-level classrooms did not teach the same content, which meant it was impossible to determine why students were not learning. Most disturbing, although the core curriculum was undefined and varied, the district and schools were identifying students as having learning disabilities or needing intervention at alarming rates.

FCS's Linda Thompson and Eugene Rutledge decided on a do-over. They redirected resources to create coherence:

- They identified essential content with scope and sequence and aligned with state standards.

(Continued)

(Continued)

- They ensured all teachers across all schools received curriculum units and materials.

- They made a massive investment in summer professional development.

- They identified site-based staff developers to support teachers in implementing the curriculum units.

- They provided instructional leadership coaches for principals.

Even with these structures in place, improving teaching and learning was a slow and steady process. But with essential content and supporting structures, district leaders could identify teaching and learning gaps with confidence. Through implementation and monitoring, district leaders could find gaps in content, teacher knowledge, and student knowledge and skills. The essential content provided a common language to build knowledge about teaching and learning. It was possible to more accurately plan professional learning and strengthen supervision. District-based coaches assigned to schools became a bridge between schools and the district. Coaches informed district professional learning by communicating the realities of schools and strengthened implementation by sharing the district's intentions directly in conversations with teachers.

As a result, student learning and performance on state tests increased in FCS, reversing a multiyear trend. The guaranteed and viable curriculum built teacher efficacy as teachers had more accurate measures of student progress toward agreed-upon grade-level expectations.

San Diego Unified School District provides an example of a different approach based on a different context.

In 2017, San Diego Unified's student performance was the highest among all large California districts. Not satisfied, Cindy Marten and Staci Monreal determined that the absence of a guaranteed and viable curriculum was the reason that gains for all students were not commensurate with the district's allocation of resources and efforts. San Diego Unified's approach to creating a guaranteed and viable curriculum differed from that used in Flint. While FCS defined essential content and provided instructional units and materials, San Diego Unified doubled-down on focusing on tasks that demonstrate student knowledge and skills that would define essential content.

San Diego Unified partnered with Marzano Research to design proficiency scales for critical concepts in English language arts and mathematics for grades K–12. Marzano Research's theory is that teachers cannot address every standard every year, so they make independent decisions about which standards to include (Simms, 2016). Critical concepts are a narrow set of standards-based essential content for each grade level, similar to previous attempts to identify power standards. English language arts could have as many as 20 critical concepts a year; mathematics could have as many as 16 critical concepts each year for grades K–8 and as many as 64 during high school mathematics (Simms, 2016, p. 24).

Proficiency scales measure student knowledge and skills on each of the critical concepts. The San Diego Unified scales ranged from 0.5 (students need help to perform foundational expectations) to 4.0 (students can exceed proficiency). Each level of the scales provides examples of the knowledge and skills expected to achieve at that level. Teachers can use the scales to measure student proficiency and identify the foundational skills necessary for students to demonstrate proficiency (3.0).

District leaders gave schools scope and sequence documents that mapped the critical concepts and proficiency scales to the grade-level instructional materials adopted by the district and available to schools. Schools could reorder the pace of learning so that students would be exposed to content on state assessments before the assessment was given. Teachers could focus on how the essential content was taught and how they would assess student progress in mastering the concepts. School leaders could ensure that students had access to the most essential content for their grade level.

Both districts used essential content to balance conflicts and achieve their equity agenda. They defined what all students should know and be able to do at each grade level for English language arts and mathematics. They provided resources and professional learning to help teachers develop common understandings about essential content. They differed in their approaches to support teaching: Flint provided instructional strategies, and San Diego Unified provided guidance on developing tasks focused on essential content. Flint expected all schools to participate fully and provided professional learning and accountability to pressure change. San Diego Unified differentiated supports and pressure. Both districts used the instructional core to build systemic coherence.

YOUR MOVE: HAVE THE BOARD COMMIT TO BACK OFF FROM PERSONNEL ISSUES.

Equity warriors know that authority over personnel decisions is critical to advancing an equity agenda.

Equity warriors know that authority over personnel decisions is critical to advancing an equity agenda. As much as we believe in the importance of professional learning and continuous improvement, having the right people in the right seats on the bus improves student outcomes. In most cities and towns, school districts are the largest public-sector employer and sometimes the largest single employer overall. School boards are tempted to use the authority to approve personnel hiring to advance political or personal agendas. It doesn't stop with hiring. We know school boards in which the interests of individual employees are championed by board members, and school board members who have intervened when an employee was feeling pressured by supervisors. School districts, including those in the largest cities, are like small towns in which the people are connected through marriage, family, neighborhood, church, or history. Not knowing employees' back stories can create problems for those who hire, supervise, or engage with them.

Board interference exists and often is offered as an excuse for not advancing equity. When someone is untouchable—whether real or perceived—that restricts accountability. School board members who micromanage or interfere in hiring or promotion limit a leader's ability to lead. We know of more than one district in which the superintendent brought the names of her direct reports to the board for approval, only to discover that board members had already determined who would be in the superintendent's cabinet. Not only did the board's action undermine the superintendent's authority to select her team, but the board's "secret" action was known widely within the district, which further undermined the superintendent's authority. The message was clear: The board, not the superintendent, was administering the district.

When factors or reasons other than a candidate's instructional knowledge or perceived ability to do the job determine hiring or promotion, districts and schools settle for whomever is in the pool. When advancement doesn't seem possible or when personal allegiances are predominant, qualified candidates are dissuaded from applying. When the demands of the positions and the rewards are not commensurate with the expectations, the candidate pool is shallow. We have worked with school boards and superintendents in searching for district leaders for the past three decades. The trend has been that the pool contains fewer candidates for positions overall, and fewer candidates who have experience that leads to success.

The superintendent's authority to make personnel decisions—in law and in practice—varies among states and districts. For example, Boston's superintendent has the "exclusive authority to make appointments" for all positions except school board staff and "community superintendents." Even in the latter case, the superintendent's recommendation of a community superintendent is considered approved unless a majority of the board members object in writing within six days of the recommendation (Boston City Charter, 2007).

By contrast, the Texas Education Code checks the superintendent's authority through policies that invest authority in the board of trustees, which has "the exclusive power and duty to govern and oversee the management of the public schools of the district" (subchapter D, section 11.151b). The superintendent is charged with ensuring the board's policies and collaborating with the board (subchapter D, section 11.1512c). The board has the authority to approve or dismiss every employee hiring recommendation made by the superintendent (subchapter 1, section 11.1513b). Further, the superintendent may not prevent a school district employee from communicating directly with a board member (subchapter 1, section 11.1513j).

San Diego Unified provides an example of a district that has written policies that clarify expectations for the board and the superintendent. The board of trustees approves all management personnel employment decisions (San Diego Unified School District [SDUSD], 2018, GC-3). But district policies clearly establish the superintendent's authority as

> the board's sole point of direction to the operational organization. The board will set the direction for the operational organization only through the superintendent, functioning as the Chief Executive Officer. However, nothing herein shall prohibit a constructive, two-way dialogue with students, staff, parents, and the community as a means to engage all stakeholders in the work of the board and the district. (SDUSD, 2018, B/SR-1)

Additional policies amplify and clarify how the board and the superintendent will work with each other:

> The board will direct the superintendent only through official decisions of the full board. The board will make

decisions by formal, recorded vote in order to avoid any confusion about whether direction has been given. The superintendent is neither obligated nor expected to follow the directions or instructions of individual board members, officers, and committees unless the board has specifically delegated such exercise of authority. Should the superintendent determine that an information request received from an individual member or a committee requires a material amount of staff time or is unreasonable, the superintendent is expected to ask that the committee or the member refer such requests to the full board for authorization. (SDUSD, 2018, B/SR-2)

The superintendent is responsible for all matters related to the day-to-day operation of the organization, within the values expressed by the board in policy. All staff members are considered to report directly or indirectly to the superintendent. The board will give direction only to the superintendent and any other employee who may report directly to the board. The board will formally and/or informally evaluate only the superintendent and any other direct reports. Any member of the board may inform the superintendent of concerns related to the performance or conduct of any individual employee and may receive communications from individual employees. (SDUSD, 2018, B/SR-3)

Equity warriors know that having policies that define authority and send clear messages are essential to advancing equity. Personnel decisions—attracting, supporting, and advancing leaders throughout the district—are among the most powerful opportunities for district leaders to advance equity. District leaders should have the responsibility for personnel decisions and be accountable for their decisions. Of course, policies that can change with a board's majority vote or are ignored have limited value. The relationships among the board, the superintendent, and district leaders are what matters most. Increasing the chances of success are relationships built on a shared commitment to an equity agenda and mutual trust in the intent to form a district leadership team that is best able to advance equity.

Equity warriors know that having policies that define authority and send clear messages are essential to advancing equity.

YOUR MOVE: CREATE WIN-WIN RELATIONSHIPS WITH EMPLOYEE GROUPS OVER WHAT MATTERS.

We have waited until now to discuss the role of employee unions in advancing equity not because the role of unions is unimportant. Nothing could be further from reality. The ability of district and union equity warriors to balance conflicts and govern effectively is vital to the success of the equity agenda. Our reason for placing the move within the politics of teaching and learning is that, in our experience, the role of employee unions in improving teaching and learning has been largely disregarded and undervalued by unions and district leaders. Equity warriors know that their equity agenda will not be advanced unless that changes.

Starting in the late 1980s and operating for 30 years, the Panasonic Foundation's district partnership program had as its theory of action that systemic improvement could be achieved only through collaborative efforts by three entities—the board of education, the superintendent or district leaders, and the teachers union or association. At the beginning of the program, it was uncommon for district leaders to involve teachers unions in discussions of systemic reform efforts. The Panasonic Foundation recognized that unions, particularly in large urban districts, often had the most stable leadership of the three entities. If unions could be convinced to play a role in improving student achievement, the resulting improvements could be sustained over time.

Convincing union leaders to collaborate was not difficult. Respect is the core issue for unions. If district leaders respected the role of the union, their opinion, and their members, then union leaders were glad to engage. They understood that engagement did not mean the union was the decision maker. Engagement meant they would have a seat at the table and a voice in decision making. Union participation in district systemic improvement began with teachers, though in some districts, representatives from other employee groups joined in discussions as well.

As attacks on educators have intensified, initial efforts to forge collaboration have suffered. The triple effect of standards-based accountability systems, economic recessions, and more recently the aggressive anti-union mindset on board-district-union relationships has reinforced industrial-era models that elevate unions' focus on working conditions. The us-versus-them climate is evident in language and actions that pit union and district in opposition, not as parts of a whole. Principals, not wishing to be left out, have formed their own associations in order to ensure that their protections and working conditions kept pace with other unionized employee groups. In our confidential conversations, union leaders shared their support for our efforts to improve teaching and learning but admitted their full attention had to be on survival and holding onto working conditions. Union collaboration with district leaders can be perceived as a sign of weakness, and in the most extreme circumstances, union leaders are called "collaborators."

Board, district, and union leaders know how to operate using industrial models to further their own objectives. School board seats have been filled by members who favor or have been supported by unions. Union bashing, working-to-rule, budget cuts, proposed strikes, and other forms of muscle-flexing occurred. In one example, of the $200 million raised in 2010 to improve Newark (New Jersey) Public Schools, $89 million was spent on labor and contract costs (e.g., back pay and incentives, buyouts) and $58 million on charter school expansions (Russakoff, 2015, pp. 223–224). Both sides gained, with dubious benefits for students.

Equity warriors know that none of us is as smart as all of us. Blaming doesn't work. It makes no sense to build a wall between employees whose purpose is to care for, educate, and serve students and those who have responsibility for providing direction, supports, and resources for that purpose. It makes no sense to identify coherence around the instructional core as key to advancing equity while also fostering and sustaining conflicts over important but secondary considerations. It makes no sense to try to attract the next generation to enter the teaching profession while also making teaching less of a profession. It makes no sense to recognize the vital role school leaders have in advancing equity yet not address the demands of the position that force principals to make life choices that affect their health and families.

Equity warriors know that to advance equity it is imperative to recognize that district leaders and teacher/administrator unions/associations have shared interests in collaborating in the design and implementation of solutions to systemic challenges.

Equity warriors know that to advance equity it is imperative to recognize that district leaders and teacher/administrator unions/associations have shared interests in collaborating in the design and implementation of solutions to systemic challenges. After decades of blame, it is time for district and union/association leaders to collaborate with each other for student success. Unfortunately, few real examples of such collaboration have been sustained over time.

Formed in the late 1980s with support from the American Federation of Teachers and the National Education Association, the Teacher Union Reform Network (TURN) is a nationwide network of 200-plus union locals. TURN's goal is to create new union models that can take the lead in building and sustaining effective schools for all students. TURN has organized into regional groups of communities of practice to better address the opportunities and conditions of districts. To this end, TURN has identified standards that define responsible and responsive teachers unions. Among its standards are considering student learning as our primary goal and assuming professional accountability for student progress and taking responsibility for teaching quality, supporting teacher professional learning, and ensuring that teachers are empowered at the school and classroom levels (Teacher Union Reform Network, n.d.).

TURN regional conferences bring together board members and district and union leaders to learn and design collaborative initiatives to improve teaching and learning. Recent conferences have focused on topics such as social-emotional development as a lever for equity, teams working jointly to plan and implement teacher evaluation systems, and college- and career-ready standards to improve teaching and learning,

Similarly, the Panasonic Foundation required or strongly encouraged union representation on district teams attending its semiannual Leadership Associates Program, a three-day event during which teams wrestled with problems of practice from their districts in facilitated sessions augmented with cross-district professional learning. In addition to participating in the formal program and discussions, there was value in the informal relationship building that resulted from late-night dinners and conversations over a beverage away from the district. Facilitated discussions helped raise points of contention for consideration, encouraged all voices to be heard, and deepened understanding of the strengths and limitations of the partners.

There are systemic and political barriers to collaboration among school boards, district administrators, and unions/associations. Equity warriors recognize the interdependence of these parts of the system and take the first steps to identify common interests. They begin by having conversations among groups to determine the possibilities and the boundaries. Genuine invitations to have conversations are required for genuine problem solving. We have watched as union and management leaders in our partner districts have resolved differences when it was mutually beneficial to do so. Also, interest-based negotiations failed when efforts to understand each other's positions were abandoned for expediency or because of the ability of one participant to apply political pressure on the other. Reaching agreements on areas of mutual interest and clarifying boundaries that include the limits of each part of the system to deliver contributes to the ultimate success, and allows leaders to support each other's work within their part of the system.

A professional growth system provides an opportunity for district and union/association leaders to find common ground on teaching and learning. Our experiences taught us that even well-intentioned parties have difficulty reaching consensus on growth and development systems that advance equity through improving teaching and learning. We have assisted district partners develop pilot programs that use multiple measures such as peer coaching, videotaping lessons, portfolios based on performance rubrics, and/or action research. Many teachers do not like or value traditional growth and evaluation methods. Teachers embrace the pilots and prefer engaging in self-directed professional learning opportunities when they trust their evaluator. Yet, administrators and union leaders could not find it in their common interest to formalize alternatives to traditional methods. Another missed opportunity to strengthen feedback and improve teaching and learning.

Equity warriors know the power of creating win-win relationships with employee groups around improving the instructional core. They do so by focusing direction, cultivating collaborative cultures, deepening learning, and securing accountability in ways that are genuine, respectful, and honest. As these examples illustrate, in spite of the larger political climate, it is possible and in everyone's best interest to build relationships among the school board, district leaders, and the union that are focused on improving teaching and learning. Equity warriors take the risk of reaching out, checking their egos, and reimagining relationships. They use their common interest in advancing equity and reclaiming educator professionalism to balance conflicts, share responsibility, and support each other.

> *Equity warriors know the power of creating win-win relationships with employee groups around improving the instructional core.*

REFLECTION: *How are our systems, structures, resources, stakeholders, and culture contributing to strengthening the instructional core? Where among these are the most positive examples of coherence?*

_____

_____

_____

_____

_____

_____

_____

_____

DIPLOMACY: BUILD EXPERTISE AND CAPACITY AROUND TEACHING AND LEARNING

In *District Leadership That Works*, Robert Marzano and Timothy Waters (2009) were interested in answering two questions: Is there a relationship between district administrative actions and student achievement, and if so, what specific district actions are associated with student achievement? The answer to the first question was, yes, there is a positive relationship from effective district leadership. They identified five district leadership actions in answer to the second question:

- Ensuring collaborative goal setting so that all stakeholders agree to support the attainment of the goals

- Establishing non-negotiable goals for achievement and instruction

- Creating board alignment with and support of district goals

- Monitoring achievement and instruction goals

- Allocating resources to support the goals for achievement and instruction, particularly for professional development of teachers and principals (Marzano & Waters, 2009, pp. 6–8)

At first glance, these actions are consistent with the moves described in the preceding dimensions, particularly how equity warriors use diplomacy—rewards, consequences, and moral persuasion—to advance equity. When it comes to teaching and learning diplomacy facing complex situations, nuances are vital to district leader success. Three quandaries pull at district leaders who want to use teaching and learning diplomacy: relevance, reliability, and responsibility.

It comes as no surprise that school communities—administrators, teachers, staff, students, and families—do not perceive district leaders as relevant to teaching and learning. In our experience, they see district leaders as middle managers who get in the way, do not add value, and operate self-perpetuating systems for their own benefit. "I am from the district office and here to help you" is often met with a smile.

Further, in complex situations, hindsight does not lead to foresight as conditions are constantly changing. Therefore, the experiences of district leaders are not reliable resources for school communities that are working through uncharted territory. To school communities, everything is negotiable, and district leaders' mandates are to be avoided, handled superficially, or considered as advice.

The third quandary is maintaining the responsibility for improving teaching and learning at the school level. The more that district leaders are directive, the more responsibility for teaching and learning shifts from the school to the district level. The transfer of responsibility has multiple effects. Paramount among them is the difficulty of motivating school leaders and teachers to see improving the instructional core as their area of responsibility.

Equity warriors resolve these quandaries by adjusting their diplomatic moves to build coherence to address complexity. They keep the focus on the equity agenda from the classroom to the boardroom, learn with school communities, and help schools learn from each other.

YOUR MOVE: EXPECT DISTRICT LEADERS TO BE INSTRUCTIONAL LEADERS AND LEARNERS.

The leap from being a school leader to a district leader with responsibilities for improving teaching and learning, particularly where one is supervising schools, is huge. District leaders who make the leap are often caught in the relevance quandary. They know too well that when they were in schools, they had little regard for district leaders' advice. Unless they are directly supervising a principal or overseeing other school-based administrators, they have little position power. They imagine their locus of power comes from what they did, not from what they are now charged to do. Principal supervisors push principals to replicate the programs and initiatives that they found successful. District professional developers push curriculum, instructional strategies, and programs they have worked with before.

District leaders are often asked to lead what they don't know. They are expected to know schools, people, and communities. Their survival depends on their success in managing the internal politics of the central office, knowing how to access resources to support their schools, and being alert to shifting trends among board members and the community at large. They continually sort through requests, trying to determine which requests are real and require responses and those that do not. District leaders quickly learn that a lack of knowledge or understanding about a situation is unacceptable. Through confidential coaching that is nonevaluative and built on trust over time, we have learned the simple truth that district leaders often share a profound sense of vulnerability grounded in a fear that a misstep will cost future advancement or loss of position.

Equity warriors know that advancing equity requires diplomacy that redefines the relationships between district offices and schools. To advance equity, district leaders recognize that the improvement of teaching and learning is their primary responsibility, that the scope of responsibility and expectations for themselves are explicitly connected to improving teaching and learning; and they are committed to learning with others, particularly principals and teachers.

Equity warriors know that advancing equity requires diplomacy that redefines the relationships between district offices and schools.

In a study for the Wallace Foundation, Meredith Honig and her colleagues examined central office practices that support schools. They were able to validate that districts generally do not experience districtwide improvements in teaching and learning without substantial central office engagement in support of schools. Their study found that central office engagement in support of teaching and learning had two primary elements: learning-focused partnerships with school principals to deepen principals' instructional leadership practice, and reorganizing and reculturing each central office unit to improve evidence-based partnerships and teaching and learning (Honig et al., 2010).

Central office leaders who were assigned to help principals full time were the point persons in shifting the principal's role to instructional leader. The partnerships included the following:

- Modeling for principals on how to think and act as instructional leaders
- Developing and using tools that supported principal engagement
- Brokering external resources to help principals

Central offices assisted the point persons by providing supports, removing issues that interfered with the partnership, working with schools through the point person, and holding principals accountable for their schools' performance. Central office staff were assigned to specific schools, learned about their assigned schools, and engaged in problem solving with the schools to help improve teaching and learning. Central office capacity building, training, and accountability shifted to focus resources, relationships, and supports in ways that affected the schools' capacity to improve teaching and learning.

Honig and her colleague Lydia Rainey continued to study how principal supervisors grow their ability to strengthen principal capacity to improve teaching and learning. Again, they found that central office and principal supervisors are critical providers of on-the-job supports that build principal capacity on teaching and learning. They also found that prior knowledge and experience in supporting principals in teaching and learning does not always translate into the principal supervisor's continued growth as a capacity builder. Supervisors who refocus job descriptions and devote their time to teaching and learning capacity building can help principal supervisors by modeling thinking consistent with the role and removing interference. Also, the disposition of principal supervisors to learn with their colleagues and to stay focused on teaching and learning contributes to their growth (Honig & Rainey, 2019, pp. 445–462).

> *Equity warriors know that teaching and learning will improve when everyone in the district advances equity by making teaching and learning improvement their personal priority.*

Equity warriors know that teaching and learning will improve when everyone in the district advances equity by making teaching and learning improvement their personal priority. Often, they use the diplomatic tools of rewards and consequences to refocus or disrupt the organization when using moral persuasion to convince others of the correctness of their cause is not enough to change behaviors. What it means to make teaching and learning a priority for each role varies by role and district. There is a great deal of pressure to let other concerns, issues, and responsibilities push out teaching and learning as a priority, even when it is explicitly stated by the district and personally held by individuals. To build coherence, conditions for success include strict guidelines and district leaders who are rewarded (rather than punished) by pushing back on interference.

One way to be explicit about guidelines and arm district leaders to keep their focus on teaching and learning is to craft job descriptions and selection processes for roles that are focused primarily on teaching and learning. Here is an example from a district of about 17,000 students.

> The newly appointed superintendent sought to increase central authority and accountability for supporting schools and increasing student achievement. He chose to do so by streamlining authority and resources with accountability within the central office. He simplified organizational reporting lines so that schools were supervised by one of the two assistant superintendents (elementary or

secondary level), who in turn reported to the deputy superintendent. The deputy superintendent's primary responsibility was to ensure that the work of the two assistant superintendents aligned with the board's and superintendent's vision, which was to prepare every student for higher education and success in the 21st century.

To shift the central office culture away from organizational silos that protected turf, the superintendent was determined to hire the deputy and two assistant superintendents from outside the organization and described their duties in great detail in the public job descriptions as a way to message the shift internally and externally. The descriptions said the assistant superintendents would be responsible for the oversight, alignment, and implementation of K–5 (or 6–12) academic programs including curriculum, instruction, and assessment; and school support and accountability systems including supervision, school improvement, and leadership and professional development.

The duties for fulfilling these responsibilities were very specific and comprehensive, vesting authority in the assistant superintendents for all decisions affecting their school levels. Though exhaustive, the list of duties and responsibilities left little doubt about where the authority and decision making lay. The job descriptions attracted assistant superintendents who wanted to be empowered to provide supervision and direct resources and staff where they decided staff were most needed. Costs for creating these three positions were reallocated from other central office positions that were determined to be duplicative or unnecessary to support schools under the new structure. Shifting staff and their responsibilities opened the opportunity for reculturing and professional learning. Staff turnover and reassignments occurred throughout the first year as staff settled into their new roles and new ways of working.

Equity warriors know that successful administrators at all levels are adept at identifying and responding to what is most important to the organization and, in particular, to their supervisors. They also know that without constant attention and push, adults will revert to their strengths and experiences. Making systemic change is like pulling at a rubber band—it stretches against pressures to return to its original shape unless scaffolds are put in place. Equity warriors stretch and redirect the organization and cement new directions by building coherence and aligning the roles of all central office leaders to the equity agenda.

Equity warriors stretch and redirect the organization and cement new directions by building coherence and aligning the roles of all central office leaders to the equity agenda.

YOUR MOVE: CREATE SYSTEMS OF SUPPORT FOR RIGOROUS LEARNING.

As complexity increases, so does confusion about the effectiveness of existing systems to support teaching and learning. Confusion is accompanied by a lack of clarity about who leads, what they lead, and for what purpose. Those who are at the extremes tug at systems in opposite ways—stepping in to a situation to exert control to build and dismantle, or standing by until the way forward is crystal clear. Equity warriors seek the middle position. Complexity offers opportunities to raise questions about how systems operate and to test and study alternatives. Equity warriors ask: Are we using our resources effectively to establish conditions for learning in which all, not some, students are achieving success?

District leaders can use rewards, consequences, and moral persuasion to begin answering the question of effectiveness and addressing the three quandaries of relevance, reliability, and responsibility. District equity warriors show their *relevance* by using their districtwide perspective, values, and data to define the strengths and challenges for the current systems. They gather information through community networks and colleagues outside their community to introduce *reliable* approaches that are relevant to their situation. They lead the design of systems that address the needs of all students, provide the supports that teachers need, and contribute—rather than take away—school-level *responsibility* for student success.

Teachers are asking for help in addressing systems of support for learning. Teachers know that students arriving at their doors are facing a wide range of challenges in their personal lives and have access to fewer external social institutions for assistance. Teachers also know these challenges affect students' ability to learn and act in ways that do not disrupt the learning of other students. In schools that serve high-poverty neighborhoods, teachers know intergenerational poverty can have a profound effect on student motivation and the support systems that produce a culture of achievement. Teachers ask for help, more support, more guidance, more learning. They wonder where the help will come from and how they fit new learning into their demanding school day and lives.

A student's peers are key ingredients in supporting their learning. Educators and families with privilege act on this knowledge in different ways: by selecting their residence to access a particular public school or district, by choosing private and religious schools, or by moving out of a public school system during the middle school years. Families know that just proximity to others is not enough and that their children will select and be selected by peers who will influence their attitude toward learning.

More astute families and educators know there are opportunities within the traditional public schools to exercise control over a student's circle of friends. School districts across the country wrestle with differentiating opportunities for students, sometimes as early as kindergarten. Gifted and talented programs are one of the ways public schools accommodate the interests of some families. On the surface, it makes sense to provide rigorous learning opportunities for students who are clearly advanced years beyond their age-level peers. However, families choose gifted and talented programs for multiple reasons—for perceived access to competitive schools, for access to better-prepared teachers, for status, or to isolate students from others who do not look like them. Families that are proactive seek out knowledge about the programs and admission process, and prepare their children for admission tests. It is also the case that families of color recognize gifted and talented programs as a systemically racist practice and are intentional in *not* applying for admission into a program they do not trust or within which their child may be the only student of color in her class.

Principals, administrative teams, and teachers are often powerless to change a system that has buy-in from some vocal and politically active families and district leaders. It is a true dilemma for public school systems that want to serve the interests of all families and recognize that there are structures that pit families and students against each other, are counterproductive, and maintain racial inequities.

Gifted and talented programs and homogeneous grouping of students are a few of many examples of *structural inequities built on assumptions that educating a few students well is ample proof that the public school system works.* As we explored in Chapter 1, a heavy reliance on closing achievement gaps as a primary policy approach continues to foster competition that pits groups against each other. Further, it stacks the deck against seeing possibilities of change, as A. Wade Boykin and Pedro Noguera (2001) suggest:

> In schools where race and class are strong predictors of achievement, where few Black or Latinx students are enrolled in gifted and honors courses but are overrepresented in special education and remedial courses, and where the link between race and achievement has been firmly established in the minds of educators, a sense of inevitability often leads to complacency about the effort to raise student achievement. In such communities, *the failure of*

students of color can become normalized as educators
and others rationalize and accept low performance as
the by-product of factors they cannot control. (pp. 32–33;
emphasis added)

We are not suggesting that students should be denied access to gifted and talented programs, or rigorous instruction. Eliminating programs seriously undermines public confidence in the traditional public schools and results in families seeking alternatives that seem a better fit for their students. Also, the conversation diverts attention, resources, and political will from the equity agenda, as if denying students access to rigorous instruction is good for anyone. Frankly, our experience is that families do not want to deny opportunities to other students. They want to be certain that opportunities for their students are available.

Equity warriors advocate for accelerated learning and rigor for all students and understand that giftedness extends to many areas beyond core academics.

Equity warriors advocate for accelerated learning and rigor for all students and understand that giftedness extends to many areas beyond core academics. At a rhetorical level, this is the point of standards-based/competency-based education. The bar is set, and everyone has the opportunity to reach the bar. If the bar is set at the right level of rigor, reaching the bar means students are successfully prepared to proceed. There will always be some students who will be motivated and able to do more, and opportunities should be open to them. Nevertheless, the public education system should not be in the position—through its structures, practices, and programs—to decide which students will be given rigorous instruction and which will not. Not only is it morally wrong, but it robs us of adults prepared to contribute to our society and economy.

Equity warriors know that the knowledge of how to educate all students to high levels is available to us. Research and practices used in gifted and talented education, and through programs such as International Baccalaureate and Advanced Placement, are known and available to any who choose to access them. Still, systems that rely solely on improving the instructional capacity of teachers will not produce the necessary supports for learning for all students. A more comprehensive approach is necessary.

There is extensive research on systems of support that— at their core—include rigorous teaching and learning strategies specifically targeted at improving the academic achievement of students of color. For example, the National Study Group for the Affirmative Development of Academic Ability describes structures and supports that contribute to academic ability. Since academic ability is developed, not fixed at birth, there are school-level interventions that are known to have impact:

- High-quality teaching and instruction in the classroom to refocus the learning process from the private understandings students acquired before coming to school. Teaching strategies include knowledge acquisition, improving comprehension through consolidation of knowledge, the ability to perform a complex task without conscious awareness or effort, deep understanding, and transferability.

- Trusting relationships in school that address mistrust of public schools as an institution, how students of color react to feedback (positive and negative) on their performance, and self-acceptance of students of color in higher academic settings in which they may be a significant minority.

- Supports for pro-academic behavior in the school and community to enhance social capital, such as particular norms that encourage student learning by addressing gaps in attitudinal and behavioral demands of high academic achievement, and the provision of supplementary education and models of academic excellence. (National Study Group for the Affirmative Development of Academic Ability, 2004)

Culturally Responsive-Sustaining Education (CRSE) is one step in addressing conditions to strengthen teaching and learning and build trusting relationships and pro-academic behavior. The New York State Department of Education's CRSE framework offers district policy makers guidance to create student-centered learning environments that affirm cultural identities; foster positive academic outcomes; develop students' abilities to connect across lines of difference; elevate historically marginalized voices; empower students as agents of social change; and contribute to individual student engagement, learning, growth, and achievement through the cultivation of critical thinking (New York State Department of Education, n.d., pp. 6–7). The framework includes four principles that define the elements of CRSE:

- **A welcoming and affirming environment** feels safe. It is a space where people can find themselves represented and reflected, and where they understand that all people are treated with respect and dignity. The environment ensures that all cultural identities (i.e., race, ethnicity, age, gender, sexual orientation, disability, language, religion, socioeconomic background) are affirmed, valued, and used as vehicles for teaching and learning.

- **High expectations and rigorous instruction** prepare the community for rigor and independent learning. The environment is academically rigorous and intellectually challenging, while also considering the different ways students learn. Instruction includes opportunities to use critical reasoning, take academic risks, and leverage a growth mindset to learn from mistakes. Messages encourage positive self-image and empower others to succeed.

- **Inclusive curriculum and assessment** elevate historically marginalized voices. It includes opportunities to learn about power and privilege in the context of various communities and empowers learners to be agents of positive social change. It provides the opportunity to learn about perspectives beyond one's own scope. It works toward dismantling systems of biases and inequities, and decentering dominant ideologies in education.

- **Ongoing professional learning** should be rooted in the idea that teaching and learning is an adaptive process needing constant reexamination. This allows learners to develop and sharpen a critically conscious lens toward instruction, curriculum, assessment, history, culture, and institutions. Learners must be self-directed and take on opportunities that directly affect learning outcomes. (New York State Department of Education, n.d., pp. 14–15)

Further, the framework recognizes that mindsets are foundational to achieving CRSE. The framework names three beliefs about teaching and learning:

- Believing that culture is not an addition but is a critical component of education

- Believing that critical and continuous self-reflection is required to dismantle systems of biases and inequities rooted in our country's history, culture, and institutions

- Believing that students and their families are individuals with their own assets, knowledge, and abilities who should be valued and consulted (New York State Department of Education, n.d., p. 16)

Equity warriors know that to reach students and engage them in high levels of learning, they must do more than "see students." They must understand and redirect the systems of support for students in ways that are culturally responsive. Even well-intended systems can be ineffective if they are inattentive and fail to recognize the gifts students and their families bring to learning. Cultural responsiveness builds trust. It is an essential foundation for differentiating support to meet the specific needs of students.

Equity warriors know that systems that address the conditions for learning are broad enough to encompass various student needs and specific enough for school-level implementation based on student needs. Many districts wrestle with versions of integrated multi-tiered systems of supports, or IMTSS (see Figure 5.2). It is another sign of deficit-model thinking that too often the use of an IMTSS is thought to be a special education strategy or is placed within the purview of a district's special education division. Creating conditions so that all students are prepared for learning applies to all students. Our schools were not designed around ensuring that all students would be successful. If that were the case, IMTSS would be in place first, rather than squeezed into an available space within the overall system.

We have borrowed from the good thinking of many districts and states in our thinking about an IMTSS that has the following components:

- Strong curriculum and instructional practices, and a student progress monitoring system
- Data tracking and a professional development system to improve teacher practices, effectiveness, and efficacy
- Tiers representing levels of differentiated services—for all students, for some, for a few
- Structured/tiered continuum of support implemented before referrals to external service providers or exclusion from school
- Collaboration among academic, special education, and student services divisions
- District- and/or community-based intervention and support teams to provide professional development, planning, coaching, and crisis support
- Partnerships, agreements, and protocols with teachers unions, city or state agencies, and insurance providers to support teachers, staff, and students based on need (e.g., Medicare, uninsured, underinsured, or unable to afford copayments)

FIGURE 5.2 ● Integrated Multi-Tiered System of Supports

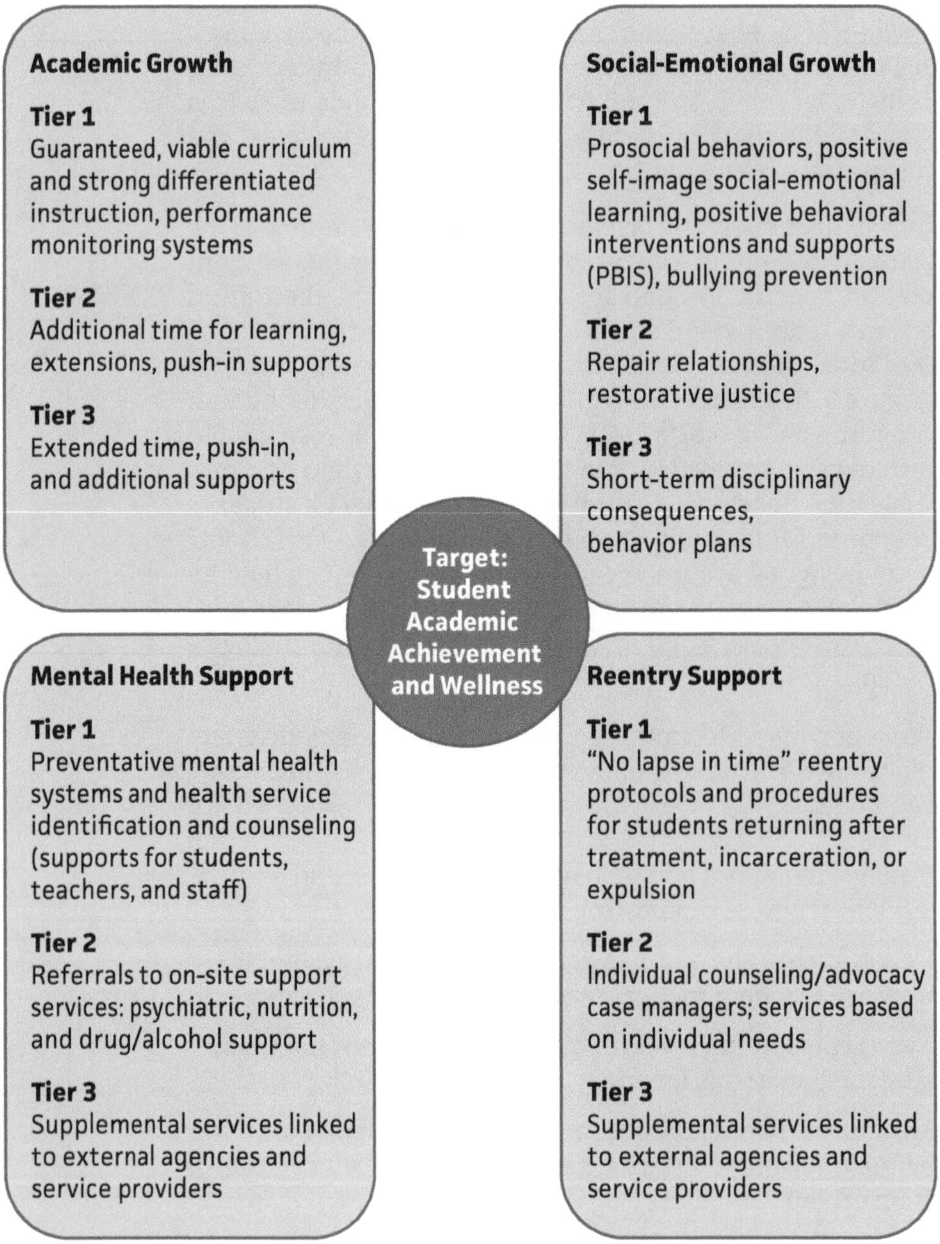

Academic Growth

Tier 1
Guaranteed, viable curriculum and strong differentiated instruction, performance monitoring systems

Tier 2
Additional time for learning, extensions, push-in supports

Tier 3
Extended time, push-in, and additional supports

Social-Emotional Growth

Tier 1
Prosocial behaviors, positive self-image social-emotional learning, positive behavioral interventions and supports (PBIS), bullying prevention

Tier 2
Repair relationships, restorative justice

Tier 3
Short-term disciplinary consequences, behavior plans

Target: Student Academic Achievement and Wellness

Mental Health Support

Tier 1
Preventative mental health systems and health service identification and counseling (supports for students, teachers, and staff)

Tier 2
Referrals to on-site support services: psychiatric, nutrition, and drug/alcohol support

Tier 3
Supplemental services linked to external agencies and service providers

Reentry Support

Tier 1
"No lapse in time" reentry protocols and procedures for students returning after treatment, incarceration, or expulsion

Tier 2
Individual counseling/advocacy case managers; services based on individual needs

Tier 3
Supplemental services linked to external agencies and service providers

There are variations on the systems of support that are dependent on the district's equity agenda and resources. Some are designed to create district-level response teams that can provide differentiated training and support to schools. For example, the mission of the Portland (Oregon) Public Schools (PPS) Multi-Tiered System of Support department is to "support schools in the development of sustainable academic and behavioral tiered systems of support through relationship building, focused training, and strategic coaching to ensure that schools have the systems needed to guarantee equitable outcomes for all students" (Portland Public Schools, n.d.).

The PPS MTSS department has eight teams that engage schools and communities to support the following areas:

- Social-emotional learning
- Restorative justice
- Distributive leadership structures, including instructional leadership teams, climate teams, professional learning communities, student intervention teams, tiered academic support, and tiered behavioral supports
- Data monitoring and analysis
- Attendance and engagement
- Rapid response for students displaying high-risk behaviors
- Student conduct and discipline (Portland Public Schools, n.d.)

Equity warriors know that their equity agenda must address the fundamental social inequities that are foundational to the current version of public education systems and structures. There is a deep database of research and practice that to this point has been used largely to tinker with existing systems and structures. That is understandable. A system's primary mission is self-preservation, particularly when the system is facing complexity. The current system's success at self-preservation is tied more closely to adult egos and interests— families, teachers, school or district administrators, and board members—than to the needs of students. Nevertheless, facing complex situations is precisely the opportunity for district equity warriors to use diplomacy—rewards, consequences, and moral persuasion—to step out on the path of reorganizing around true and accurate conditions of learning. By doing so, equity warriors demonstrate their relevance and reliability and act on their responsibility so that others can do the same.

Equity warriors know that their equity agenda must address the fundamental social inequities that are foundational to the current version of public education systems and structures.

YOUR MOVE: DESIGN DISTRICT PROFESSIONAL LEARNING THAT RESULTS IN IMPROVED INSTRUCTION.

Our shelves are lined with books about professional learning for educators. Each of them—sometimes strongly and sometimes subtly—sends a similar message: Superintendents and district leaders design and use professional learning poorly. For example, researchers cite professional development programs that

- are not learner centered—do not ask the audience what they need;
- are not knowledge centered—lack the opportunity to understand why, when, where, and how the learning might be valuable to them;
- are not assessment centered—introductory sessions are not followed by opportunities to experiment and receive feedback; and
- are not community centered—learning is conducted in isolation without continued contact and support (National Research Council, 2002, p. 27).

Experienced practitioners encourage superintendents and district leaders to

- both direct and empower;
- create a common language;
- monitor the implementation process as they develop principal capacity to lead;
- limit initiatives; and
- communicate priorities effectively (Dufour & Marzano, 2011, pp. 28–46).

As much as it troubles us to admit it, large-scale, district-level professional development systems have been ineffective in helping adults examine their beliefs and biases and develop the knowledge, skills, and dispositions to advance equity by improving teaching and learning.

Equity warriors know that continuous, meaningful, and effective professional learning is critical to advancing equity and improving teaching and learning.

The three quandaries for superintendents and district leaders are most apparent in the area of professional learning. As researchers and practitioners above suggest, district-led professional learning is provided to diverse audiences without defining the purpose, considering the context, following up after learning sessions, and monitoring outcomes. Professional learning follows a generic formula applied to generic content. Time is not devoted to creating clarity and understanding before participating in professional learning. The answers to questions about relevance, reliability, and responsibility are simple—district leaders have decided what is relevant to the participants' work and have determined that the content is reliable. The district leaders' responsibility is to provide the information; the recipients' responsibility is to receive it. Session over. Check. Done.

Equity warriors know that continuous, meaningful, and effective professional learning is critical to advancing equity and improving teaching and learning. They strive to develop professional learning around effective practices that apply to their objectives, context, resources, and where district and individual needs are met. They do so in three ways: by embedding professional learning in the district culture or ways of working, by motivating and encouraging everyone to engage in professional learning, and by creating structures to have schools direct professional learning.

Equity warriors build an organizational culture in which everyone is expected to be a learner, and everyone applies their learning to their work.

Culture

Equity warriors build an organizational culture in which everyone is expected to be a learner, and everyone applies their learning to their work. The possibilities and directions are endless when considering how to fill gaps in knowledge around equity and improving teaching and learning. Therefore, district leaders begin the process by naming a specific purpose that will advance their equity agenda. Defining the direction helps district and school leaders set parameters for their initial professional learning. We have mentioned the importance of purpose often. Applying purpose to learning, adults are more successful when they understand the reasons for learning and what success looks like.

One of our learnings is that processes and content need to be simplified. In our work with district leaders, we help design simple processes and protocols that do not require much time to learn. We have found that the energy spent on learning processes decreases energy available to apply the protocol. For example, we have been guilty of spending too much time and engaging too many people to create strategic plans. The plan was the goal. Frankly, the plans were never good enough for the participants to feel that they accomplished something of value. We lost reliability.

We had more success working with partners in designing protocols that fostered strategic thinking rather than strategic plans and more success in designing guidelines rather than the just-right model. For example, we found it more important for district leaders seeking consistent implementation of professional learning communities to focus on critical questions that define the work than to prescribe models that focused on membership, meeting protocols, schedules, communications strategies, and other ways to operationalize the model. Again, we learned the hard way that rather than designing detailed hybrid, remote, and in-person learning models, it was better to assist each school to clarify objectives and design models given their specific context.

In addition, we have learned the effectiveness of integrating learning into workstreams. School board meetings or quarterly retreats provide blocks of time for board member learning. Superintendents have led board members through deep data dives and sample state assessment questions so they can gain a better understanding of the changing expectations for students. Superintendents have engaged board members and staff in restorative justice circles to deepen understanding. Cabinets have reserved time for weekly, biweekly, or monthly book studies. In Norfolk, superintendent John Simpson selected books that reflected his leadership beliefs. His monthly 90-minute learning sessions were devoted to deep discussions of assigned chapters led by cabinet members as well as identification of applications for their management systems. More than once, cabinet members asked to repeat the book for even deeper reflection on the learnings and to review the applications that had been piloted.

Once a culture of professional learning begins to take hold, individuals will create structures for learning with others that fit their time and interests. When San Diego Unified established a districtwide focus on reading, schools began to buy classroom sets of books, and district leaders responsible for middle schools organized book clubs to discuss adolescent literature. As they met after school hours and sipped beverages, they became familiar with the nuances of the genre and developed questions to discuss with students during their visits. The district's culture changed.

Motivation

Equity warriors know that some adults need motivation to be learners.

Equity warriors know that some adults need motivation to be learners. For some, finding time for learning is just like a New Year's resolution—well intended and difficult to achieve. Nevertheless, meaningful professional learning to advance equity and improve teaching and learning should cause a change to occur. The change can be increased understanding or starting or stopping something. Personal ownership for learning is necessary to move beyond participation and awareness about the learning to application.

Executive coaches begin their process by helping clients determine the objectives or desired outcomes. Similarly, growth and development systems target objectives and actions that demonstrate the objectives were met. Yet, threat of consequences is only one diplomatic tool that can be used to motivate learning.

District leaders often create voluntary professional learning for middle-level district leaders interested in deepening their instructional knowledge and leadership. Participants engage in learning in synchronous and asynchronous sessions, and join collegial groups of three or four with the support of a mentor to design and present a project to address district priorities. School supervisors have designed similar programs for assistant principals. The assistant principals volunteer to meet with the supervisor, engage in professional learning, and join in triads to design and execute schoolwide projects in a yearlong program. In all cases, supervisors become more familiar with the participants' skills and are able to judge participants' readiness for advancement. Typically, there is no promise of promotion, although these programs are known to be stepping stones. District leaders benefit from advancing leaders with demonstrated experience in district priorities as well as the possibility of launching new ideas.

Structures

Equity warriors know that the effectiveness of any strategy, particularly those targeted at improving teaching and learning, depends on the human and social capital of the school where the instructional core lives. Therefore, district leaders begin creating structures to engage schools in analyzing their needs against their equity agenda and objectives and having school leaders drive professional learning. In other words, district leaders create structures to help clarify and prioritize their needs, understand their current capacity, set learning targets, and plan professional development. If schools are responsible for implementing adult learning that results in changes in practice, then schools are the drivers. District leaders are supporters.

Equity warriors know that the effectiveness of any strategy, particularly those targeted at improving teaching and learning, depends on the human and social capital of the school where the instructional core lives.

In our partnerships, we have helped district leaders create reciprocal and horizontal structures to alter top-down relationships between district and school leaders. Our intention has been to foster an organizational culture in which school principals are concerned about the success of other schools in the district, not just their own. Here, we offer two examples of engaging principals in reciprocal learning.

At the time, the high schools in Long Beach Unified School District had coprincipals. One benefit was the ease in gathering principals for multi-hour blocks of professional learning. A principal from each of the schools volunteered for one of two groups, one focused on

(Continued)

(Continued)

English language arts and the other on mathematics. The groups met monthly with central office curriculum/professional development leaders in their content area. The groups' objectives were to learn about the curriculum and to bring questions and concerns from their department heads and teachers as well as requests for support.

Over the months and years that the groups met, principals deepened their content knowledge and understanding of trends and proposed changes in state and district policy. The meetings were a place for principals to share their walk-through observations and key results visits and learn to identify strengths and challenges and coaching techniques in a professional setting. Principals and district leaders discussed and collaboratively developed priorities for district-level support for professional learning.

There were times when the exchanges between principals and district leaders were heated. It was through these dialogues over time that school leaders were able to help district leaders design and provide supports that were better aligned with the schools' needs. It also helped district leaders test receptivity to policies and curriculum changes before final decisions were made.

In San Diego Unified School District, we were asked to support 13 middle schools that had been identified as in need of assistance. In California at the time, schools that did not make annual progress on state growth targets had five years to improve or face sanctions. Some of the 13 schools were new to the list; others were in their third or fourth year. Principals from these 13 schools were not happy about being on the list or receiving "support" and, in particular, being called together once a month to meet with district leaders.

We knew that the schools had strengths as well as challenges. We also knew district leaders were pushing programs, supports, and resources on schools to show they were doing their part to help schools make adequate progress and escape the list. As part of our support, we asked the 13 principals and the district curriculum/professional development leaders to meet with us once a month. Our intent in bringing them together was to create a dialogue for schools to learn from each other, for district leaders to learn from the school leaders, and to inform the district leaders' decision making.

The first meeting was rocky. Each principal shared a rosy description of her school's English language arts and mathematics programs. Everything was going well. Nobody needed district support! Over time, the dialogue became more honest, open, and real. Principals had a lot of questions, brought challenges, engaged with each other, raised complaints, and vented. The agenda was split to give equal time to English language arts and mathematics. Before long, we realized that there was not enough time to delve deeply into both content areas, so the content alternated each month.

We had observed principals asking questions and taking notes. Principals asked to bring a teacher leader and their vice principal with them to one of the content meetings. Principals who traveled with the colleagues reported that they used the time to prepare and plan together, which helped shape next steps. As in the Long Beach example, there were times that discussions were heated. On more than one occasion, the district's chief academic officer introduced a draft policy and recommendation for a new instructional program. The feedback was strong in opposition to the policy, and she objected to having her judgment questioned. Nevertheless, over time, these meetings deepened principals' knowledge of, and support from, district leaders.

These two examples show some of the possibilities and difficulties in changing district culture to support professional learning that improves teaching and learning. When principals are brought together with district leaders in dialogue over time, principals gain a deeper understanding of the resources available to them and the outcomes they can expect from the effective use of the resources. When principals have a platform to engage with colleagues and voice their opinions about the professional learning support they need, they have stronger ownership and responsibility for ensuring implementation. However, district leaders are not completely comfortable with confrontation or having their work questioned. Rather than accepting dialogue and questioning as productive, they may be inclined to react or withdraw.

Equity warriors know that addressing the digital divide in teaching and learning may be the most significant of equity challenges and possibly the greatest opportunity to reimagine the district and school relationship around professional learning.

As a final note, equity warriors know that addressing the digital divide in teaching and learning may be the most significant of equity challenges and possibly the greatest opportunity to reimagine the district and school relationship around professional learning. At a minimum, we have learned the uses of Zoom/Team meetings and conference calls for communicating, conducting business, and learning. Just the savings of travel time in some districts contributes significantly to effectiveness. In New York City, after the pandemic began, system leaders communicated directly with more than 2,500 principals and district and central office leaders in regularly scheduled video meetings as easily as they could with 10 people. Even before the pandemic, some districts were far ahead in one-to-one learning and reestablishing district offices as clearinghouses of openly licensed educational resources and sharing teacher-created materials. Most districts have yet to unleash the potential for providing just-in-time supports for teachers in designing lessons and interschool collaboration in learning from and with each other. A great opportunity for district and school leaders to build systems that work is waiting to be seized.

Equity warriors use professional learning to advance equity and improve teaching and learning.

Equity warriors use professional learning to advance equity and improve teaching and learning. They know that since the desired outcome is to strengthen the instructional core in each classroom, school leaders need to own responsibility for professional learning that addresses the context of their school. They clarify the roles and responsibility of district leaders to embed professional learning in district culture or ways of working, motivate and encourage everyone to engage in professional learning, and create structures in which schools direct professional learning. They help school leaders act on their knowledge and implement changes in practice so that everyone is learning and growing.

YOUR MOVE: GET THE BEST POSSIBLE TEACHERS INTO EVERY CLASSROOM.

This country desperately needs the best and brightest to become teachers. Teacher shortages and long-term vacancies are occurring even in communities that have not been hard to staff traditionally. District leaders can do little to address the economic, social, and political factors that affect the teaching profession nationally. District leaders continue to commit substantial resources to recruiting and hiring teachers, particularly teachers of color and men who are underrepresented in a profession that is 76 percent female and 79 percent white (National Center for Education Statistics, 2020). Yet, their efforts are often undermined by specific practices and by not using fully the diplomatic tools available to them.

District leaders own responsibility for providing a pool of qualified candidates for school leaders to consider. Equity warriors can take steps to advance equity in attracting candidates to work in the district: develop and monitor human capital placement practices, recruit effectively, attract and mentor student teachers, and induct new teachers. While savvy school leaders are proactive and take on these steps, they do so because district leaders have not been reliable.

Placement

Equity warriors know they need to have their own house in order to recruit effectively. Human resource/capital officers influence placement decisions by the candidates they send to the school and in their interactions with candidates. Some human resource officers have strong relationships with school leaders and refer candidates who they feel are the best fit for the leader or school. Others "help" candidates decide which schools would be the best fit for them. Unfortunately, sometimes district leaders advise the strongest candidates against accepting a position in high-need schools. At the same time, school leaders can make it difficult for human resource officers to place candidates. Principals withhold posting vacant positions so that teachers considered problematic or without assignment are not transferred to or placed in their schools. Principals wait until the last opportunity to post a vacancy that can be filled by someone to whom they have promised the position or a new teacher still available weeks before the school year begins.

There are many reasons behind these maneuvers, and the reasons vary by district. The result is that schools with the greatest needs are not guaranteed the best candidates, districts that spend time recruiting may not be able to offer contracts to the best candidates before other districts do so, the newest principals often scramble to fill positions at the start of school, and schools may not be fully staffed until weeks after students have begun their school year. Chaos in hiring contributes to principals "settling" for candidates or granting tenure to teachers who they feel are not strong teachers.

Equity warriors can institute policies and practices to change the chaos of placement.

Equity warriors can institute policies and practices to change behaviors and reduce the chaos of placement. Superintendents and district leaders in our partner districts have used their relationships with principals and union leaders to repair the problems that create the workarounds. When there is trust and a shared commitment to advancing equity, temporary fixes can become permanent over time. For example, a district repeatedly lost candidates because vacancies were not posted until late summer. The superintendent exercised a clause in the contract and convinced principals that if they did not wait to post vacancies, they would have more control over the selection of candidates. Making the shift required a leap of faith by the superintendent, principals, and union leaders.

District leaders have created and monitored protocols for placing the strongest candidates in the neediest schools. School supervisors have worked with principals to ensure that they share the wealth so that schools with new principals are fully staffed. The extent to which these policies and practices are successful and sustainable depends largely on having support structures for teacher recruitment and induction.

Recruitment

Equity warriors know that in a competitive market, particularly in parts of the country that have been traditionally hard to staff, aggressive recruitment is critical. In all parts of the country, especially but not exclusively for schools that serve students of color, recruiting men and women of color has been an unattainable goal. District leaders with contracts to offer have recruited at colleges and job fairs. They have established alternative pathway programs with colleges and universities to attract and support candidates. The New York City Department of Education, like many other school systems, offers a variety of grow-your-own programs for aspiring teachers with certification, for those without certification, for men of color, for school-based staff without certification, and for paraprofessionals. These efforts are costly and come without a guarantee of success. Districts spend $20,000 per recruit and much more for participants in alternative pathway programs.

Equity warriors know that in a competitive market, particularly in parts of the country that have been traditionally hard to staff, aggressive recruitment is critical.

Student teachers

While some school leaders use student teaching as a recruiting strategy for traditional teacher candidates, districts rarely do so. Student teaching assignments, in which an undergraduate or master's candidate completes a semester or longer classroom-based internship, are typically negotiated between a school and the candidate's higher education supervisor. Typically, universities are not preparing teachers for individual districts and are likely to be unresponsive to superintendents and district leaders who seek to shape the college of education's program to be aligned with their equity agenda. However, district leaders could increase their leverage if they are willing to ensure that student teachers are placed with strong teachers, are willing to supplement the student teachers' learning, and can commit to offering positions upon successful completion of the student teaching experience. To do so, district leaders would need to be willing to wrestle from schools the primary responsibility for relationships with colleges of education.

Induction

The policies and practices for successfully attracting and retaining teachers depend on more than just recruitment. Induction, which we define as starting on the day teachers sign the contract and continuing until they've earned tenure, may be the most important time for shaping a teacher's career. Teachers new to the profession want to make a difference and give students the opportunities to learn and grow that their teachers gave to them. Unfortunately, they are stunned by being dropped into the deep end of the pool and told to swim. They do not have and are not provided with the tools tied to their passion for advancing equity. Yet, the novice teacher is expected to have the same result on her first day in a classroom as veteran teachers for their students. What other profession has that expectation? Studies have shown that one-half to two-thirds of new teachers work in isolation, with little support from other teachers (Kardos & Johnson, 2007, p. 12). Equity warriors know that has to change.

In our experience, few districts have robust induction programs for new teachers. In many districts, new teachers simply show up at their assigned school on the first day of school and are shown to their classrooms. The most robust teacher induction programs have some universal elements:

- New teacher summer orientation for at least two weeks to learn about district policies and procedures, curriculum, and preparatory and transition activities for the first days of school

- Buddies, mentorship, or coaching from school-based teachers tailored to the teacher's needs such as observations, problem solving, classroom management, and instructional practices

- Participation in learning communities with school-based colleagues in grade-level or content areas

- A professional learning in curriculum, instruction, and assessment series presented by district leaders or university partners, which may assist new teachers in fulfilling state continuing education or certification requirements

- Principal support that includes goal setting, feedback, and guided reflection in a growth and development model

Some programs provide differentiated support for teachers over two or three years based on their preparation/certification program, experience, or success teaching. For example, there may be different levels of support for new teacher graduates from a teacher preparation program, new teachers without an education background, and experienced teachers who are new to a district.

Equity warriors understand that teachers require continued professional learning in their content *and* instructional practices, as well as in district initiatives. Their approach details expectations for principals, mentors, and teachers and has systems in place to monitor progress. To reduce isolation, they ensure principals have new teachers learn from and with experienced teachers, and with other teachers in site-based experiences. The learning and supports are differentiated based on experience and assessments of teachers' needs. Mentors participate in district professional learning and support to improve their coaching. The learning is also developmental, embedded into the school, and continuous over two or three years.

> *Equity warriors understand that teachers require continued professional learning in their content* and *instructional practices, as well as in district initiatives.*

Not everyone who enters the teaching profession is meant to be a teacher. Even in the best situations where systems and supports are in place, some beginning teachers are unable to continue to learn and improve their practice starting with classroom management. District leaders have an obligation to focus attention on first- and second-year teachers and to hold principals accountable for using the evaluation process to motivate teachers to improve or reassess whether teaching is a good match for them. While growth and development of individuals is the responsibility of school leaders, we have witnessed their reluctance to confront teachers without the encouragement from district leaders.

Equity warriors recognize that effective teaching takes years of learning subject matter content, constant reflection on teaching and instructional strategies, and deep knowledge of students as learners. They understand the importance of beginning to develop teachers from the moment a contract is signed. To do so, they design and monitor human resource systems aligned with their equity agenda. They strive for win-win strategies that limit school competition for teachers by building a culture where school leaders are concerned about the success of all schools, not just their own. District leaders take responsibility for creating a pool of qualified candidates, particularly teachers of color, and ensuring that they land in schools with the greatest needs. They ensure that new teachers have the supports needed to be successful teachers. They monitor progress and ensure that new teachers are held to high standards for continuous improvement before earning tenure.

REFLECTION: *Are district leaders expected to be instructional leaders able to design and execute reliable systems of support that result in rigorous learning for all students? Are they intentional in using professional learning and providing a pool of high-quality teacher candidates that make possible school-level responsibility for student success?*

Equity warriors recognize that effective teaching takes years of learning subject matter content, constant reflection on teaching and instructional strategies, and deep knowledge of students as learners.

WARFARE: ACT WITH A LASER-LIKE FOCUS ON TEACHING AND LEARNING

So it is said that if you know others and know yourself, you will not be imperiled in a hundred battles; if you do not know others but know yourself, you will win one and lose one; if you do not know others and do not know yourself, you will be imperiled in every single battle.

Sun Tzu, about 500 B.C. (Cleary, 1988)

Ultimately, students decide what they will learn, and they bear the responsibility for learning. Teachers decide how they teach and reach students, and the responsibility for engaging students rests with them. School leaders decide how they will create a learning community in which teachers and students learn, and the responsibility for nurturing the community rests with them. What happens if students, teachers, and school leaders do not do their jobs?

Teachers need to know their students as well as themselves if they are to be successful in engaging students. When they know themselves but not how their students learn, they "win one and lose one." This is the essence of the teacher side of the instructional core triangle. It is also the most deeply confrontational part of improving teaching and learning. If students do not respond to the instructional strategies, not only will students not learn, but situations can be toxic. When learning does not occur, teachers label students as unmotivated or difficult and claim nothing can be done. When that happens, the student says the teacher "doesn't like me," "thinks I am stupid," or has a bias against people like me.

Teachers may be open to following the administration's direction on the content and standards they are expected to teach. But they often are not as open to directives or suggestions about instructional strategies. Successful teachers are confident in their toolkit of instructional strategies. Their strategies are consistent with their philosophy of teaching, their beliefs about how a teacher is expected to teach, and/or how they learned as students. They are reluctant to move outside their comfort zone. Lines are drawn. Situations can be toxic when they are pushed.

School leaders are reluctant to challenge teachers who know themselves but not their students. They know these teachers have had success with some students over the years. It is much easier and also a higher priority to focus on teachers who don't know themselves or their students. Still, it is troubling when school leaders ignore or avoid teachers who are not successful with all of their students.

So, if responsibility for teaching and learning rests with those in the school, what is the district leaders' responsibility for improving instructional strategies? The moves earlier in this chapter point to the district leaders' responsibility for bringing system coherence around a focus on teaching and learning and creating conditions that support learning. As district equity warriors prepare for a long campaign in pushing the adoption and use of instructional strategies shown to have the greatest impact on student learning, they, too, heed the advice to know themselves and know others.

YOUR MOVE: CREATE SAFE LEARNING ENVIRONMENTS FOR EXECUTING YOUR EQUITY AGENDA.

John Hattie (2009), after 15 years of studying evidence-based research on student learning, proposed a model for what he calls visible teaching and visible learning. His summary of the research includes six guideposts for excellence in education:

- Teachers are among the most powerful influences in learning.

- Teachers need to be directive, influential, caring, and actively engaged in the passion of teaching and learning.

- Teachers need to be aware of what each and every student is thinking and knowing, to construct meaning and meaningful experience in light of this knowledge and have proficient knowledge and understanding of their content to provide meaningful and appropriate feedback so each student moves progressively through the curriculum levels.

- Teachers need to know the learning intentions and success criteria of their lessons, know how well they are attaining these criteria for all students, and know where to go next in light of the gap between students' current knowledge and understanding and the success criteria of "Where are you going?", "How are you going?", and "Where to next?"

- Teachers need to move from the single idea to multiple ideas, and to relate and then extend these ideas so learners construct and reconstruct knowledge and ideas. It is not the knowledge or ideas, but the learners' construction of this knowledge and these ideas that is critical.

- School leaders and teachers need to create school, staffroom, and classroom environments where error is welcomed as a learning opportunity, where discarding incorrect knowledge and understandings is welcomed, and where participants can feel safe to learn, relearn, and explore knowledge and understanding. (Hattie, 2009, pp. 238–239)

The first impulse of superintendents and district leaders is to concentrate on the sixth guidepost, supportive learning environments for adults. After all, it is consistent with two of Fullan and Quinn's (2016) drivers for whole system change: cultivating collaborative cultures using relationships and shared expertise to produce strong groups and strong individuals; and deepening learning by clarifying learning goals, building precise pedagogical practices, and building collective capacity. This first impulse is not wrong. It is incomplete.

Creating environments safe for learning and relearning depends on superintendents and district leaders understanding some version of the other five guideposts as part of their equity agenda. For example, understanding the instructional strategies that promote construction of knowledge and ideas rather than inculcating knowledge and ideas is necessary to imagining the elements of a learning environment. Depending on the context, the learning environment might require having teachers challenge their beliefs, question their practices, and/or commit significant time to relearning. The same is true for district leaders and staff. Without creating safe learning opportunities, district leaders cannot test their assumptions about their equity agenda and the appropriate tools available to advance equity.

Reaching agreement on the importance of creating safe learning is easy. Yet, implementation is difficult to accomplish. We have been guilty of mandating professional learning communities in our partner districts and schools as a way to create environments for collegial learning. By mandating, we disregarded professional judgment of central office staff and teachers, dictated the learning that must take place, and created artificial communities of adults who may not like or respect each other. After we mandated the structure, we tried to address lack of traction by measuring compliance with implementation or helping adults understand our intent of creating safe, trusting, and self-directed learning groups. We did not treat adults as professionals with responsibility for their own learning. We failed in creating the ideal environment for learning and diverted attention from our equity agenda to implementing structures for learning.

Equity warriors know district and school leaders are responsible for creating safe learning environments that foster adult learning.

Equity warriors know district and school leaders are responsible for creating safe learning environments that foster adult learning. Superintendents and district leaders help central office and school leaders to do so by being clear about the equity agenda, by setting expectations for leaders of learning, and by removing obstacles that divert attention from the agenda. Most of all, they accomplish these responsibilities by learning what it means to live them.

Clarity about the equity agenda requires consensus and calibration among superintendents and district leaders on what it means to improve teaching and learning. Reaching clarity is complex and difficult work. Even in districts that have a strong organizational culture and where district leaders have had similar experiences growing up professionally in the district culture, consensus is not automatic. In San Diego Unified, Cindy

Marten and Staci Monreal convened their instructional cabinet for a full day every week. The cabinet included the supervisors of schools and district leaders responsible for supporting schools with teaching and learning resources. The supervisors of schools were selected for their knowledge and proven success in improving teaching and learning. They devoted considerable time to shared learning and reaching consensus on supports for schools. Yet, disagreements and differences continued. In addition to horizontal collaboration, Marten and Monreal needed to closely supervise individual members of the cabinet to reinforce coherence around the shared agenda.

Equity warriors face the difficult and delicate task of steering the direction while respecting the individual experiences of district and school leaders. Invitations to learn collaboratively are not truly invitations if they cannot be declined. Equity warriors are required to listen, question, and guide while staying focused on outcomes. They listen and raise questions about conditions that support learning. They practice learning and removing obstacles.

Equity warriors face the difficult and delicate task of steering the direction while respecting the individual experiences of district and school leaders.

We were asked to assist Montgomery County Public Schools' supervisors of schools in aligning their support for schools to improve teaching and learning. The supervisors had deep instructional knowledge, operated within a strong organizational culture that promoted excellence, were experienced, and had considerable authority over the schools they supervised. They also knew that instructional practices and student achievement varied within and among schools.

We introduced instructional rounds (City et al., 2009) as a process for supervisors of schools to learn together and reach consensus on collective actions to advance equity by focusing on the instructional core. Instructional rounds have four parts: define a problem of practice, observe practice, debrief observations, and determine the next level of work. One of the distinguishing features of successful instructional rounds is the capacity of participants to suspend judgment and collect and report evidence objectively. It takes practice to avoid inserting judgment into observations and separate that which the observer sees from that which he thinks about what he sees. For example, saying students were not engaged in the task is an interpretation of evidence based on professional judgment. That the teacher said "You need to get to work"

(Continued)

to seven students is description without judgment. Objective reporting of evidence by several observers allows for a more accurate assessment of situations, from which judgments can be applied.

The supervisors participated in half-day sessions over four months in which they reached consensus on a problem of practice that focused on their core concerns about teaching and learning, and practiced collecting and reporting evidence. Why so long? Even though supervisors knew each other well, they were not comfortable sharing their knowledge of instruction with colleagues, they were unaccustomed to having their knowledge challenged, and, most of all, they delayed school visits because they were uneasy about showing vulnerability to school leaders. Eventually, they were able to move beyond their reservations and conduct instructional rounds at schools. However, their uneasiness remained.

Over the years, we have become increasingly aware of the difficulty of creating environments where participants can feel safe to learn, relearn, and explore knowledge and understanding. We observed district leaders, when experiencing discomfort, question the value of sacrificing mission expediency in the service of reaching consensus and building coherence. We observed them change directions for reasons that on the surface seem reasonable. Their decisions represent either-or solutions rather than yes-and approaches that would accommodate learning and doing. Repeatedly, we have observed that district leaders are more comfortable with managing up and down in the organization than horizontally. They are blind to operating in a different way. Competition and pressure to perform are strong drivers. Yet, by accepting these drivers in their own work, they are unable to help those they supervise to become leaders of learning. *Do as I say, not as I do* is a failed approach because the supervisor has failed to solve the dilemma that subordinates will face—how will I stay focused on the equity agenda, lead learning, and remove obstacles that are in the way?

Equity warriors know that if they continue to repeat strategies that have not advanced equity, they will not achieve a different result.

Equity warriors know that if they continue to repeat strategies that have not advanced equity, they will not achieve a different result. They understand that when district leaders are unclear in their messages about advancing equity through improving teaching and learning, their efforts will fail. They know that if they do not understand how to create safe learning environments, they will be unable to help those they supervise to do so. Equity warriors understand that by knowing themselves, their agenda, and the people they supervise, they are able to ask questions that will drive thinking and solutions. They also know to stay with the questions until the answers are evident.

YOUR MOVE: VISIT SCHOOLS ONLY TO LOOK AT TEACHING AND LEARNING.

Superintendents and district leaders walking through classrooms to understand teaching and learning is not a new idea. In *The Search of Excellence*, Thomas Peters and Robert Waterman (1982) identified Managing By Wandering Around (MBWA) as a way successful corporate leaders improve communication vertically within the organization and show respect for frontline workers. Subsequently, countless articles applying MBWA to education flooded journals and publications. Walk-throughs, learning walks, drop-ins, and multiple variations became vogue. It is hard to believe that visiting classrooms to understand teaching and learning first-hand was a revolutionary idea. Unfortunately, in some places it still is.

Context and conditions matter. Early on, I received a call from a superintendent of a small Midwestern district. Two district schools had implemented walk-throughs, and the results were positive. Teachers welcomed administrators into their classrooms, and the ensuing dialogue fostered collegial learning. Based on the positive reception, the superintendent directed all schools in the district to institute regular walk-throughs. It was a disaster. The teachers, the union, and the school communities pushed back. The superintendent was stunned and confused by the unanticipated response.

As when introducing any initiative, leaders need to ensure that they understand the context and determine the fit for the current situation. Over the decades, through various iterations, walk-throughs gained acceptance by instituting guidelines and resolving issues. There is a separation between supervisory evaluations and nonevaluative walk-throughs. Feedback to teachers is carefully crafted. Teachers and students are comfortable with visitors. Visitors make efforts not to interrupt instruction. Union leaders are consulted and understand the purpose. Administrators are more knowledgeable about instruction and better able to communicate with teachers. Teachers are encouraged to use walk-throughs for their own learning.

Walk-throughs by superintendents and district leaders are rarely collegial. Unlike MBWA in corporate settings, teachers do not relish the opportunity to meet with their superintendent or school supervisors to discuss teaching and learning. They do not view classroom visits as an indication of respect by the organization's leaders. District leaders rarely invite teachers to debrief a visit or to share their thoughts about what happened in their classrooms, their purpose, and their teaching moves. Teachers question what a visitor can understand by a single 5- to 10-minute visit to their classroom. They question the visitors' knowledge and expertise.

There are good reasons for limiting interactions with teachers. In our visits to classrooms, we have learned to be cautious about providing even general compliments to teachers after visiting classrooms. Some teachers have used our comments to rebuke constructive feedback from school administrators. We have also learned that providing warm and cool feedback is rarely well received. Even when there are 25 positive reflections, teachers home in on the three wonderings or areas to grow.

Equity warriors use walk-throughs for their learning about school leaders and the context of the school.

Equity warriors use walk-throughs for their learning about school leaders and the context of the school. Their walk-throughs have a clear purpose anchored in their learning, their purpose is communicated to all members of the school, they are accompanied by school leaders, and they visit as many classrooms as possible regularly.

Over time, we adopted three fundamentally different approaches to walk-throughs with our partner district leaders. Sometimes, we used a highly structured approach to provide external accountability for program or initiative implementation. Other times, we introduced a simple, loosely structured approach to explore the leaders' knowledge or to push their thinking. We also used a school as a learning laboratory to calibrate the instructional lens of district leaders. Our intention for each was for district leaders at all levels to learn about and understand their schools to inform their coaching and supervision of school leaders. Examples of the three approaches follow.

> Our work in supporting the adoption and implementation of common curriculum and instructional strategies by Flint Community Schools was mentioned earlier. The strategy to improve teaching and learning included rallying all parts of the district around the essential content and units of study common across schools. Walk-throughs by school supervisors were a key component in creating accountability for implementation.

Principals in FCS, like many other school districts at the time, were not selected for their instructional leadership. FCS's community school model relied on administrators who could manage the school building as well as after-school community programs. The design of essential content and units of study that contained daily lessons implemented across all schools was as much for the benefit of district and school leaders as it was for teachers and highly mobile students. Teachers were given a pacing chart specific to the grade level and school calendar. Pacing charts divided the year into six or eight units for English language arts and mathematics, respectively, and included a few unscheduled days between units for presentations, grading, extensions, and catching up.

District leaders carried the pacing charts with them as a learning tool when they visited schools. Adherence to the pacing charts was an initial step in helping teachers and leaders become comfortable and confident in trying new curriculum. Each visit began with a 15-minute conversation with the principal about the school's data and follow-up from the previous visit. Principals sometimes included their assistant principals and/or curriculum coach on the walk-throughs. Before entering any classroom, the district leader had a conversation with the principal that was intended to reach consensus about the purpose of the unit and the learning objectives they should expect to observe in the classroom, based on the pacing chart. Visits to the classrooms included matching the lesson objective to the lesson in the pacing chart; finding evidence of student work that showed progression through the unit; noting the teacher's comfort with the content and instructional strategies; and, most important, talking with students about their learning, the day's lesson, and lessons preceding that day's lesson.

The pacing guide is a tool to anchor the debrief in objective evidence. There was no need for alarm if a teacher had fallen behind the pacing guide by a few days. The evidence of student work and student feedback enabled the district leader and principal to discuss the principal's feedback to individual teachers, and the principal's leadership moves. While there was little judgment exercised in determining the feedback to teachers, district leaders gathered evidence and made judgments about the principals' leadership capacity.

District leaders watched for principals who were surprised to find that teachers were not keeping pace or seemed unfamiliar with

(Continued)

the objectives, units, and lessons. Such unfamiliarity demonstrated that they were not visiting classrooms and supporting teachers in implementing the essential content. Principals who could not accurately assess whether the teacher was on pace demonstrated their lack of understanding of the units. The walk-throughs enabled district leaders to assess whether principals were making an effort to understand the key elements of the essential content, were hammering compliance with the pacing guide, or were not being accountable for implementation.

To understand how best to support schools, district leaders had to be comfortable with the essential content and units. In FCS, district leaders were reluctant to hold principals accountable and were not comfortable enough with the unit design to brainstorm feedback to teachers and differentiate supports. Further, they were reluctant to use their monthly meetings with principals to deepen their learning together. Principals who were able to build supports within their schools for teachers accelerated implementation and gains in student learning. Most important, principals who could use the visits to calibrate, understand, and communicate with teachers earned their teachers' respect.

It is now more common to find school leaders knowledgeable in curriculum and instructional practices. Even those without considerable classroom experience know the importance of bolstering their instructional knowledge in order to be effective. District leaders can use questioning to push thinking, build capacity, and strengthen the internal accountability of veteran school leaders who know instruction.

Strong instructional leaders know how to make their expectations for teaching and learning explicit. As we have seen, a charismatic leader is able to impose his expectations on teachers through the force of personality or relationships. Other successful leaders strive for teachers to reach consensus and are able to enforce compliance through gentle reminders to implement their shared agreements. In either case, walk-throughs can provide evidence by looking through three lenses—teacher actions, student actions, and supportive classroom environments.

Some teachers are surprised to learn that what they are doing at the moment is not the main interest during a walk-through. Teachers are quick to tell visitors, "You should have been here five minutes ago. . . ." While important, the teacher's actions are only one side of the instructional core triangle. Emphasizing the teacher's actions creates the most confrontation and defensiveness. Often, focusing on the teacher's instructional moves is unproductive and unnecessary. It is unproductive because ultimately external pressure does not change teacher practice. Motivation for meaningful changes in practice comes from within. It is unnecessary because by focusing on the other lenses—which generate evidence of results—debriefs are depersonalized and more objective.

Looking at the task students are asked to perform reveals a lot about a teacher's instructional moves. School leaders and teachers can deepen their understanding of the outcomes of instruction by questioning the purpose of the task, the level of rigor, and the ease or difficulty students have in performing the task. Students provide a lot of information about instruction when we ask them simple questions about what they are learning, why it is important, whether it is difficult, and what is next. Students also provide us with information when we observe them perform the task.

Analyzing classroom environments tells us about the supports provided to students for the day's lesson and the trajectory of learning. Are objectives and instructions clear? Are units clear? Are examples of student work present as teaching aids? Are there note-taking protocols? The environment is not only what is seen by the visitor but also what students have as supports. When examples of successful student work are present, students can develop their analytical skills to determine the expectations for their work. Student notebooks contain clues about learning objectives, study guides, and student understanding. Notebooks should provide students with evidence of their learning and whether the lesson is building on the prior day's lesson. Students, particularly those who are underperforming, need constant reminders about why they are learning and how they are growing as learners.

District leaders use evidence gathered through walk-throughs to assess a principal's knowledge of her teachers. They also use the evidence to ask questions of school leaders that suggest leadership moves, not to provide answers. Asking the right questions repeatedly over time and pushing school leaders to understand the meaning behind the questions stimulates problem solving appropriate to the school leaders' capacity and the school content. It also models for principals how they lead the improvement of teaching and learning while distributing leadership and responsibility for analysis and actions to school leaders and teachers.

Equity warriors use questioning rather than telling to improve teaching and learning. Using questioning rather than telling is especially important in using walk-throughs as learning laboratories to calibrate school leaders. Cross-school learning opportunities are most effective when they are extensions and aligned with the other two types of walk-throughs.

We have supported district leaders to design and execute cross-school learning opportunities for school leaders. Long Beach Unified's use of Key Results Walk-Throughs (discussed in Chapter 1) is the most comprehensive and consistent approach adopted in our experience. Long Beach is not unique. District leaders take the opportunity to use cross-school visits within a district, or team visits to a school in another district, to provide learning removed from personal ownership for the teaching and learning that is observed.

The learning begins with a clear purpose connected to professional learning themes. In our experience, these walk-throughs are most effective in calibrating school leaders as they process how instruction and student performance at the visited school compare to their own. On occasion, district leaders structure visits by asking principals to schedule teams to visit three classrooms—a teacher whose teaching is considered exemplary, one considered typical, and one whose work is subpar. The teams discuss the differences without identifying which teacher is which and the questions they would ask to have each teacher reflect and improve his practice. Depending on the level of trust, collegial discussions that ensue help school leaders think through options from different perspectives. Their analysis is aided—as well as hampered—by their objectivity in assessing teachers based on observations that are not clouded by their relationships or experiences with the teachers.

Effectiveness of using cross-school walk-throughs as a learning experience hinges on facilitation during the visits. District leaders often include all the school leaders they supervise in the visit. School leaders rarely know each other well enough to engage in meaningful analysis and push each other's thinking. Conversations tend to be superficial, unless participants are assigned to three- or four-person teams with mixed experience levels and a facilitator. Small, targeted visits facilitated by district leaders—though time consuming—are more effective in exploring and transferring learning particularly until the relationships and conditions are established for teams to self-facilitate.

Equity leaders use various forms of walk-throughs to know the school leaders they supervise and support. Through exploring questions about teaching and learning together and not directing or telling, district leaders are able to sharpen the problem-solving ability of school leaders who hold responsibility for improving teaching and learning. Through being consistent and reflective in asking questions, they are able to better know themselves as leaders and remain open to their learning.

> *Equity leaders use various forms of walk-throughs to know the school leaders they supervise and support.*

YOUR MOVE: HOLD CENTRAL OFFICE AND SCHOOL LEADERS ACCOUNTABLE FOR TEACHING AND LEARNING.

Equity warriors recognize that true accountability starts with knowing oneself. Fullan and Quinn's (2016) fourth and final driver in building coherence is securing accountability, which they describe as creating conditions to maximize people's internal accountability that is reinforced by external accountability. Their summary of research on school and system effectiveness and improvement "suggests that internal accountability must precede external accountability if lasting improvement in student achievement is the goal" (p. 111). Experience has taught us that internal accountability sustained over time is the only means for lasting improvement in student achievement, and external accountability is just a means to that end.

> *Equity warriors recognize that true accountability starts with knowing oneself.*

In previous chapters, we explored the shortcomings of external accountability systems, particularly those designed to foster competition among groups. Competition is helpful when it provides a standard for comparison and lets us know how we are doing in relation to others. Lacking the tools for comparison—such as data—hampers growth and development. At the same time, competition can be divisive or used to subjugate others. When superintendents and district leaders do not believe in the efficacy of district accountability systems, they will disregard the systems and choose other ways to advance their agenda.

Accountability systems, internal and external, are built over time and are deeply embedded in organizational culture. Accountability systems define what leaders value or hold as important, help fix their actions relative to standards of behavior or actions of others, frame the decision making for their actions, and identify rewards or consequences for meeting expectations or not. Beyond replacing leaders with others who have demonstrated internal accountability for advancing equity, the primary leverage for superintendents and district leaders in designing accountability systems is in creating the external stimulus for motivating internal accountability. Creating external systems that motivate internal accountability is made easier by having a focus on improving teaching and learning to advance equity.

We cannot add much more to what we have said about the importance of using purpose, values-enhanced leadership, and clear expectations as the starting point for accountability systems. Still, determining that a focus of accountability systems is on improving teaching and learning to advance equity simplifies a complex challenge. Superintendents and district leaders begin by asking how I hold myself accountable for improvements in teaching and learning that will advance equity? Self-reflection as well as processes for collegial conversations, horizontally and vertically, to test assumptions begin to build the foundation for gaining a realistic assessment of what each individual, from her position of responsibility, can accomplish through a long campaign. Self-reflection and honest feedback are essential to establishing efficacy.

Knowing one's values and having clear expectations set the stage for building systems to motivate others. The authors of *Leadership and Self-Deception* (2010) argue that the choices leaders make are either consistent with or in opposition to their beliefs about how they should act with others. Simply stated, when choosing to act in opposition to their expectations, leaders betray themselves. The act of betrayal leads down a slippery slope to distorting reality to justify the leader's action. Ultimately, betrayals lead to other betrayals, which leads to blaming others and having various negative reactions—lack of trust, lack of commitment, lack of accountability—depending on the context (Arbinger Institute, 2010).

We have experienced similar behaviors and reactions from leaders at all levels—from the boardroom to the classroom and back again. Equity warriors committed to improving teaching and learning to advance equity have high expectations for themselves that can be smashed when facing overwhelming odds. Recognizing that the journey will be long and there will be setbacks can help identify the few, strategic actions that leaders will use to leverage improvement and to which they will hold themselves accountable.

Equity warriors understand the conditions they face and eliminate feelings of guilt when they experience temporary setbacks. Guilt is implicit when feeling that an act of betrayal has occurred. Success depends on acting in a guilt-free environment, free of blaming and shaming. Advancing equity is too hard as is, without carrying the baggage of guilt for past mistakes. Advancing equity is literally to advance. Mistakes have been and will continue to be made. Fear of making mistakes and guilt over mistakes prevent equity warriors from learning. Equity warriors move on and do not use past missteps to influence their actions and perceptions of others. Otherwise, they are not able to establish the conditions that enable collaborative cultures and foster deep learning.

> *Equity warriors understand the conditions they face and eliminate feelings of guilt when they experience temporary setbacks.*

Accountability systems help leaders frame their decisions for their own actions. To do so, leaders reflect on and understand the strengths and shortcomings of their decision making. In *Decisive: How to Make Better Choices in Life and Work*, Chip Heath and Dan Heath (2013) identify four villains of decision making:

- **Narrow framing:** the tendency to define choices too narrowly, to see them in binary terms
- **Confirmation bias:** developing a quick belief about a situation and seeking information that bolsters the belief
- **Short-term emotion:** the loss of perspective due to temporary emotion
- **Overconfidence:** the unshakeable certainty about how the future will unfold

Superintendents and district leaders who fall victim to these villains rarely are successful in advancing equity. The authors suggest decision-making processes that are the opposite— widen your options, reality-test your assumptions, attain distance before deciding, and prepare to be wrong. These processes depend on a shift from self-contained decision making to decision making informed by others. To state the obvious, listening to others helps leaders consider alternatives and test assumptions. Doing so is at the heart of designing external accountability systems. In other words, external accountability systems are effective in motivating internal accountability when the systems create opportunities for inclusion of different points of view and ownership of decision making for improving teaching and learning to advance equity. The processes are not divorced from the intended outcome. They are one and the same.

Following this reasoning, pressures to act are embedded in internal accountability, to the extent possible. While quantitative data can measure progress in improving teaching and learning, superintendents and district leaders will have to rely on their knowledge of others to determine whether a leader's internal accountability is evident and/or growing. At some point, equity warriors will face a decision about whether the investment of time and effort is yielding results and what they will do. In most cases, leaders will not be surprised.

We have experienced multiple examples of external accountability that have failed to support levels of internal accountability necessary to improve teaching and learning, and only a few that have been successful.

In our experience, successful approaches fall into two categories: differentiating opportunities and defining expectations. Differentiating opportunity to expand the scope of responsibility of leaders who show promise has been a common approach across districts. Here are some examples:

- Central office leaders who have demonstrated a high degree of internal accountability are given more challenging assignments through promotion, expansion of program responsibilities, and/or temporary assignments to restructure or redesign systems and departments.
- Central office and school leaders are invited to participate in policy advisory groups or ad hoc committees or are selected for special recognition (e.g., principal of the year).
- Principals have been tapped to lead or mentor other school leaders.
- Principals are selected to share their experiences through professional learning sessions and hosting visitors to their school.
- Central offices and schools are given more autonomy over decision making and less interference and supervision.

Another approach common across districts is to define expectations that give leaders permission to act in ways consistent with shared beliefs around improving teaching and learning to advance equity. Some examples follow:

- Providing resources and permission for regular professional learning on teaching and learning
- Providing executive coaches to division leaders and central leaders in management development programs

- Assigning central office leaders to support or case manage specific schools

- Requiring central and school leaders to submit annual personal growth goals and learning plans at the start of each school year

- Requiring principals to observe instruction in classrooms for at least 90 minutes per day

- Separating teaching and learning from operations

Each of these examples reinforces districtwide expectations, allows leaders to reserve time for self-reflection and strengthening their knowledge and skills, and strips away obstacles that can be excuses.

Equity warriors understand that clarity about their own accountability for improving teaching and learning to advance equity provides them with the awareness needed to design systems for others. Formal external accountability systems are worthwhile when they can be made to contribute to developing internal accountability. Otherwise, external accountability systems are worse than a waste of time—they distract attention from advancing equity and diminish the authority of those who enforce them.

> *Equity warriors understand that clarity about their own accountability for improving teaching and learning to advance equity provides them with the awareness needed to design systems for others.*

YOUR MOVE: CREATE A CULTURE OF INQUIRY ABOUT INSTRUCTION.

In *Organizational Culture and Leadership*, Edgar Schein (1992) wrote that "organizational cultures are created in part by leaders, and one of the most decisive functions of leadership is the creation, management, and sometimes even the destruction of culture. . . . [O]ne could argue that the only thing of real importance that leaders do is to create and manage culture and that the unique talent of leaders is their ability to understand and work with culture. . . . [L]eaders create and change cultures, while managers and administrators live within them." Schein recognizes that cultures are difficult to change, that culture "refers to the elements of a group or organization that are the most stable and least malleable. Culture is the result of a complex group learning process that is only partially influenced by leader behavior. But if the group is threatened because elements of its culture have become maladapted, it is ultimately the function of leadership to recognize and do something about the situation" (p. 5).

Equity warriors know that pitting groups against each other and competition are maladapted to learning organizations. Implicit in competition is that there are winners and losers—that there is not enough room on the podium for everyone. While competition may be an inherent and unextractable part of human nature, the era since *A Nation at Risk* has shown that competition does not improve teaching and learning. Competition stands in the way of having all students achieve and all teachers being the best they can be. Further, competition that limits opportunities for students to reach their potential alienates families and students.

Competition over ideas and expertise shows up when questioning instructional strategies. Teachers are most resistant to suggestions that hint at devaluing or changing their instructional strategies. Removing winners and losers from exploring the effectiveness of instructional strategies begins with supporting educators—leaders and teachers—to be learners with particular attention on building cooperative, collegial relationships. Our experience has been that, more often than not, providing genuine and authentic learning opportunities around improving understanding of the instructional strategies has motivated and excited adults. One approach that has shown promise is turning classrooms into learning laboratories for adults as well as students.

Equity warriors know that pitting groups against each other and competition are maladapted to learning organizations.

Digging through student data, we found that improving reading comprehension for middle and high school emerged as a focus for our partner schools in Corpus Christi, Texas. Middle school principals and literacy coaches studied various approaches to teaching reading and were influenced by Cris Tovani's instructional strategies for adolescent struggling readers. At the time, Tovani taught in a Denver-area high school. We learned that Tovani opened her high school classroom for visitors interested in seeing the instruction strategies she wrote about in practice. So, we took a five-person team to see her.

Much to our surprise, we were ushered into a room with about 20 other visitors there for the same purpose. Tovani welcomed us, asked for introductions, and shared her lesson plans for the two classes we were to observe. One class was a heterogeneous group of students of average reading ability. The other class was a group of struggling readers, some of whom began the semester reading years below grade level who had survived to their senior year by "fake reading." Tovani encouraged us to interact with students, to take notes, and to be ready to debrief after the observations.

The classroom was large enough to hold 30 students sitting most of the time in discussion groups and 25 observers around the perimeter. Students smiled and were friendly and unintimidated by the visitors. Tovani explained that they liked to have visitors from across the country watching them learn. Tovani moved through her lesson as planned, and students moved in and out of groups, eager to answer questions when asked.

As remarkable as the visit had been to that point, the debrief was amazing. Tovani asked everyone to share an observation or a question. As visitors took turns, she took notes. She clarified and explained her rationale for her teaching moves in response to questions and probed the observations made by visitors as she added their comments to her notes. Our team was impressed not only by the richness of the learning opportunity but also by Tovani's genuine stance as a learner.

Our partner districts and many others have encouraged school leaders to create learning laboratories to examine instruction in their schools. In Flint Community Schools, for example, each school was invited to identify one or more laboratory classrooms. Teachers who volunteered to lead one of these laboratory classrooms also were assigned to have a literacy coach work with them. The teacher benefited from having a thought partner who could model and coteach as well as coplan lessons regularly. The coach accompanied other teachers to observe a lesson that the laboratory teacher and the coach planned. District and school leaders visited the laboratory classes to assess progress in implementing the curriculum and the readers/writers workshop instructional model. Doing so enabled them to learn from teachers who were committed to implementing the curriculum and model and to anticipate rough spots that other teachers might encounter.

Districts have adopted variations of laboratory classrooms. The success of laboratory classrooms as a promising practice depends on leadership that supports a culture of inquiry, not judgment. Schein (2013) defined inquiry as an attitude based on curiosity. He said inquiry is asking questions to which you do not already know the answer and building relationships based on curiosity and interest. Inquiry is believing that asking the right questions will move things forward.

Equity warriors know the importance of curiosity in the face of uncertainty and of asking the right questions rather than rushing to judgment. Schein (2013) reminds us of the importance of gathering data as we encounter cultural diversity in our lives and work. Judging and acting without having the data to inform our understanding of teachers, students, and classrooms is misguided. Additionally, to build collaboration and create open communication, asking the right questions out of a sense of genuine curiosity can lead to finding the less-than-obvious interdependencies among people and parts of the organization and contribute to safe spaces for learning.

Laboratory classrooms provide opportunities to practice inquiry around instructional practices. A laboratory classroom positions the teacher to be the expert learner. As it was in the Tovani example, she was the person whose actions were the focus of the inquiry, and her position was respected and trusted. Regardless of what we might think about an individual teacher or school leader, he holds a position of respect within the classroom or school. Having a laboratory classroom allows reflective relationships to develop over time and builds a collegial learning network. Again, in Tovani's case, she was gathering data from the observers as much as—if not more than—they were gathering data from observing her. If observers continue to notice similar actions and reactions by students over time, their comments should trigger action or reaction by the teacher. In answering the questions, the teacher is able to clarify her beliefs and actions. Reciprocal learning happens without hierarchy.

Laboratory classrooms and similarly structured laboratory schools that are typically reserved for university-school partnerships built on inquiry are able to reinforce the professionalism of teachers and school leaders and the centrality of the classroom and school as the place where teaching and learning happens. These structures raise the importance of teaching and learning in ways that motivate teachers to learn and motivate students to do their part in reflecting on the learning when they see their teachers learning. These structures give district leaders the opportunity to learn beside school leaders and teachers as they reflect on their own beliefs about teaching and learning. They learn to know themselves and others.

REFLECTION: *What systems and structures are in place for district leaders to learn from and with school leaders and teachers? Are the opportunities for learning translating into deeper understanding of effective teaching and learning? Are relationships fostered to continue inquiry and learning?*

CHAPTER 6

School leaders ensure each and every student succeeds

POLITICS: BRING COHERENCE
TO PROVIDE ACCESS TO
RIGOROUS LEARNING
FOR ALL STUDENTS

Equity warriors struggle with balancing conflicts that define the role of school leadership in improving teaching and learning. Principals and school leaders struggle to meet expectations that are often in conflict. Depending on the district and the moment, principals are expected to be leaders and managers, planners and executors, instructional gurus and operational geniuses, change agents and sources of stability, supervisors and developers, disciplinarians and advocates, marketers and collaborators, and leaders in the community and in the classroom. It is little wonder that principals often feel like the "tuna in the sandwich." It is also little wonder that principals do not have a focus on teaching and learning. Successful principals know their supervisors' priorities. Frankly, principals are more likely to be disciplined or replaced due to a lapse in a safety protocol or conflicts with the teachers union than because of failure to increase student achievement.

Equity warriors balance conflicts and govern effectively by bringing coherence to teaching and learning systems and structures.

School-level equity warriors balance conflicts and govern effectively by bringing coherence to teaching and learning systems and structures. They keep the main thing—teaching and learning—the main thing. They do so by integrating and augmenting teaching and learning directions set by the district; cultivating collaborative cultures of strong groups and individuals; strengthening the instructional core through continuous and deep learning; and creating conditions to maximize administrator, teacher, staff, and student accountability for student learning. They share a deep belief that they hold the most strategic lever for advancing equity: knowing and educating each and every student so they have the tools that will enable them to think, learn, and act independently and to apply their skills in school and elsewhere.

The moves in this section are examples of those used by equity warriors to strengthen the instructional core across their schools. The moves target content, teachers' knowledge and skills, and students' contributions to learning. Equity warriors ensure that moves, while presented separately, are made in concert. They know that making a shift in one part of the core requires shifts in the other two to improve teaching and learning.

YOUR MOVE: BRING COHERENCE TO TEACHING, LEARNING, AND INITIATIVES BY DEFINING RIGOR.

By partnering with more than 100 elementary, middle, and high schools, we learned the power of simplifying focus and consistent messaging to bring coherence. We organized our approach to school improvement and leadership coaching around three goals:

- Improve teaching and learning of rigorous standards in mathematics and English language arts
- Implement a system of interventions to accelerate the learning of students performing below expectations and/or students who have specific language development or developmental needs
- Build an organizational culture of preparing all students for rigorous academic work to meet graduation requirements

The three goals simplify messaging about an equity agenda that is robust, coherent, comprehensive, and focused on teaching and learning. The goals require careful unpacking to find strategic points of entry depending on the school's context. To do so, our partner school leaders and coaches assess the context continuously while keeping mindful of a research-based improvement framework that incorporates our lessons learned. Our framework contains seven elements:

- Distributed leadership
- College-readiness culture, including engaging families and community
- English language arts achievement
- Mathematics achievement
- Intervention systems, particularly supports for students with disabilities and multilingual learners
- Professional learning
- Data-based decision making

Each element represents a body of work and protocols of its own. Typically, assessment begins with the principal determining the leadership capacity and willingness of adults and students—including families and community members—to lead. Identifying allies who can lead, be responsible for executing on the equity agenda, and learn to use data effectively is part of the assessment as well as the ongoing work.

Further, a focus on mathematics and English language arts that includes an honest appraisal of instructional capacity and responsive professional learning is an immediate priority. Although academic achievement, not performance on any single measure, is the ultimate objective, performance gains are essential in the short term. Schools that can increase student performance in state testing benefit by building efficacy and trust and decreasing external scrutiny.

Improvements in student performance provide short-term wins. Focus on the core instructional program through regular assessment of student progress and professional learning in English language arts and mathematics builds confidence in the curriculum. Confidence in the core curriculum enables leaders to identify gaps in student learning that benefit from additional supports. Building a college-readiness culture that enhances student efficacy and garners the attention of families and community partners contributes to improving student achievement for the long term.

Equity warriors keep the interconnectedness in mind as they simplify messaging around the goals for others.

Equity warriors keep the interconnectedness in mind as they simplify messaging around the goals for others. Simplifying allows other leaders to focus on the intended outcomes and not confuse outcomes with the processes for achieving them. The processes—such as data-based decision making or distributed leadership—become clearer as the way we do the work naturally through practice, experience, and reflection.

Our partner schools use the goals and agenda to create action plans anchored in short-term objectives, possible activities, and gathering evidence of success. In our work, the objectives are heavily weighted toward capacity development that engages others in contributing to and owning responsibility for progress. Activities described in previous chapters—equity visits, walk-throughs, data collection and analysis, and instructional leadership teams—are used regularly.

A critical and often overlooked part of plans is identifying and collecting evidence of success along the way. In the early stages, having a schedule of meetings or a year-long professional learning schedule is something to celebrate. As the work deepens, finding evidence of success that can show incremental growth may be more difficult to quantify. Qualitative measures—such as monthly celebrations with student stories—provide inspiration as well as build collective efficacy.

Collecting evidence inevitably uncovers differences in teaching and learning. Equity warriors are kept awake nights by knowing that academic opportunities for students vary within their school—sometimes widely. They know that assigning a student to one teacher rather than another may give the student an advantage—or reduce their advantage. Variance is a flaw in social systems, not just education. To address the variance, equity warriors engage other school leaders in reaching agreement on rigor.

Educators know that rigor is defined by school culture and individual relationships between teacher and student. Again, teachers cannot force students to learn. They motivate students to learn by setting expectations, establishing rewards for meeting expectations, and using conditions—school culture, peer groups, and families—to influence students. Rigor is contextualized—what is considered rigor in one school or for one group of students is not considered rigorous enough for another or too rigorous for a third. Behind closed doors, teachers criticize their peers for their lack of rigor or for having standards that are too high.

Equity warriors create strategies to determine a common definition of academic rigor that goes beyond *knowing rigor when we see it*. They bring school communities together to clarify academic expectations, they adopt programs that reinforce college-readiness attitudes and skills from the earliest grades, they open classrooms to peers, and they post student work that shows progress in meeting academic standards. They also engage teacher leaders in creating a schoolwide definition of rigor, as the following example of distributing leadership illustrates.

> *Equity warriors create strategies to determine a common definition of academic rigor that goes beyond knowing rigor when we see it.*

Principal Carmen Garcia's theory of action for San Diego High School's Instructional Leadership Team (SDHS ILT) and examples of the team's leadership processes and products are mentioned in Chapter 4. Among her responsibilities as principal, Garcia was intent on *providing opportunities and access to rigorous courses for all students*. SDHS combined several high schools on a single campus, including one of the highest-performing high schools in the country and one of the lowest-performing high schools in the San Diego Unified School District. The student populations of the schools differed, as did the opportunities afforded students after graduation. Defining rigor became the SDHS ILT's first task.

(Continued)

(Continued)

By the end of the first SDHS ILT daylong retreat, its 25 members had reached consensus on the following definition of rigor by brainstorming answers to a simple question: What is rigor?

Rigor is purposeful and relevant learning that honors student voices and encourages them to tackle challenging work by providing supports that foster intellectual curiosity and perseverance in a culture of achievement.

They accepted responsibility for this definition as schoolwide leaders. They also accepted responsibility to share the definition with their academic departments and to ask them to brainstorm the following:

- List five elements that you would expect to see in a curriculum that would be examples of academic rigor.

- List five characteristics of instructional materials that you would expect to see in an academically rigorous classroom.

- List five teacher behaviors that you would expect to see in an academically rigorous classroom.

- List five student behaviors that you would expect to see in an academically rigorous classroom.

- List five ways that you would assess student knowledge in an academically rigorous classroom.

Within three retreats and regular academic department meetings spread over three months, the SDHS ILT of 25 people, most of whom did not know each other at the start, created consensus on schoolwide examples of rigor in curriculum, materials, teacher and student behaviors, and assessment practices. In the following months, they also identified areas of learning for the SDHS ILT and their academic departments. Teachers demonstrated instructional strategies the school had named as best practices. Members led collegial walk-throughs to see teacher and student behaviors. They studied practices together to identify the criteria that made them best practices.

A key discovery in the first months came when SDHS ILT members admitted to being unfamiliar with curriculum design. Though they were aware that their curriculum—largely relying on the textbook and their introductory understanding of the common core standards—was not effective with their students, they did not know how to correct the situation. That discovery kicked off a three-year, schoolwide curriculum design process in which learning and application informed curriculum units used by all those teaching the course. The processes and systems created and implemented in the SDHS ILT's first two years set the foundation for accelerating the work in year three, when San Diego Unified adopted proficiency scales as the basis for a districtwide guaranteed viable curriculum.

The SDHS example is one of how an instructional leadership team can balance conflicts and enable the principal to govern effectively. The principal was part of the SDHS ILT, but she let the members, with facilitation, take the lead and reach consensus. Had the principal imposed or even suggested her definition for rigor, the members would have resisted and likely not been enthusiastic about leading their colleagues. Members were selected for their standing within their schools and their academic departments. Respecting their positions and giving them the opportunity to lead with supports enabled them.

Equity warriors know that teachers who are isolated and/or focused on their own classroom are not certain that their teaching and student learning are rigorous. Analyzing and unpacking common standards provides part of the answer, though the activities are often too abstract to have application for teachers. Visiting classrooms with an eye on student performance on a task, or comparing student papers across classrooms in a looking-at-student-work protocol, offers some insights. Nevertheless, teachers have opinions about rigor and are often aspirational in defining it. Like the SDHS example, teachers can be encouraged to avoid misconceptions that rigor simply means more time, words, pages, or difficulty. Having consensus on a definition is a step forward on the important and most relevant question: How do we help students demonstrate rigor?

> *Equity warriors know that teachers who are isolated and/or focused on their own classroom are not certain that their teaching and student learning are rigorous.*

We will address this question later in this chapter.

YOUR MOVE: ARTICULATE A TEACHING AND LEARNING CHANGE STRATEGY.

What leaders do and how they do it profoundly affects people's actions. Certainly, context and the times call on leaders to bring different skills to different situations. To balance conflicts to improve teaching and learning, successful leaders have clearly defined priorities for improvement and a change strategy based on the school's assets and challenges. The specific change or improvement strategy matters less than simply having and executing a strategy that matches the principal's knowledge, skills, and dispositions and the school's context.

An equity agenda that aims at improving teaching and learning and the achievement of all students requires that equity warriors prioritize learning *and* have an effective change strategy to describe the journey. Athletes and artists are able to improve their crafts by using clear expectations for the next level of performance. Having expectations provides objectivity, which can depersonalize feedback and bring attention to improving skills. Being transparent about expectations allows for individuals to self-assess and for ownership of change by knowing what the next level looks like. Thinking about personal development as stages encourages thinking about continuous growth. A 7-year-old knows that someday she will physically be able to run as fast as her older brother. She is just not there yet.

> *Equity warriors adopt and adapt whole-school change strategies as they observe and learn from the actions and reactions of teachers, staff, and students.*

Equity warriors adopt and adapt whole-school change strategies as they observe and learn from the actions and reactions of teachers, staff, and students. We have found the Concerns-Based Adoption Model (CBAM) a universally helpful approach to leading curriculum and instruction change (Hall & Hord, 2001).

CBAM was developed specifically for leading school-level change. Two components of the model—Stages of Concerns and Levels of Use—are particularly insightful tools for analyzing readiness for change and planning professional learning for teachers and staff. The model recognizes that change doesn't happen by flipping a switch or attending a workshop. Change that leads to teacher mastery or successful program implementation comes from systematic growth through various stages. Specifically,

- growth happens from personal reflection and coaching;
- reflection and coaching can be helped by measuring a teacher's use of the desired curriculum and/or instructional practice or a staff member's implementation of an initiative or program; and
- a person's readiness for systematic growth can be measured by her feelings, preoccupations, thoughts, and consideration of the change, or what Hall and Hord have called *concerns*.

Gene Hall and Shirley Hord (2001) define seven Stages of Concern (pp. 61–64), illustrated in Figure 6.1. The lowest three stages are about convincing oneself to be interested in adopting the proposed change. Too often, approaches to professional learning do not move beyond awareness or even to conversations about

FIGURE 6.1 ● Stages of Concern

0. Awareness
● "I think I heard something about it, but I'm too busy right now with other priorities to be concerned about it."

1. Informational
● "This seems interesting, and I would like to know more about it."

2. Personal
● "I'm concerned about the changes I'll need to make in my routines."

3. Management
● "I'm concerned about how much time it takes to get ready to teach with this new approach."

4. Consequence
● "How will this new approach affect my students?"

5. Collaboration
● "I'm looking forward to sharing some ideas about it with other teachers."

6. Refocusing
● "I have some ideas about something that would work even better."

Source: George, A. A., Hall, G. E., & Stiegelbauer, S. M. (2006; 3rd printing with minor additions and corrections, 2013). *Measuring implementation in schools: The stages of concern questionnaire*. Austin, TX: SEDL. Reprinted with permission from the American Institutes for Research.

why any teacher or staff member would be interested in learning how the proposed change will affect them. Workshops that are one-and-done, whether an hour or two days, do not gain traction unless teachers and staff are hooked and begin to internalize interest in the proposed change.

When the teacher or staff member reaches the stage labeled "management," they begin to pilot the change. At this point, they are concerned about how to implement. An expression of concern is "I seem to be spending all my time getting materials ready." At this stage, the person is trying and may be struggling, which often happens with teachers or staff members who become convinced that the change may be of value and/or are attempting to please the principal or coach.

When teachers and staff members reach the highest three stages—consequences, collaboration, and refocusing—they move beyond just implementing and begin to consider effect.

Using the Stages of Concern, we learned why relying solely on professional learning communities or collegial groups—department or grade-level teams—fails as an approach for implementing curriculum, instructional strategies, and programs. For example, we learned that focus on the concerns through one-on-one coaching in the early phases of adoption is critical for most adults to feel comfortable and confident in trying on content or practices. We learned that expecting change to happen early on is unrealistic and counterproductive as adults become frustrated.

Equity warriors understand that successful change requires a commitment to the long term so that teachers and staff can comfortably move through the stages—from awareness, to early use, to regular use, to mastery. Some adults will move faster through the stages than others. Those who move faster may struggle with the confidence to collaborate with others. If they can overcome their lack of confidence, they will be the ones who are best able to adapt and innovate based on their students' needs.

The second component of CBAM—Levels of Use, illustrated in Figure 6.2—provides a tool for measuring progress toward mastery (Hall & Hord, 2001, pp. 81–86). As the Stages of Concern focus on feelings or readiness for change, the eight Levels of Use name what change looks like. The lowest three levels describe nonuse as learning and preparation. Thinking about teachers who exhibit the behaviors in the lowest three levels as nonuse is helpful. Though it is important to recognize that getting ready to change takes effort, getting ready should not be confused with doing. Users are those who learn by doing with students. The top five levels classify users from early use to mastery.

The Levels of Use help school leaders, teachers, and staff develop a common language around action. It is important to learn and be comfortable while changing practices. However, equity warriors know that staying in lower Stages of Concern and Levels of Use will not advance their equity agenda. Action matters.

The strength of CBAM is its specificity in naming the concerns, actions, and behaviors in school change. We have had success in using Stages of Concern and Levels of Use with school leaders

FIGURE 6.2 ● Levels of Use

0. Nonuse

- "I've heard about it, but, honestly, I have too many other things to do right now."

1. Orientation

- "I'm looking at materials pertaining to the innovation and considering using it sometime in the future."

2. Preparation

- "I've attended the workshop, and I've set aside time every week for studying the materials."

3. Mechanical Use

- "Most of my time is spent organizing materials and keeping things moving as smoothly as possible every day."

4a. Routine Use

- "This year, it has worked out beautifully. Basically, I will use it the same way I did this year."

4b. Refinement

- "I recently developed a more detailed assessment instrument to gain more specific information from students to see where I need to change my use of the innovation."

5. Integration

- "Not everyone has the skills needed to use the program so that it has the greatest effect on student learning. I've been working with another teacher, and recently a third teacher began working with us."

6. Renewal

- "I am still interested in the program and using it with modifications. Frankly, I'm reading, talking, and even doing a little research to see whether some other approach might be better for students."

Source: Hall, G. E., Dirksen, D. J., & George, A. A. (2006). *Measuring implementation in schools: Levels of use.* Austin, TX: SEDL. Reprinted with permission from the American Institutes for Research.

as a framework for planning school professional development and program implementation. We return to the SDHS ILT to illustrate a process.

Into the third year, the SDHS ILT was deeply involved in designing and implementing rigorous curriculum units across all content areas. Many teachers, but not all, had moved beyond the management stage (stage 3) to wrestling with assessing student understanding as feedback on the units and their use of the instructional best practices (stage 4). Concurrently, many were concerned about how to work effectively with colleagues and learn collaboratively (stage 5).

While the SDHS ILT's purpose and the desired outcomes had been communicated and understood from the beginning, the change process had not. The administrative team and the leadership coaches had designed the change process keeping in mind the Stages of Concern and Levels of Use. Developing knowledge and practice over time and naming Levels of Use were embedded into the planning for the meetings and the design of protocols. The time for sharing explicitly the change process had long passed.

SDHS ILT members were growing impatient and frustrated by the lack of transparency in understanding the change process. Some leaders were interested in deepening their skills. Some members thought the process was stalled as the work of curriculum design became spiraled. Some were frustrated that they did not have the tools to combat the resistance. Others were comfortable being led but needed confidence that they were on the right path.

Simplifying and introducing the CBAM tools created a common language. By explaining the Stages of Concern and asking SDHS ILT members to place themselves and each of their colleagues in one of the eight Levels of Use, they compiled more objective data about the status of the change process. Members were accustomed to using data and evidence, so charting data was not a stretch.

The SDHS ILT focused on one of their instructional improvement strategies, using measurable lesson objectives to monitor student progress, to learn to apply the tools. They answered three questions:

- Identify where you and members of your department are in the Stages of Concern in using lesson objectives (e.g., awareness, informational, personal, management, consequence, collaboration, and refocusing).

- Map the steps the department will take during the next six months to lead through the Levels of Use of

(1) orientation, (2) preparation, (3) mechanical use, and (4a) routine use in implementing lesson objectives.

- Schedule presentations to department/course-alike teams (e.g., first meeting and monthly meetings, PLCs, pull-out days).

There were three outcomes from introducing and using the tools. First, members developed a way to assess readiness. Rather than thinking of resistance to change generically, they could classify readiness. Second, the stages and the levels helped define the next steps in addressing concerns and implementation. Using the tools in concert, team members could ask questions about use. Third, they shared a common language to articulate their struggles and plan next steps.

Equity warriors apply a change strategy to guide their teachers and staff in improving teaching and learning for all students. To do so, they have tools that articulate pathways for progress. Not every adult is at the same place. Adopting a change strategy that differentiates support while articulating common expectations balances conflicts inherent in achieving an equity agenda. The agenda is achieved when everyone is on the pathway to reach mastery—students and adults. Successful change strategies recognize that not everyone will reach mastery in the same way or at the same time.

Equity warriors apply a change strategy to guide their teachers and staff in improving teaching and learning for all students.

YOUR MOVE: PRIORITIZE STUDENTS WITH DISABILITIES AND MULTILINGUAL LEARNERS.

Even a cursory review of achievement data shows that students with disabilities and students whose first language is not English are more school dependent and underperforming than their peers. They also know these characteristics are not unitary—race and poverty, language and years in school, and expectations and ownership all show up and influence beliefs, assessments, and supports provided to students. While there are important differences among the learning needs of individual students, we believe there is one universal truth: Strengthening teaching and learning in the general education classroom—anywhere across the country—leads to increased academic achievement for students with these characteristics.

Existing district and school systems and structures are to blame for our failure to improve achievement of students with disabilities and multilingual learners. Consider the following:

- As we discussed in Part I, expectations for students based on achievement gap data reinforce stereotypes that students with disabilities and multilingual learners having performance gains consistent with those of their peers is the exception to the rule.

- Low expectations for students by adults and students themselves stick to students over time.

- Students with disabilities and multilingual learners are often the responsibility of adults in the system other than their school's principal and general education teachers. These adults may have a personal interest in maintaining students in those designations for as long as possible or until transition grades, when students are miraculously redesignated.

- Attention to the letter of the law rather than the spirit and intent of federal and state mandates results in resources being diverted into compliance measures and programs rather than services meeting student needs.

- Often, instructional materials such as multiple texts and manipulatives to scaffold instruction are not available.

- Students are assigned to interventions—homogeneous grouping of students with similar designations or into available interventions rather than ones that target a specific learning need deprives students of instruction in core content with a general education teacher.

- Performance on new standards—such as those that emphasize text complexity, language (academic vocabulary and function), and building knowledge from informational texts—does not accurately show struggling students' progress in language acquisition.

Performance on standards, in particular, shows the system's failure. Designated students are removed from instruction with their peers for varying amounts of time and receive support from adults who do not have content knowledge. In practice, special education and multilingual support teachers are not included in professional learning about the academic standards—nor do they have the background or confidence in content knowledge. In addition, adults do not often have instructional materials that assist in language acquisition in academic subjects. Adults do not have time to plan individualized instruction, and teachers do not have time to collaborate on instruction and supports. As a result, structures reinforce isolation rather than inclusion, and students have limited meaningful interaction with students whose example contributes to learning and language acquisition.

Equity warriors have not been helped by the lack of political and other pressures to improve systems for educating students with disabilities and multilingual learners. Disagreements about approaches to language acquisition *and* special education services teeter between full immersion without supports—the sink-or-swim approach—and full-time isolation. Where progress monitoring occurs, experience suggests that too often lack of progress is blamed on not enough services and supports, not on the wrong type of supports and expectations. More of the same is the result.

Equity warriors have not been helped by the lack of political and other pressures to improve systems for educating students with disabilities and multilingual learners.

Research on schools that have been successful in raising achievement among designated students identifies some of the moves we have discussed—teachers with knowledge in core content as well as special education/sheltered instruction strategies, progress monitoring, collaboration among teachers and support providers, ongoing professional development, and differentiated interventions and supports (American Institutes for Research, 2017). The most compelling research has focused attention on the importance of direct academic vocabulary development, listening, speaking, scaffolding lessons, accessing core content, and reinforcing academic identities. We know schools where students spend entire days rarely asked to speak, have limited exposure to academic language, and/or are in substantially separate classrooms in which they have no exposure to grade-level content.

Equity warriors begin by owning responsibility for the continued progress of each student in their school.

Equity warriors begin by owning responsibility for the continued progress of each student in their school. This is no small step. In our partnerships, district leaders are able to name principals who have built a climate of inclusion and have success with students with disabilities and multilingual learners. These schools are—once again—the exceptions.

To learn how schools with a reputation for providing a high-quality education for all students, particularly students with disabilities, we studied 15 "best practice schools" as part of a multiyear study of special education reform in New York City public schools (Perry and Associates, Inc., 2014). Across these schools, we reported the following (pp. 26–27):

(Continued)

(Continued)

The character of school life is enthusiastic and engaging, not demoralizing or disillusioning. These schools have strong leadership that fosters a positive schoolwide culture with culturally competent staff. Staff promote a positive schoolwide culture by focusing on academics as well as students' social-emotional needs and expectations. Teachers are fair and create academically and emotionally safe learning climates with high and clear expectations about academics and behavior so every student can reach their personal best. Teachers are respectful and sensitive to race and class inequities, empowering them to better identify students' needs and potential. Further, school staff are culturally competent. That is, they address race and class openly, manage dynamics of difference in the school, and keep open lines of communication with students, families, and the communities they serve.

High-quality teaching and instruction are prioritized, and school leaders find ways to deliver it. These schools recognize that flexible and relevant instruction leads to better student outcomes. The quality of outcomes for any school is based, in part, on the quality of the instruction that its teachers deliver. Leaders understand which interventions and strategies are effective in achieving improved outcomes—targeted professional development focused on classroom practice, collaborative staff and teacher trainings, curricular coherence, development of stronger school leaders, and opportunities for teachers to learn from each other—and have found creative ways to deliver them.

High expectations are set for what each child should achieve, and then performance is monitored against these expectations, intervening whenever they are not met. Getting the right people to become teachers and developing them into effective instructors gives schools the capacity to deliver appropriate, targeted, and differentiated instruction that leads to improved outcomes. Schools that are successful with students with disabilities go further. They use strategic staffing assignments that make the most of individuals' strengths and weaknesses and put in place processes designed to ensure that every child is able to benefit from this increased capacity.

Data are integrated into the school improvement process. Data on student progress are gathered and used regularly and are understood as an empowering tool for school staff. Data provide information that guides decisions about instruction, curriculum, and programming. Data-driven assessment, analysis, and action are deeply embedded in the school's culture and are a top priority for better student achievement and school-wide improvement. Student achievement data by demographics, racial groups, and ability groups provide an opportunity to reflect on institutional policies and practices that may unintentionally perpetuate differential achievement patterns of different student groups.

Funding is provided to maintain services in the event of fluctuations in student enrollment. Principals understand that funding levels vary according to the child's needs and can be spent flexibly. These principals are savvy at weighing inputs, programs, activities, and staffing with results. They often customize educational services and by design are more transparent about their funding practices.

Equity warriors know that best practices apply across schools and student populations. Schools like these gain a reputation for providing high-quality education—based on student achievement results and family interest—by emphasizing that students with disabilities and multilingual learners are a priority and contribute to the uniqueness of the school community. Equity warriors also know that leadership is an active ingredient in building a supportive culture that will help teachers, staff, and students seek and use instructional approaches, scaffolding, and authentic progress monitoring that demonstrate student success. The starting point is understanding the challenge and deploying resources.

Equity warriors know that best practices apply across schools and student populations.

In San Diego Unified, Roosevelt International Middle School principal Christina Casillas differentiated the data on the multilingual learners that were nearly 50 percent of the school's student population. Of the total multilingual learner population, 64 percent had been reclassified, meaning they were no longer receiving supplemental supports. Yet, Casillas knew that although they had tested proficient, their academic success would depend on continued attention to language development. Of the students still designated as English learners, more than half had been in public schools more than six years without testing language proficient. The school also had another group of students who were considered at-risk.

(Continued)

Helping teachers and staff understand the different language abilities of students was followed by recognizing that groups of students needed different levels of support. Casillas assessed her staff capacity to design a combination of professional learning, supports for individual students, and in-classroom supports. She deployed staff and resources while settling on activities and instructional strategies, including in-class supports for high-needs groups of students, organizing school and family events, and providing opportunities to learn through multiple modalities such as the arts and community partnerships.

Equity warriors flip the script by valuing multilingual learners and students with disabilities.

Equity warriors flip the script by valuing multilingual learners and students with disabilities. They know that English and academic language acquisition and fostering academic identities are at the core of all learning and are exemplified in the rigorous academic standards. They plan with intentionality by using data to identify strengths. They balance conflicts between and among groups over limited resources by building a school culture that brings students, teachers, and staff together to learn from each other rather than keeping them in separate or isolated tracks.

YOUR MOVE: CREATE A LEARNING ENVIRONMENT CONSISTENT WITH YOUR EQUITY AGENDA.

Equity warriors know the importance of consistency in their talk and walk to build collaborative cultures that support teaching and learning. Organizational cultures and learning environments are dynamic in most schools. Each year, students and often teachers and staff arrive and become members of schools, bringing with them their strengths, experiences, beliefs, and fears. Even in the most stable environments, school leaders struggle to create safe, fair, and accountable structures to ensure that conflicts between and among adults and students are resolved consistent with their espoused values and in ways that advance their equity agenda.

Just having everyone get along does not seem to be part of the human condition. As it is with any other community, schools are required to harness the energy that is a natural outgrowth of people coming together. More to the point, schools are the social institutions where we send our children to learn how to get along with others—adults and peers—who are different from them. Learning from and with others is a vital part of individual development and is vital to our democratic form of government.

School leaders strive to make schools safe places for all students to learn. They keep aware of happenings in the neighborhood and with families that may carry over into the school. They build alliances with law enforcement officers, social workers, and other support providers to exchange information. They create discipline codes and procedures to set norms for behavior and expectations. They react when expectations are not met. Maintaining a safe community is not easy, and the consequences for a mistake—for whatever reason—can be grave.

Equity warriors are aware of the conflict inherent in using power and authority in a social institution dedicated to advancing equity and the success of every student. Students, even the youngest, watch how authority is exercised. Students learn from and mimic adult behavior. Students learn who cares for them and who does not, who to trust and who not to trust, and how and when to act. Behavioral systems and structures are opportunities to reinforce key messages that advance equity.

Data tell us that behavioral systems and structures are not used wisely to advance teaching and learning. Detention, suspension, and expulsion, which remove students from learning opportunities and contribute to academic failure, are ineffective in changing behaviors (Losen & Whitaker, 2018). More to the point, research has shown that nearly 20 percent of the achievement gap between Black and white students can be attributed to disproportionate suspension rates (Morris & Perry, 2016, pp. 80–81). Disproportionality in the rates of suspension, expulsion, arrests, referrals to law enforcement, restraining, and/or secluding students of color, particularly Black males, begins at preschool and continues through high school (U.S. Department of Education, 2014). Fear of in-school violence has led to zero-tolerance policies and the regular presence of school-based police officers. Together, these policies and practices have been described as contributing to a school-to-prison pipeline for men of color.

Experience has taught us that aligning behavior management and support systems to an equity agenda is not a simple matter. School leaders have an obligation to keep adults and students safe. We don't need to repeat the demands on teachers, some of whom are personally dealing with the effects of trauma and social pressures. When teachers feel unsafe or threatened, they react by distancing themselves from students who are perceived to be a threat. Alternatives are few. There are not enough

Equity warriors know the importance of consistency in their talk and walk to build collaborative cultures that support teaching and learning.

resources to hire and prepare staff to provide necessary support services to students and adults who need them. Parents and community members, rightfully, abandon schools considered to be unsafe for alternatives that are.

In addition to building collaborative cultures based on shared values, as discussed in Part II, equity warriors establish conditions that improve teaching and learning by fostering relationships. School leaders establish such conditions through visioning, modeling, and acting in ways that are consistent with the equity agenda. However, while essential, these steps are not enough. Behavioral systems and structures that equip adults and students with the tools to balance conflicts are required.

Designing systems and structures to support teaching and learning and advance equity begins with the assumption that people act as they do because they do not have the tools to act differently. Beginning with and holding on to this assumption enables school leaders to be objective and withhold judgment until adults or students demonstrate that they know the difference but choose to continue to act in ways inconsistent with the equity agenda. Further, operating with this assumption helps avoid creating systems and structures that are reactionary. For example, if a school has found it necessary to have school-based police officers, school leaders must have the authority to select and supervise the officers and ensure that officers have received training in working in a school setting. Insisting on authority and training are structural changes that address the problem, and ones that may be more effective than removing officers.

Equity warriors design systems and structures consistent with their equity agenda and their school's needs. There are organizations and resources that offer various personal and group development tools. For example, our partner schools have used schoolwide Positive Behavior Intervention and Supports (PBIS) to reset a school's tone and climate. PBIS is a multi-tiered system that begins with all adults and students learning and acknowledging prosocial expectations and behaviors. PBIS emphasizes a schoolwide culture, but students who are unable to meet expectations are identified for more intensive attention and skill development to prevent disruptive behaviors. A strength of PBIS is that adults and students are encouraged to assist each other in acknowledging prosocial behavior. Students who exhibit prosocial behavior do not miss instructional time and are rewarded by teachers.

Social-emotional learning offers a comprehensive and more resource-intensive, systemic approach. The Collaborative for Academic, Social, and Emotional Learning (CASEL) framework

FIGURE 6.3 ● CASEL's SEL Framework

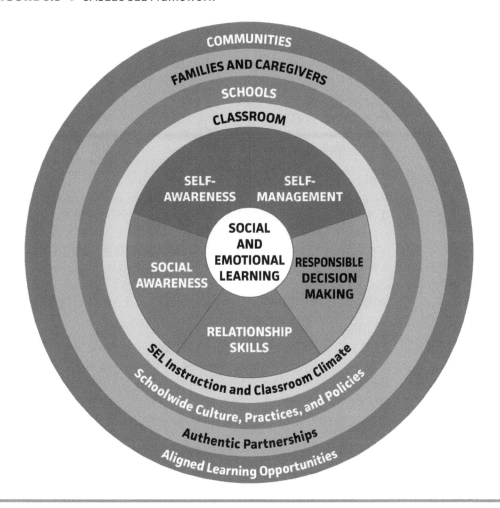

Source: Collaborative for Academic, Social, and Emotional Learning, https://casel.org/selframework/

identifies five elements: self-awareness, self-management, responsible decision making, relationship skills, and social awareness (see Figure 6.3). The framework defines competencies that can be taught to students at all ages and adults. Increased awareness of the importance of social-emotional development has contributed to an expansion of program models and providers targeting specific audiences.

Restorative justice in schools encompasses a range of practices intended to build self-awareness, self-advocacy, and community. Restorative circles and restorative conferences are two of the most common practices to help participants make safe choices and solve problems productively. Restorative circles, which are used by a classroom of students or groups of adults, engage participants in activities to understand and acknowledge their emotions and develop language to discuss and understand their feelings and the feelings of others. Circles are also used to strengthen community by providing opportunities to engage in problem solving on matters that affect the group. Restorative conferences are dialogues, tightly facilitated by a practiced adult or peer mediator, between a person who has been harmed and the person who caused the harm. The facilitated protocol helps participants understand the harm caused, take steps to repair the harm, and make plans to avoid future mistakes.

Equity warriors understand that establishing conditions that help students and adults settle conflicts is an essential ingredient to improving teaching and learning. To state the obvious, students who are removed from the classroom or the school are deprived of learning time, and students and adults who do not have opportunities and skills to know themselves and others can't create community. School leaders build systems and structures that show adults and students how to settle conflicts that get in the way of advancing equity.

Equity warriors understand that establishing conditions that help students and adults settle conflicts is an essential ingredient to improving teaching and learning.

REFLECTION: *Does your school have an explicit and shared definition of academic rigor supported by a theory of action and an implementation plan? Is your change strategy articulated and intentionally focused on balancing conflict between and among interests? Does your equity agenda prioritize the most vulnerable students?*

_____

_____

_____

_____

_____

_____

_____

_____

DIPLOMACY: USE PROTOCOLS AND PROCESSES TO BUILD CAPACITY

Equity warriors know that focusing on the instructional core—content, teacher, and student—is the way to advance equity. They use the tools of diplomacy—rewards, consequences, and moral persuasion—to bring coherence in applying processes and systems that push teachers to know students as learners and respond to each student's learning needs. To know when it is appropriate to use the tools, school leaders jump into the fray and work side by side with teachers and students to improve teaching and learning. There is no other way.

Equity warriors know that focusing on the instructional core—content, teacher, and student—is the way to advance equity.

The good news is that school leaders have access to processes and protocols that are effective in strengthening the instructional core. Effective processes take ideas, concepts, and programs and transform them into actions that can be immediately applied to the classroom. Effectiveness is measured in the engagement of students and the effect on their learning. The processes, when they are applied in concert and tailored to the situation and school culture, close the circle from idea to results.

Equity warriors assess the strengths of their teachers and staff to know students as learners. They stay focused on strengthening the instructional core and know that affecting one part of the core affects the other parts. Equity warriors are vigilant in applying the protocols and process repeatedly until they are embedded into the school's culture and become the way things are done.

YOUR MOVE: INSTITUTE UNIT-PLANNING PROCESSES TO DELIVER A GUARANTEED VIABLE CURRICULUM TO EVERY STUDENT.

Articulating a change strategy, such as CBAM, helps school leaders understand the big picture direction and reduce conflict inherent in leading the school in the difficult work of advancing equity. While some teachers will benefit from knowing the strategy, many teachers are most comfortable with being shown the way step by step. Equity warriors use their knowledge of teachers to lead through the process of teaching rigorous curriculum and meeting the needs of all students.

Equity warriors know teachers are reluctant to abandon familiar curriculum and instructional materials. Minimally, teachers need a year just to become familiar with new materials and adjust their instruction. That assumes teachers are required to use new materials or at least are receptive to taking the risk of doing so. So, it is no surprise, even when improved curriculum materials are provided, that instructional improvement doesn't happen immediately. Nevertheless, when one side of the instructional core changes, the other sides are required to change as well.

Our partner schools have had success in chunking curriculum to help teachers make the shift from teaching to student learning. Having a guaranteed viable curriculum that articulates essential learning is the starting point. Whether the guaranteed viable curriculum is districtwide with prescribed units, or based on a school-adopted text, unit planning provides a data-based change process that helps teachers manage their pacing, their teaching, and their monitoring of student progress.

Equity warriors use unit planning to take their vision for students and realize the vision in teaching and learning. Unit planning is the process of taking the grade-level curriculum and standards and mapping teaching and learning to the academic calendar. There are multiple versions of unit planning that are familiar to school leaders. Our partner schools adopted approaches that help teachers develop a cycle that spiraled learning over time. The steps are as follows:

Equity warriors know teachers are reluctant to abandon familiar curriculum and instructional materials.

- Divide the year into units of instruction based on themes/content in the state standards, and determine the number of days for each unit. Typically, six to eight units are enough for the year.

- Identify the essential content and big ideas that students are expected to learn by the end of the unit.

- Identify and match the learning targets (specific knowledge, concepts, and skills) within the unit.

- Create an end-of-unit assessment for students to demonstrate the expected learning.

- Create a unit preassessment to administer at the beginning of the unit to determine student prior knowledge.

- Map the days of instruction and the formative tasks students will accomplish along the way.

- Launch and adjust the days of instruction based on the unit preassessment.

Unit planning is not counting which lessons and pages to cover. It intends to organize teaching around essential learning. Equity warriors know that while the process is familiar and straightforward, changing mindsets to help teachers embrace the process takes time. Equity warriors apply rewards, consequences, and moral persuasion to situations that require facilitation, collaboration, and discipline in adhering to the cycle.

Equity warriors use unit planning to take their vision for students and realize the vision in teaching and learning.

Initially, unit planning can feel overwhelming. Facilitation by school leaders is important to instill confidence that the process is manageable and to help teachers gain momentum. We have seen the most success when school leaders, either administrators or content coaches, calendar half-day planning sessions for grade-level/course-alike teams throughout the year and facilitate their planning. Facilitators lead through the process and seek agreement on the essential learning for each unit. When units are provided, facilitation is most helpful in unpacking the essential learning and the knowledge and skills required by the end-of-unit assessment.

School leader facilitation also may be necessary to build collaboration among the team. Equity-focused unit planning depends on teachers helping each other analyze the results from previous units and sharing instructional strategies. Some of the most sophisticated and confident teams are able to think creatively about how they use their strengths to benefit students. For example, we have watched teachers within grade-level teams who have a strength engaging students in a particular content or lesson teach combined classes or rotate groups of students while other teachers focus on another part of the content or expected learning. Collaboration in this way comes from understanding the expectations embedded in the essential learning and analyzing student data.

Sticking to the plan and repeating the cycle takes scheduling and discipline. Unit planning that includes reviewing data from the previous unit requires constant monitoring and commitment. Again, since teachers often find it difficult to hold each other accountable, school leader facilitation applying the tools of diplomacy to particular situations may be necessary to overcome excuses and have teachers show up ready to plan. Ideally, strong teams self-monitor when they have a commitment to each other and a belief in a systems approach to improving student achievement. Staying committed, particularly when the team changes, may require nudging.

Returning to our example from Flint Community Schools, district leaders decided to adopt a unit-based approach for its guaranteed viable curriculum to increase rigor and consistency and build teacher and student efficacy. They knew teachers were not keeping pace through their curriculum. With a highly mobile student population, teachers repeated lessons and revisited content in the hope that students would demonstrate mastery before moving on. Students fell further behind as they grew frustrated by repetitive lessons and were not exposed to essential content from year to year.

The district K–8 curriculum was divided into six English language arts (ELA) and eight mathematics units each year. All teachers had access to the K–8 curriculum map, which showed how the essential learning spiraled each year. ELA units were aligned to the themes in the state standards. Not all units were the same length. Each unit included reading skills, word study (vocabulary, academic language, and grammar), and writing skills. There was a research unit each year beginning with kindergarten. Initially, teachers balked at introducing the research unit for the primary grades. They did not believe students would be successful, even though state standards called for instruction in research skills at each grade level. Delving into the units, primary grade teachers learned that students were quite capable of grasping basic research concepts and skills, and they enjoyed being scientists and historians! Teachers also understood that students would have the opportunity to be researchers nine times over nine years. No need to be perfect in kindergarten!

The district pacing chart scheduled planning days between units. These days were available for students to make up missed work and for enrichment, and for teachers to participate in unit planning. ELA teachers analyzed student writing to discover which skills in the writing process would need to be reinforced for individuals or groups of students. Since every unit required a published writing piece, teachers could be confident that students would make progress through the 54 end-of-unit writing opportunities they would have over nine years.

Similarly, the mathematics units were aligned to the state standards, spiraled each year, and were of different lengths. Algebraic concepts were introduced in the primary grades. Analysis of the end-of-the-unit assessment by mathematics teachers led to isolating specific skills and knowledge that needed to be reinforced. Rather than delaying the next unit, teachers planned minilessons and routines that could be inserted into the next

> units to reinforce skills lacking for groups of students as well planned supplementary instruction for students who had specific gaps. They also knew that students would have the opportunity to master difficult concepts—such as fractions—over multiple years.

Equity warriors lead teachers through the planning processes to help teachers define the essential content, measure student progress, and reinforce learning. Equity warriors know that students fall behind if they are not exposed to rigorous grade-level content. Teachers who wait for students to demonstrate mastery at each step before moving on disadvantage students unintentionally. Unit planning helps teachers ensure that time is devoted to essential grade-level learning. Unit-planning processes keep teachers and students from being overwhelmed by chunking learning. Unit planning provides for the deliberate collection and analysis of data to measure outcomes and to individualize instruction based on student needs.

Equity warriors know that students fall behind if they are not exposed to rigorous grade-level content.

We have watched teachers, once convinced, embrace unit planning and make it part of the school's culture. It becomes the way that teachers own control of the curriculum and their teaching. A unit-planning approach helps teachers understand that they are part of a multiyear system of student learning. In our experience, there is no other way to advance equity through improving teaching and learning than to have adults work together over the years as a system.

YOUR MOVE: LINK PEER COACHING DIRECTLY TO STUDENT LEARNING.

A few months after we introduced instructional walk-throughs to a school's administrative team, it was time to begin collegial walk-throughs. One of the teachers whose classroom we had visited several times told us that she was very anxious about being visited by other teachers. She had not seemed anxious during our visits. When asked for clarity, she said other teachers could not be fooled by what they saw. Her comments reinforced two perceptions we have found true: Teachers typically do not give credence to the instructional leadership role of school leaders, and they value the opinions of their peers a great deal.

That teachers don't value principals' instructional knowledge is not surprising. Just as principals value learning from the experiences of their current peers more than district supervisors and leaders, teachers are no different. Principals, particularly those who have been administrators for some time, rarely show their instructional knowledge and skill. Nor should they. Teachers can easily dismiss the prowess of school leaders or others who are not in the classroom every day. They dismiss it regularly.

That teachers value the opinions of their peers requires consideration. In spite of efforts over the past two decades, teachers rarely see other teachers in action. Schedules must be intentionally planned to enable teachers to visit each other. Creating schedules that make time for visits comes at the cost of limiting time for collaborative planning. Furthermore, teachers have little knowledge about the expertise of their peers. Teachers rarely celebrate the teaching expertise of their colleagues. Nor do teachers want to be celebrated. Teachers' own philosophies and experiences shape their instructional approach. Also, they know that teaching and learning depend on the teacher's relationship with her students. Therefore, they believe there is little to learn from a colleague.

We have promoted and learned from peer-coaching models as a way to advance equity for more than two decades. Peer coaching holds the promise of flexibility in applying rewards, consequences, and moral persuasion depending on the persons and situation. Our understanding evolved over time. Initially, we learned with our partner principals that their role as evaluator was getting in the way of building relationships with teachers that could lead to changes in instructional practices. Teachers were unaccustomed to being vulnerable, particularly when there might be consequences. So, principals selected a teacher whose instructional practice they respected to be a peer coach. The model had principals as supervisor, peer coach as confidential mentor to the teacher, and teacher as learner.

We experienced several problems with this model. Peer coaches were reluctant to engage colleagues without an invitation. Since trust was lacking and asking for coaching would be considered a sign of weakness, teachers invited peer coaches into their classrooms reluctantly, if at all. To build relationships, peer coaches gathered materials and/or ran copies for teachers. Still, invitations didn't follow. In some schools, teachers resented coaches because they did not have responsibility for students, and creating the coaching position increased the teaching load for others. Some principals assigned peer coaches to teach students part-time. Predictably taking the path of least resistance, coaches filled the time they were to coach with preparing for their teaching. In addition, we learned, as did the peer coaches, that coaching adults required different skills than teaching students.

Learning from initial experiences, our partner principals added structures to strengthen peer coaching. Principals used their evaluator role to identify areas of improvement and offered confidential peer coaching to teachers to help them improve. In Flint, staff developers were charged with supporting the district's curriculum implementation. Staff developers were assigned to two schools specifically to support all teachers implementing the readers/writers workshop model and units of instruction. In other places, lab classrooms and other formal structures with defined roles were in place to model instructional practices.

As testing and accountability pressures mounted, principals were reluctant to remove their strongest teachers from directly working with students, which enhanced teacher resistance. Further, with the introduction of common core standards, peer coaches struggled to learn the standards along with other teachers. Tight budgets and lack of clarity about the standards and the instructional materials pushed principals to try different models of whole-school professional learning. Districts that had resources for professional learning during the summer and pull-out days supported teachers. In many places, teachers were left on their own.

We continued to provide external peer coaches to our partner schools to analyze data and improve instructional strategies known to be effective in raising student achievement. Our success depended on the ability of our highly skilled coaches to build relationships with teachers. Though our coaches engaged and had the full support of principals, and had deep content knowledge and classroom experience, our success was sporadic. It wasn't until—following the lead of San Diego Unified's district leaders—we learned about the power of learning targets and coaching cycles, that we could link the peer-coaching model directly to student achievement.

Learning targets are student-friendly descriptions of what teachers expect students to learn or accomplish in a given lesson (Moss & Brookhart, 2012). The lesson could be completed in one day or over multiple days. The keys to learning targets are that they are specific sets of knowledge and skills that can be measured by students and teachers. In other words, they name the task or the elements of the task that students will accomplish to demonstrate proficiency.

The learning target's power is this: Learning targets push teachers to clarify expectations for themselves and their students by defining the essential learning, and learning targets generate data for each student that are observable by students and the teacher. Teachers use the learning targets to guide the selection of instructional strategies. When teachers observe students reaching the target, they know their instruction has been effective. Efficacy for teachers and students grows as they measure learning.

Identifying learning targets requires teachers to unpack grade-level content standards and set specific and measurable expectations for student learning. Diane Sweeney's (2011, 2013) student-centered coaching approach provides structures for guiding teachers through the process. The coaching cycle is the heart of the process. As the following example illustrates, teachers work with a coach to set learning targets based on rigorous grade-level standards. Coaching helps push teachers to stretch their expectations for students. To begin the coaching cycle, teachers administer an assessment to determine levels of student proficiency. Following instruction, the teacher again assesses student proficiency in meeting the targets.

We return to Bethune K–8 School in San Diego Unified School District, which we introduced in Chapter 4. Our support for Bethune included principal leadership coaching as well as coaching in mathematics instruction. Although increasing student achievement in mathematics was recognized as high need, Bethune's largely veteran staff did not welcome coaching. Principal Valerie Jurado's attempts to convince staff to engage in professional learning were successful only for short stretches.

The Bethune staff liked, worked with, and respected our colleague, mathematics coach Holly Culbertson. However, they did not take responsibility for sustaining the use of instructional strategies that Culbertson modeled with their students. Teachers acknowledged that the strategies were engaging students and effective in introducing higher-level thinking and solving word problems. Yet, they rarely integrated the instructional strategies into their lessons because the strategies required more planning and effort than they were willing to expend.

Jurado and Culbertson convinced teachers at two grade levels to participate in a series of three, three-week coaching cycles. The coaching cycle plan included identifying specific student goals (e.g., writing an equation that matches the problem) that were within the grade-level content standards. The precycle planning included analyzing preassessment results to determine the learning targets for the next set of lessons. Culbertson's questions for the teachers helped her understand and, when necessary, challenge their expectations.

The plan also articulated instructional goals for the teacher (e.g., the use of explicit purpose and learning targets throughout the lesson) as well as goals for teacher, coach, and principal learning (e.g., clarify and connect standards to big mathematical ideas). Teachers administered the mid- and postcycle assessments. Culbertson analyzed the data with teachers and cotaught 15-minute thinking and problem-solving routines nine times during the three-week cycle. Teachers and students continued the lessons without coaching on the other times. In all cases, students showed growth on the learning targets across the grade levels.

Student-centered coaching proved to be the most effective approach to peer coaching in our experience. Drawing a straight line from content standards to student performance on specific tasks provides that which most teachers want: learning that can be applied in their classrooms immediately. Examination of data on student growth builds teacher and student efficacy and challenges beliefs that students are unable to master rigorous tasks. Defining roles for school leaders, teachers, and coaches clarifies expectations and supports for a defined time. Coaching time and resources are linked to high-leverage actions that affect student learning. Accountability and the credit for success are with the teacher and student who own the process and the data.

Equity warriors know that systems and structures are necessary to help teachers lead each other in improving teaching and learning and advance equity. Their intention to build capacity rather than fix a "bad teacher" is clear. They select strong-willed teachers who can bring others along as peer coaches. They reexamine and allocate their resources for site-based professional learning. They recognize that linking professional learning tightly to demonstrations of student learning increases buy-in, effectiveness, and personal accountability. Peer coaching from within the school—using department and grade-level teams—unleashes collegial leadership and ownership for advancing equity.

Equity warriors know that systems and structures are necessary to help teachers lead each other in improving teaching and learning and advance equity.

YOUR MOVE: DESIGN
AND PILOT PROTOCOLS.

Whether it is having teachers and staff agree to plan professional development, participate in collegial walk-throughs, embrace an approach to restorative justice, or launch another initiative, school leaders know that reaching agreement to start a journey is not the hardest part of achieving their equity agenda. It is only the beginning! Often the most sincere and earnest intentions are abandoned as details and implications unfold. The devil is in the details.

Equity warriors use protocols to help teachers and staff plan, implement, and assess progress of ideas and initiatives.

Equity warriors use protocols to help teachers and staff plan, implement, and assess progress of ideas and initiatives. School leaders and facilitators often carry with them dog-eared copies of *The Power of Protocols* (McDonald et al., 2007) or have the School Reform Initiative (https://www.schoolreforminitiative.org/protocols/) among their favorite links. There seems to be a protocol for every occasion. Effective protocols are simple to understand and follow, they lead participants to the desired outcome, and—most important—they generate the knowledge necessary to reach a level of understanding about the task.

Simplicity and success in leading to the outcome need little explanation. If the protocol is complicated to learn or if the purpose is unclear, its effectiveness diminishes. Also, if the protocol doesn't lead to informing the outcome, then the result will be at best incomplete or at worst misguided. Creating protocols that inform as well as lead to accomplishing a task is not uncommon. Teachers familiar with constructive and/or experiential learning know student tasks can be designed that help students learn content as they demonstrate mastery. In this way of thinking, assignments that have students read, explore, and consider what they are learning along the way are more effective than having students recall information after sitting through a series of presentations. The same concept applies to working with adults.

Protocols that push learning new practices can be direct and/or subtle. We have experienced success working with school leadership teams in developing curricula or assessments by assigning readings that prepared and guided teams through sessions in which they discussed and applied the readings to their work. Participants knew their ability to use the work time effectively depended on their preparation. At other times, we asked teams to answer questions that pushed teachers to self-initiate their inquiry. For example, one protocol for looking at student work asks teachers to identify the learning standard measured by the assignment. To be successful, teachers need to know and apply their knowledge of the standards. They can't complete the protocol without demonstrating their knowledge.

Equity warriors advance equity by using protocols that deepen teacher knowledge of content, sharpen their teaching skills, and address student learning needs. Further, they facilitate the process for developing protocols that allow school leaders to have pride of ownership of the process as well as the product so they can lead others. Building a series of protocols creates culture change, as the following example from the San Diego High School Instructional Leadership Team illustrates.

Equity warriors advance equity by using protocols that deepen teacher knowledge of content, sharpen their teaching skills, and address student learning needs.

Over three years, every time agreement was reached on what needed to come next, SDHS ILT members were asked to devise an approach. The facilitation steps became familiar as they were repeated with each task:

- Reach consensus on the desired outcome
- Identify guiding questions
- Facilitate whole-group or department/course-alike teams in protocol design
- Align group protocols
- Pilot
- Reflect and modify as necessary

At times, facilitators identified protocols to start the discussion. For example, in designing a sample protocol for reviewing the results of common assessments, the facilitators offered an eight-step protocol designed by another district. Following an overview of the protocol and the reasons for recommending it, the department teams took over. Teams conducted their own analysis of the protocol and adjusted the steps and discussion questions to fit their content areas. After reporting back to the SDHS ILT, they edited the draft protocol for their own use.

Members used their familiarity with the intended outcome and the protocol questions to introduce the protocol to their non–SDHS ILT department colleagues. By the next meeting, the protocol had been piloted, modified, and prepared for use as a campuswide tool. Teacher ownership and the members' championing of the protocol reduced resistance.

(Continued)

(Continued)

Members were encouraged to share sample protocols of their own making. Agenda planning guides for course-alike common preparation meetings, course outline feedback templates, department updates on unit design, and professional learning scheduling templates emerged from teachers who were willing to share tools they developed to address an identified need as efficiently as possible. Of course, colleagues tend to be easier on each other. As quality assurance, school leaders worked to encourage collegial discussions that would produce products that met established criteria and could achieve consensus.

Equity warriors know it is not enough to select a protocol and encourage others to use it to accomplish a task. They choose or codevelop protocols with intentionality.

Equity warriors know it is not enough to select a protocol and encourage others to use it to accomplish a task. They choose or codevelop protocols with intentionality. They create conditions for collaboration in learning and analyzing protocols. They guide participants in deepening their learning as they apply the protocol to their purpose. They build muscle memory and consistency through adopting protocols and reinforcing their use. In this way, they build a school culture in which the equity agenda is advanced step by step.

YOUR MOVE: SELECT, ONBOARD, AND RETAIN TEACHERS AND STAFF INTENTIONALLY.

In effective systems, district leaders own responsibility to develop and monitor human capital placement practices, recruit effectively, attract and mentor student teachers, and induct new teachers. School leaders own responsibility for selecting and developing teachers and staff, which is critical to the school's culture and to advancing its equity agenda. Therefore, equity warriors do not leave teacher selection and development to district leaders. They are intentional in who they select, develop, and retain.

Given the importance of developing a team of equity warriors, we're surprised when school leaders are not more proactive about selecting and inducting teachers and staff. There are reasons for not being proactive, for settling for less-than-perfect candidates, particularly in schools perceived as hard to staff. We have partnered with schools that are in such disarray that they started the school year with few certified teachers. It was sad to watch a revolving set of substitute teachers without content knowledge and lesson plans lead classrooms. Students knew coming to school was a waste of their time, and they acted accordingly.

Yet, these situations are the extreme exceptions, the result of failures on multiple levels. More often, the absence of a strong organizational culture draws energy and attention away from selection and induction. Schools with strong equity cultures withstand leadership and staff transitions, and maintain a continuity of practice over time. Strong equity cultures recognize the importance of peer and collegial support. Strong equity cultures are learned, and those joining the culture are indoctrinated. Most important, cultures that advance equity are intentionally nurtured and explicit in their actions. They don't invite every applicant to join the team. They certainly do not wait until the school year begins to start induction.

Equity warriors do not leave teacher selection and development to district leaders. They are intentional in who they select, develop, and retain.

Schools with strong equity cultures invest in selecting teachers and staff who can contribute to the equity agenda. While the principal's and school's reputations are major considerations in attracting teachers and staff to join the school community, teachers and staff use their informal networks and relationships to attract colleagues. Activating informal networks and relationships is particularly important given the competition for equity-focused teachers and teachers of color.

Research on teachers and teaching describes the positive effects on Black and Latinx student achievement when the teaching force closely approximates the demographics of the student population as a whole (Simon et al., 2015, p. 7). Studies on school efforts to attract teachers of color suggest the process begins with developing a strategy that articulates the school's mission and vision and defines the characteristics of teachers and staff who could contribute to the school's agenda (p. 26). Aggressively recruiting within networks that have a pool of candidates of color—Teach for America and historically Black colleges—is a common strategy. Schools seem to have the most success when they engage their Black and Latinx teachers actively in the recruiting (p. 26). Further, Black and Latinx teachers are more likely to remain in a school if they have collegial relationships with other teachers and staff of color (p. 26).

Although the benefits of having teachers and staff of color in schools serving students of the same populations are undeniable, the pool of eligible candidates is inadequate for the number of classrooms where they are needed. Further, school leaders cannot assume that teachers and staff of color will understand the community or a student's experiences just because they share the same race or culture as a student (Shafer, 2018). Everyone in the community shares responsibility for the success of every student. Equity warriors know they need to exert the same level of effort to network and attract the best available teachers and staff who share their equity agenda as they do for teachers of color and hard-to-staff positions.

Building a culture of teaching to advance equity is hard work. Retaining teachers is a constant challenge. Sixteen percent of teachers leave the profession or change schools every year (Goldring et al., 2014). New teachers, even those who have undergraduate degrees in education *and* have joined programs like Teach for America that provide additional support, tell us they felt inadequately prepared for their initial teaching experience. When we ask those who have remained what enabled them to do so, support from other teachers is at the top of their list.

Susan Villani (2002) surveyed mentorship efforts and identified four ways that colleagues mentor new teachers: providing emotional support and encouragement, providing information about the daily workings of the school and the cultural norms of the school community, promoting cultural proficiency about students and the families, and peer coaching. Similarly, studies about administrators' role in retaining teachers reiterate the importance of administrative support to ensure that teachers have necessary resources; communications channels; instructional leadership that strategically hires, and regularly and fairly evaluates teachers and staff to support continuous improvement; and inclusive decision making that involves listening to and engaging teachers and staff and that provides appropriate autonomy (Learning Policy Institute, 2017).

Equity warriors know that induction and onboarding are among the protocols and processes that reinforce the school's culture among veteran and new teachers and staff.

Equity warriors know that being transparent about protocols and processes provides the frameworks that facilitate learning for adults as well as students. Implicit in protocols and processes is the expectation for continuous improvement and learning. Being transparent and articulating that processes and protocols are part of the school's equity agenda enables teachers and staff to understand the ways of working that define the school. So, understanding the protocols and processes through onboarding and induction of teachers and staff is vital to their success and retention.

Equity warriors know that induction and onboarding are among the protocols and processes that reinforce the school's culture among veteran and new teachers and staff, as the following example illustrates.

The New York City teacher contract requires each school to have a New Teacher Induction Committee. The committee includes the principal and the school's union representative (called a chapter leader) and teachers. The committee is charged with designing and executing a plan for mentoring new teachers.

School induction plans vary by school and grade level. In some schools, committees compile handbooks with information about how the school works. The handbooks are practical references with policies and practices intended to clarify expectations, answer questions, and keep teachers out of trouble. The handbooks tend to evolve over time, and some contain nearly 100 pages.

Some New Teacher Induction Committees take an active role in leading induction and mentoring teachers, beginning with planning and leading orientations before the school contract year starts. In these schools, the handbooks and other materials describe the school vision and mission as well as the new teacher support plan before and during the school year. Mentors are assigned to teachers who introduce them to the school, help teachers set up their classrooms, and explain school initiatives that underscore priorities and expectations while not overwhelming new teachers.

Mentoring takes multiple forms. New teachers may be scheduled to observe an expert teacher, participate in inquiry processes, and receive support from administrators and grade-level or department lead teachers. They participate in new teacher team meetings regularly to build relationships with an affinity group and participate in grade-level and department teams. They also receive formal feedback from administrator supervision.

Some schools have each of these multiple forms of induction and mentoring in practice. The strongest cultures embrace teachers into the community from the day they are hired.

Equity warriors are as purposeful about selecting, onboarding, and retaining teachers and staff who share their agenda for advancing equity as they are about their other areas of responsibility.

Equity warriors are as purposeful about selecting, onboarding, and retaining teachers and staff who share their agenda for advancing equity as they are about their other areas of responsibility. They harness the enthusiasm and commitment of teachers and staff for advancing equity, and show them how they can contribute by improving teaching and learning every day. Most important, equity warriors mold teachers and staff new to the school into a community that shares responsibility for each student's success.

REFLECTION: *What protocols and processes define your school's culture? Are these protocols and processes intentional in raising expectations as well as shifting mindsets from an emphasis on teaching to an emphasis on student learning?*

_____

_____

_____

_____

_____

_____

_____

_____

WARFARE: HOLD EVERYONE IN THE SCHOOL ACCOUNTABLE FOR STUDENT LEARNING

Let's start with the assumption that teaching and learning are the focal points of the school's equity agenda. We might stretch the assumption to be that every day we have with students, particularly those who are school dependent, matters in their journey to graduating high school prepared for higher education and/or a career. Then, let's further assume that the keys to improving teaching and learning are in analyzing and strengthening the instructional core—the content's rigor and complexity, teachers' knowledge and skills, and students' role as measured by their performance on daily tasks. That leads us to the question: What moves must principals and school leaders make to pressure teachers, staff, and students into strengthening the instructional core?

Equity warriors are present. They are in classrooms where teaching and learning take place. They meet with teachers to discuss their curriculum, instruction, and data. They articulate continuous improvement and change strategies. They introduce and lead processes and protocols that reinforce an organizational culture of collegial learning. They know that politics and diplomacy can take time to yield results. Equity warriors have a sense of urgency about the students who enter their schools every day. They know there is not a moment to lose!

Equity warriors trust in their strategies, protocols, and processes and are cautious not to take short-term actions that will undermine efforts to build a shared culture to advance equity. They remember that using pressure to reach an objective produces results in the short term. Nevertheless, they do not shy away from challenging teachers, staff, and students when their actions do not contribute to advancing their equity agenda. They particularly do not shy away from challenging teachers, staff, and students in their classrooms.

Equity warriors trust in their strategies, protocols, and processes and are cautious not to take short-term actions that will undermine efforts to build a shared culture to advance equity.

YOUR MOVE: USE THE TASKS STUDENTS ARE ASKED TO DO AS YOUR ACCOUNTABILITY SYSTEM.

Equity warriors understand the power of having a laser-like focus on demonstrating understanding as a measure of learning. Elmore's fifth principle of the instructional core, "the real accountability system is in the tasks that students are asked to do," is the lever to do so (City et al., 2009, pp. 31–33). Principals and school leaders can determine the effectiveness and appropriateness of instruction in any content area or grade level by seeking answers to two questions:

Equity warriors understand the power of having a laser-like focus on demonstrating understanding as a measure of learning.

- What task are students asked to perform at the end of the lesson?

- What do students need to know in order to complete the task?

Equity is measured in outcomes. Students and families expect preK–12 education to prepare students to graduate ready for success in higher education and/or a career. Teachers and students know that when climbing from one grade level to the next they are on a journey; and like on all journeys, they look for mileposts to determine if they are there yet. The most satisfaction comes from arriving. Certainly, the route taken on a journey is important. Yet, the route's effectiveness is measured by arriving at the predetermined destination.

Good instruction is a route to a destination. Instruction can be fun, rigorous, engaging, disciplined, personalized, or generalized. Instruction can inspire or be boring, can motivate or discourage. Whether instruction is good depends on perspective. School leaders, teachers, students, and families often have different perspectives on good instruction. Making good instruction concrete requires agreement on shared outcomes. The answer is found by looking in the instructional core. Or, more precisely, the answer is found in student performance on a task that helps students and teachers measure objectively the effectiveness of instruction.

Research on learning in complex, rapidly changing environments emphasizes doubling-down on thinking rather than remembering. For students to develop the intellectual tools and learning strategies needed for flexible adaptation to new problems and settings, the goal is to help students transfer what they learn into solving problems. In addition to agreement on the essential learning contained in the curriculum units, principals and school leaders form consensus on instructional approaches to guide the design and execution of daily lessons.

There are multiple approaches to designing lessons. Some are content specific, such as the four-step—launch, explore, summarize, and practice/apply—lesson design for teaching mathematics, or the "I do, we do, you do" gradual release of responsibility (Pearson & Gallagher, 1983). Research on teaching and learning across instructional models has identified common elements. Among them are the following:

- Teachers must draw out and work with the understandings that students bring with them.

- Teachers must teach some subject matter in depth, providing many examples in which the same concept is at work and providing a firm foundation of factual knowledge.

- Teaching metacognitive skills should be integrated into the curriculum in a variety of subject areas.

- Classrooms incorporate a community-centered approach that develops norms for the classroom and school, as well as connections to the outside world, that support core learning values. (National Research Council, 2002, pp. 14–25)

These elements underscore the importance of knowing students well and planning opportunities to give voice to the rich diversity of cultures in the classroom. Gholdy Muhammad (2020) builds on these common elements. Her four-layer equity framework includes the following as learning goals: identity development, skill development, intellectual development, and criticality. She explains that "criticality is the capacity to read, write, and think in the context of understanding power, privilege, and oppression. Criticality is also related to seeing, naming, and interrogating the world to not only make sense of injustice, but also to work toward social transformation" (Muhammad, 2020, p. 12).

Tasks that conclude the lesson inform students and teachers about whether the intended learning was mastered. To this end, effective tasks make visible the steps students take to complete them and the level of understanding they should exhibit to demonstrate mastery. This is the key—effective instruction and assessment are not separate. Instruction and assessment are two parts of the whole. Here is an example.

Students were expected to complete writing assignments long before the adoption of the Flint Community Schools (FCS) districtwide English language arts (ELA) curriculum based on the readers/writers workshop model. School visitors could expect to see student writing posted in the hallways outside of every K–8 classroom. Writing assignments were commonly connected to a seasonal theme or topic. Posted writings were replaced periodically as the seasons changed or in advance of family conferences that followed a marking period. Occasionally, the original assignments were posted with the papers so that observers could understand what was asked of students. Often, the student-produced works were slight variations of each other. The papers were written about the prompted topic and followed the same five-paragraph format. The students' opening sentences varied among three or four options. Papers were not graded.

The FCS districtwide adopted ELA curriculum had six, genre-based units. A published paper, a personal narrative, a work of historical fiction, a poem, or a research paper was the summative assessment at the end of the unit. Visitors walking the halls and observing classrooms could expect to see papers in progress, not finished papers. These might be opening sentences in various forms or working drafts of papers stapled together showing progression.

(Continued)

(Continued)

Student work was posted not to celebrate—that would come later—but to contribute to instruction. FCS's workshop model encouraged students to jot story ideas in a journal, analyze the writing style of the authors they were reading, experiment with different openings intended to grab the reader, tell their stories orally before writing a draft, edit their drafts, peer edit other students' drafts, and see the progression of writing over time.

Students used their work and the work of other students to build their writing. On one visit, as the administrative team stood in the hall debriefing a classroom walk-through, a 3rd grader walked by and began examining the posted writing. When asked, he said he was looking at other students' writing for ideas on catchy openings. After a minute or two, he smiled at one of the openings and ran back into the classroom holding a fresh idea.

Teachers used student work to provide feedback to individual students and to identify trends across students. Teachers frequently pulled students to the front of the room for a minilesson if they noticed students needing additional support. Direct instruction was more evident at the start of the unit when introducing the genre to students. As the unit progressed, students were expected to work independently with teacher direction and monitoring.

At the beginning of the unit, part of the instruction is about understanding the rubric. With a little practice, students can readily suggest the elements of good work that populate the scoring rubric. Conversations about rubrics in each unit help students understand concepts and skills that remain constant—such as clarity and sentence structure—across writing assignments, as well as those elements highlighted in the genre, such as differences between fiction and nonfiction writing. Understanding what is the same and what is different activates students' preexisting knowledge. Writing in different genres allows for multidisciplinary experiences through which students connect their analysis of writing and skills with scientific and historical content.

We have observed variations of instruction that have similar elements as the workshop model across content areas. Project-based or student-centered learning in mathematics, social studies, science, health, and languages have versions of the model. The task drives instruction, and student demonstrations create opportunities for students and teachers to measure progress.

Unfortunately, we have also observed classrooms in which students were engaged and enjoyed the activities; however, the task was not purposeful or rigorous.

Analysis of the task and what students must know and be able to do to demonstrate mastery places accountability directly on what matters. If students need a body of knowledge to complete the task, instruction must close the gap. For example, if a task calls on students to analyze a historical event and describe its significance, then reading a three-paragraph textbook summary of the event does not offer enough content for students to be able to analyze the event and describe its significance.

Equity warriors know that asking even simple questions about the task will make teachers uncomfortable. Teachers may not have the answers, they may not have enough knowledge, or, like many of us, they were not taught to plan lessons with the end in mind. Assessments, like the state assessments that do not measure what students are learning, reinforce the disconnect between teaching and learning. The disconnect can undermine an equity agenda by reinforcing what students don't know because they are not being asked what they know nor given the tools they need to demonstrate mastery. Equity warriors know that accountability begins with the task as the real measure of student progress and instruction that enables all students to have success.

Equity warriors know that accountability begins with the task as the real measure of student progress and instruction that enables all students to have success.

YOUR MOVE: STRENGTHEN TEACHERS' CAPACITY TO TEACH SUBJECT-MATTER CONTENT.

Principals and school leaders assume teachers know the content they are expected to teach. Sometimes their assumptions are wrong. We have learned from working side by side with teachers as they learn and implement the district curriculum that even the strongest teachers have gaps in their knowledge of key concepts and content. Yet, the lack of deep content knowledge is rarely discussed as an area of professional learning. Leaders find it more convenient to focus on improving instructional strategies that can be observed rather than on content knowledge.

Teaching something well is not possible if you do not know the content, yet we ask teachers to do just that. We shouldn't be surprised that teachers do not start their careers with deep content knowledge. Teacher preparation programs, teacher certification requirements, and in-service professional learning are poor substitutes for the years of dedicated learning required to know content well. Shifts in student enrollment require schools to move teachers among grade levels and content areas. Updates in curriculum standards may require teachers to learn new content or shift from factual knowledge to conceptual understanding. Teachers respond by not attempting to teach what they don't know, whether it is a new concept at the elementary level or in a content area.

Principals and school leaders are not required to have content knowledge in specific areas. Some elementary and middle school principals have extensive classroom experience, and some have very little. Large middle and high schools can have an administrative team with expertise in several content areas. Small schools that have one administrator are not so fortunate. Principals tend to supervise and teach that which they know. The most resourceful principals find content specialists to advise them on a teacher's expertise and to support teachers. Some stay clear of interactions about content rather than appear vulnerable.

Equity warriors use the tools at their disposal to deepen teacher content knowledge and place teachers in a position to use their knowledge to the best advantage of their students. Among these tools are targeted professional learning, content coaching, and scheduling and teacher assignments. Each of these tools requires principals and school leaders to know their teachers and to place the interests of students ahead of the interests of adults.

Engaging school leaders in planning professional learning for teachers in content areas yields results. However, that is not easy. At the high school level, teaching content includes the knowledge and processes that are part of the discipline as well as the approaches to learning the discipline. Not only is the content fundamentally different across content areas, but the ways information is presented is different in, for example, a science text and a history text. Teachers are expected to teach the content in addition to *how* students can access the content.

Bringing teachers together in instructional leadership teams to direct and lead professional learning is challenging. Teachers who specialize in different content areas think differently. We learned this by making mistakes. Our earliest work in helping high schools improve teaching and learning included facilitating instructional leadership teams consisting of two or so representatives from each discipline. We had difficulty facilitating any agreements on standards-based approaches or identifying instructional strategies. We could have teams reach agreement on concepts—for example, student engagement—but could not reach agreement on more specific details on how it would look in classrooms. There were passionate dialogues where it became obvious that team members did not share a common language and thought differently. Finally, we decided to have team members work on the specifics within their departments rather than across departments. We watched as they brought more energy and accountability to curriculum design and identifying effective instructional strategies and could reach agreement more easily.

Equity warriors are attuned to recognizing the differences in how people think, and they strategize for improving teaching and learning based on those differences. Effective approaches to engage teachers in collaborating and learning are as different as the content areas. Dividing and conquering is more productive! To do otherwise is as frustrating as hammering a square peg into a round hole.

> *Equity warriors are attuned to recognizing the differences in how people think, and they strategize for improving teaching and learning based on those differences.*

Recognizing the differences, principals and school leaders who have resources and expertise available to them can undertake content coaching. A comprehensive content-coaching system helps teachers to do the following:

- Deepen their understanding of content
- Design and implement lessons
- Anchor their approaches in core beliefs on learning and teaching
- Foster professional habits of mind
- Expand their pedagogical knowledge
- Work together with others in content-related teaching and learning (West & Staub, 2003)

Content coaching is a more transparent approach to tackling the problem of understanding whether teachers have adequate content knowledge. Therefore, we have found content coaching most successful when working with new teachers and elementary or middle school teachers when there is consensus that students are underperforming in a particular content area. At the elementary and middle school levels, a case is often made for content coaching in mathematics.

Students struggle with mathematics chiefly because their teachers do. Mathematics anxiety or phobia is real in students as well as adults. For some reason, adults accept the myth that some people are just not good at mathematics and that that is okay. While the myth is self-perpetuating, such a myth is harmful to students, especially students of color. Robert Moses identified algebra as a civil right. In his words, the most urgent social issue affecting poor people and people of color is economic access. In today's world, economic access and full citizenship depend crucially on math and science literacy. . . . [M]ath literacy—and algebra in particular—is the key to the future of disenfranchised communities. (Moses & Cobb, 2001, p. 5)

Algebra and math literacy is a gate that keeps students out of higher education. Math literacy is a real hurdle but one that can be overcome if faced directly.

Mathematics is about thinking and conceptualizing. Teachers as well as students need to learn to understand mathematics as mathematicians. Teachers and students must believe that learning mathematics is important to students' futures and that they—teachers and students—can be successful. For elementary and middle school teachers, content coaches introduce and model instructional strategies so that students can demonstrate their thinking and understanding. Our colleague Holly Culbertson is masterful at stepping into a classroom—even for the first time—and showing how students can demonstrate their understanding of mathematical concepts, often to the disbelief of their teacher. Holly has deep knowledge and deeply held beliefs that students can be proficient mathematicians. Students know when teachers believe in them. They call her the "math lady."

Although elementary and middle school teachers are willing to admit they may lack content and conceptual knowledge, high school teachers are different. Changes in standards, particularly when connected in terms of student performance on state assessments, may increase teacher openness to content learning. However, effective content coaching confronts high school mathematics teachers' attitude about their students. In very simple terms, which I admit may be unfair, mathematics teachers need to be teachers first, mathematicians second. They need to convince students that algebra is important, not just something they learn so that they can do higher mathematics, like eating broccoli because it is good for you. Effective teachers supplement and address shortcomings in student computational skills and conceptual knowledge by using technology and other tools to expand learning time rather than blaming the teachers who came before them for not properly preparing students. Most of all, mathematics teachers must stop perpetuating the myth that some students can't learn as a defense for their lack of success with students.

Though unfair, I came to these conclusions while struggling to help high school mathematics teachers improve student achievement. I don't have a background in mathematics, but I do understand the data that show student underperformance across grade levels. I observed mathematics classes for hours looking for clues used by teachers who are successful with students and student reactions. I watched as school leaders sentenced students to repeat courses they failed, only to fail them again in classrooms with the same teachers using the same lessons that didn't work the first time. We doubled the time allotted to algebra classes, only to watch students do more of the same work unsuccessfully. We watched homogeneous grouping fail dreadfully for students and teachers.

Equity warriors use all the tools they have to help students be successful. They navigate through numerous challenges to reshuffle their master schedules and teacher assignments—key leverage tools—to match students with teachers best able to help them. Here are some tools shown to be effective:

> *Equity warriors use all the tools they have to help students be successful.*

- **Departmentalize elementary teachers as early as 2nd grade.** Rather than hope for the best, assign teachers and hold them accountable to teach mathematics and science, or literacy and humanities, throughout the day. Principals have allowed departmentalization at the primary grades when asked by teachers who know their strengths and interests and are willing to share students. Departmentalization more commonly begins at 4th grade. In our experience, departmentalization has been shown to improve student learning, sometimes dramatically.

- **Assign your strongest teachers to work with underperforming students.** Principals are responsible for scheduling teachers. They have an obligation to live their promise of "students first" by making decisions that are best for students. Heterogeneous grouping of students and positioning the strongest teachers at transition grades are ways to be fair to teachers, to challenge them, and to honor their experience.

- **Have the same teachers teach prehonors and advanced courses.** Teachers assert that students are unprepared for advanced classes. Challenging these same teachers to offer a course that prepares students for more rigorous courses will build teacher empathy and efficacy, as well as student confidence.

- **Hold departments responsible for content-based professional learning.** Teachers are the ones responsible for student learning. They can read the data as well as administrators. The questions are: What will teachers do to improve student success? How will departments use their time for planning to improve their content knowledge? Where are the resources to help? As content experts, they should have the answers to these questions.

Equity warriors do not let teachers make decisions solely for their benefit. Of course, they strive for ideal win-win situations. Nevertheless, equity warriors cannot advance equity and achieve their equity agenda if they don't use the levers at their disposal. Frankly, neither teachers nor students benefit when school leaders repeatedly make decisions that do not hold teachers accountable for the professional responsibility to help all students achieve. Continuous learning for teachers, especially in their content area, is indivisible from continuous improvement. There is too much at stake to let fragile egos about content expertise, or fear of losing teachers, get in the way of advancing equity.

YOUR MOVE: CHALLENGE STUDENTS TO BE RESPONSIBLE FOR THEMSELVES AND OTHERS.

We surveyed families of incoming 9th graders in a newly launched high school about their expectations for their children. Almost every family said they expected their children to graduate ready for college. We posed the same question to the incoming 9th graders. The answers were almost identical. We showed the survey results to the school's instructional leadership team and asked for their reactions. To a person, they said those expectations were unattainable. Students, they said, were unprepared, unmotivated, not supported at home, and unwilling to do the work necessary to graduate prepared for postsecondary academic success.

This pattern was repeated in other schools, particularly schools that serve students who are the first generation to graduate from high school. In our experience, students fall into two groups. The majority believe that if they do what they are asked, put in the time, and complete the courses, they will graduate high school ready for postsecondary success—a job, community college, or four-year college. The second group, smaller in number but considerable, attend school because it is an obligation—imposed on them by law, family, or social pressures. They have moved from grade to grade and don't understand the implication of credit-bearing courses in high school until it is too late. These are the 16- and 17-year-olds who lack enough credits to graduate. At some point, they are told to leave.

Teacher and staff engagement of students also can be placed in categories. There are those who teach and support, and their efforts work for students or not. They do their job—teach their content well or make time for counseling students. They are committed to helping students, though they know the limits of what they can do. A second group are those who make no excuses for themselves and students, and are constantly pushing students. They are the ones who expect students to be successful in their classes. They require students to come to their classrooms or offices during lunch and after school to make up work or for extra support. They remind students that they will be looking for them to review their grades in an after-school study session. In the middle of these two extremes are those who continue to reach out and negotiate with students to demonstrate their learning. They measure student willingness to engage in their learning, and adjust their lessons and support for students. Sometimes the offerings are rigorous. Sometimes they demonstrate what has been called the soft bigotry of low expectations.

We have found these categories of students and adults in every school regardless of grade level and student demographic. The systems in place—the informal systems, such as adult and student attitudes, as well as formal systems that sort students by judgments about their interest and ability—make a difference for students. For example, we have seen Advanced Placement teachers who do not accept student failures because student performance reflects on them. They hold weekend study groups in coffee shops to prepare students for exams. They push students to learn. They don't accept failure. This is not tough love. It is evidence of the interdependence of learning—my success as a teacher depends on your success as a student, and vice versa.

Students of all ages share the blame when they don't learn. I watched a first-year teacher spend the first month acting on high expectations for her 10th-grade U.S. history students. She required students to read, be prepared for classroom discussions, and complete homework assignments. At the end of the month, she began the class with her admission that she heard their complaints, and those of their families, that she expected too much from them. She would lower her expectations. Students smiled. They knew a first-year teacher was vulnerable, they tested her, and they showed their power. Unfortunately, by the end of the first semester, her classes were deadly dull. Students and the teacher were bored with a steady routine of completing worksheets based on the textbook. Students won the battle and lost the war.

There are extreme situations in which students are out of control. Like *Lord of the Flies*, it doesn't end well for anyone. These are the exception. However, students always have control over their learning. Fortunately for them, under the right conditions, they are willing to learn. The right conditions rely on having adults who value students, value the learning, and use instructional strategies that keep students engaged in learning with peers.

Looking into the instructional core, students are key players in their learning, as David Cohen and Deborah Ball describe so well:

> Much research shows the students' experiences, understandings, interests, commitments, and engagement are also crucial to instructional capacity. One way to consider the matter is that the resources that students bring influence what teachers accomplish. Students bring experience, prior knowledge, and habits of mind, and these influence how they apprehend, interpret, and respond to materials and teachers. . . . When teachers say, "My student could never do that," they do not recognize the ways in which students could learn or change. Students—and interactions among students—shape the resources for their own learning. (Cohen & Ball, 1999, p. 3)

Effective teaching requires recognizing students' power over their learning. Adults can begin by understanding their students, knowing their students as learners—their strengths and interests—and how they learn. It is not easy to do so with 35 students, or 180 students, but there it is. Fortunately, teachers and staff have instructional strategies to enable them to learn about their students by breaking them into groups and sharing their thinking. Some strategies are simple and time-tested such as think-pair-share, turn-and-talk, jigsaw, station rotations, reciprocal teaching, and brainstorming. All of these require students to express their thinking. When done with intentionality, they reinforce for students that their opinions matter and should be heard. In any case, students must show up to learn. Whether they are reading silently or listening, their opinions must be shared. Otherwise, they do not fulfill their obligation to be a resource to others.

Equity warriors have high expectations for students.

Students learn from other students. Heterogeneous grouping of students allows students with different strengths to be in the same room. Yet, unless they have an opportunity to interact with each other, peers are robbed of the opportunity to learn from them. Students are deprived of the opportunity to be valued and to learn from wrestling with ideas that are different from their own. This may be obvious. However, independent work or teacher-student interactions constitute the majority of time in the classroom at all grade levels.

Teachers have control over the content, their knowledge, instructional strategies, and assessments. Equity warriors exercise the control. Equity warriors have high expectations for students. They ignite in all students high expectations for their own learning and being part of a learning community. They challenge students to apply their learning in ways that are relevant to them. They help students of all ages see the consequences of choosing not to learn. They know students learn at different rates, so they don't give up on any of them.

It is a mistake to minimize the role of students in their learning and the learning of their peers. Students watch adults. They learn from our deeds more than our words. Our deeds tell them who cares for them. They appreciate when adults attend to their safety and security. They also know when they are being challenged and when their time is wasted. They know that teachers who waste their time during the school day are not to be trusted with their time after school. They know when their voice, experiences, and strengths are appreciated. They act accordingly.

Equity warriors know the instructional core provides a lens on the adult and student roles in learning. Equity warriors know the moves that advance equity through improving teaching and learning for all students. They lead change processes to create school cultures that support learning, adjust policies and practices to improve access, define rigor, and support teacher professional learning. They know these efforts alone are not enough to raise teachers' expectations unless they teach students to be advocates for their own learning.

YOUR MOVE: HOLD ADMINISTRATORS AND COUNSELORS ACCOUNTABLE FOR THE EQUITY AGENDA.

Equity warriors know that teaching and learning happen not only in classrooms. Interactions that result in decisions that shape lives occur in the school's halls and offices as well as in the classroom. In this warfare of teaching and learning section, we have referred to adults, teachers, and staff intentionally. Though their roles are different, they are connected in their support of students.

Equity warriors know that teaching and learning happen not only in classrooms.

It comes as no surprise that schools are embracing their role in providing for the social and emotional development of students. While school counselors can provide much-needed support to teachers, staff, and students, the availability of counselors is rarely adequate to respond to the demand. The American School Counselor Association (2018) recommends a 250-to-1 student-to-counselor ratio. Actual staffing ratios, estimated at 430-to-1, have hovered around more than twice the recommended number. Recognizing both the demand for supports and the certainty that the number of counselors will not come close to meeting the need, teachers are asked to assume greater responsibility for students' social-emotional development.

Counselors and administrators at the elementary and middle levels work with students who require additional targeted support when they have been recommended for services by student support teams or special education services, or when they have violated school behavior expectations. At the high school level, in addition to targeted support, counselors devote considerable time to course scheduling, monitoring credits, and postsecondary counseling. Too often, counselors at all levels perform clerical tasks such as scheduling and record keeping. Often, the clerical and record-keeping tasks are necessary because more efficient systems and personnel are not in place. Counselors also are asked to take on administrative tasks that divert them from counseling responsibilities when they are not working directly with students.

In addition to the support role that counselors have in students' social-emotional development, they are gatekeepers. Educators of color often tell us their personal stories of counselors who refused them access to college preparatory courses and/or made it clear that they did not have what it takes to be a success. These stories are too frequent and common across the country to be dismissed as isolated incidents. Additionally, counselors' failure to support students, for whatever reasons, stands in the way of advancing equity. Here are just a few examples:

- High school counselors who did not activate an early warning system for 9th-grade students in danger of failing a course or reach out to meet with students at the end of the semester when they failed a course. They were preoccupied with helping seniors graduate and submit college applications.

- High school counselors who assigned multilingual learners to non-credit-bearing courses.

- Counselors who are not monitoring student transcripts to determine who is on track to graduate on time and offer assistance as needed.

- Counselors who do not inform students about entry examinations for gifted and talented programs or specialized programs, or who prevent them from taking these exams.

- Counselors who do not investigate student absences to understand the reasons and work on solutions.

- Counselors who meet with students during instructional time, which creates additional learning loss.

- Counselors who are quick to refer students for special education evaluation or services solely at a teacher's request.

- Counselors who do not ensure that student support teams and teachers have implemented interventions.

- Counselors who do not educate families about learning supports that will extend learning time and address learning loss.

These are system failures. When they occur, policies, protocols, supports, and accountability that set expectations and guide actions are not in place. In addition, awareness of the problems and failures to act often signal problems in the schoolwide culture. Not acting undermines access and robs students of the knowledge and incentives necessary to reach their potential. Failure to act breeds hopelessness among adults and students. If not corrected and the systems work against them, only the most resilient or lucky students will succeed.

Equity warriors hold counselors and themselves accountable for correcting system failures and supporting students to advance equity. Correcting systems begins with assessing the strengths and shortcomings of existing programs, technology, and personnel. There are innovative practices and long-established programs that are available as examples that can be applied to the school context. The following are among the actions taken by principals and school leaders in our partner schools:

Equity warriors hold counselors and themselves accountable for correcting system failures and supporting students to advance equity.

- School leadership teams redesigned the role of counselors to focus on student achievement. The redesign included using school funds for technology updates and clerical staffing for scheduling and monitoring attendance and performance, as well as systems for teachers and staff to support counseling functions.

- Administrators and counselors collaborated with students in designing and monitoring behavioral contracts that include developing self-discipline skills.

- Counselors took the lead in hosting child and adolescent development professional learning sessions for teachers and staff.

- Administrators and counselors created academic pathways beginning in the middle grades that increase enrollment and success of underrepresented students in Advanced Placement and honors courses.

- Teachers and staff created mentor programs that ensure students connect to at least one adult at the school.

- Counselors, teachers, and students designed and implemented transition plans beginning in 6th grade for every student.

- Every adult participated in an advisory program for middle and high school students for daily check-ins and continuous mentoring and monitoring the progress of students.

- Administrators, counselors, and teachers offered extracurricular programs and classes to support career planning and vocational interests and required or scheduled students to participate in at least one per semester.

Equity warriors create, monitor, and hold all adults accountable to consistent execution of their equity agenda, no matter how difficult or uncomfortable confronting the actions may be.

Equity warriors know that counselors and counseling are vital to helping students and adults feel connected to the school community. They attract counselors who understand the important contributions they are able to make and provide them with expectations and necessary resources. They help establish the mindset that adults are gate openers, not gate closers.

Students are keenly aware of inconsistent messaging. When equity warriors espouse their equity agenda and speak about the success of all students, students know which adults do not share the agenda. Equity warriors create, monitor, and hold all adults accountable to consistent execution of their equity agenda, no matter how difficult or uncomfortable confronting the actions may be.

REFLECTION: *How do you know that every adult and student understands and acts on the school's equity agenda? Are expectations clear? Are formal and informal accountability systems in place?*

_____

_____

_____

_____

_____

_____

_____

_____

Epilogue: Juan's story

We return to the challenge. Imagine a reality different from Jesse's.

As we walk down the corridor to the 6th-grade English class, we notice that learning has spilled out of the classroom and into the halls. Students have posted book reviews and QR codes to their finished and in-process writing samples hanging on the hallway walls. Messages of encouragement accompany the samples. Small groups of students sit in the hallway near the classroom door, huddled over their books, notebooks, and computers.

I'm in this hallway because I asked to join a principal supervisor's monthly visit to the middle school. On this day, visitors will be exploring this question: How are teachers using standards-based grading and proficiency scales to communicate expectations with students? The visitors include the supervisor, the principal, one assistant principal, and two resource teachers from the district office. The supervisor assigned the resource teachers to schools to learn about and coach students as well as support site administrators who are planning the teachers' professional learning experiences.

I enter the room and, at first, do not see the teacher. The room itself is bright and not very large, but the walls are painted, and the teacher has added plants and lamps. Many books and various supplies are at the ready, available to students and the teacher.

When we arrive, students are already working in groups. The groups can choose a space that works best for their study. Some work together at circular tables; others sit on large pillows scattered around the room.

Although this gives students flexibility, this seemingly loose arrangement also enables the teacher to see a variety of groups throughout the lessons.

Students are in heterogeneous book clubs where they focus on reading together, writing responses, and working through the more complex analysis of the texts together. Over time, they have focused on how to listen to one another and how to develop thinking together. Students have structured notebooks filled with their thinking and notes from reading lessons in class. The notebooks are designed to help students use new strategies, learn and reflect on new content, and develop discipline to refine their thinking. The notebooks also give the teacher data to better know her students.

The teacher has been at this school for six years, but she has taught at both middle schools and high schools in this district for many years. This diversity of experience has enabled her to develop an understanding about the city as a whole and about how students grow across grades 6 to 12. She has a teaching credential in the subject area plus advanced degrees and additional certificates for teaching language and reading. She continues to attend district-sponsored professional development and participate regularly in learning opportunities offered by English language arts professional organizations. She has been recognized as a National Writing Project fellow.

District leaders are intentional in their support for teaching and learning. The district leadership team identified standards-based grading and proficiency scales as the right next steps to advance the district's equity agenda. The superintendent and school board then endorsed that plan and set the necessary policies in place to make them happen. Those two practices have changed how teachers plan and communicate learning to students and families. As part of their support for that work, the district encourages principals to schedule common planning time for teachers and offers protocols to support teachers when they plan together and compare student work against expectations. Supervisor visits are scheduled throughout the year to inform district learning and track progress.

On the board, the teacher has projected a list of "I can" statements from all of the lesson objectives. She also has posted on the board a list of students who have signed up for a "self-reflection conference." The teacher circulates the room, checks in with several book clubs quickly, and then quietly lets a student know she is ready to meet. I sit near enough to hear but off to the side as Juan brings his notebook up and sits next to the teacher under the list of learning objectives. He takes the lead in the conference, thumbing back through his notebook and using the list of objectives to show the work he has done for each. As he does this, he reflects on what he learned, how he will use this process as a reader, and any aspect of the learning that he thinks he needs to continue to work on in the future. Through the whole process, the teacher takes notes and asks questions but does not offer judgment or evaluation. She does point out some notes from previous conferences where she did reteach and clarify ways to improve the work, but this conversation was intended to allow Juan to explain how he used this feedback to improve his work for this summative meeting.

It is striking how much the students work together independently and how Juan, a long-term multilingual learner, leads the conference and is clearly aware of the objectives. He appears confident and a little hesitant. As the conference concludes, I wonder how often he has had the opportunity to take the lead in an academic conversation with a teacher or anyone in a position of authority.

As he is about to make his way back to his book club, Juan tells me that the conferences help him to know what he is learning and where he is improving as a reader. He reports that he didn't really like reading and didn't read well when he began 6th grade. He says he found it difficult to slow down, sit and read, and know what he was thinking about a book. Now he can do that and even has a few favorite authors.

The teacher surveys the class before turning to me. She explains that Juan started the year as a reluctant reader, often wandering the library, trying to disappear, and then just pulling a book off the shelf when prompted with questions about reading. As she began to know Juan as a learner, she recognized his frustration and his desire to learn, and she was able to approach him by building on his strengths, not his deficits. The school invested in sets of culturally responsive books by a diverse group of authors so that students could have real choice in what they read. By allowing students to choose books together and read and discuss in groups, and with constant encouragement, she has seen students like Juan change from reluctant readers to seeing that they have an important voice in a reading community. She also says that using lesson objectives with students in an assessment conversation gives them power over their learning, hopefully increasing agency, but also allowing for a more authentic reason to use academic language and to reflect on their own growth.

The teacher explains that her work with the National Writing Project, which started years ago, clarified for her that the classroom is the center of learning about teaching. Everyone can learn about teaching in a classroom by reflecting with students. She encourages her colleagues to observe her, and she visits them to learn how Juan and her other students respond in different contexts and environments. The data from observations inform her grade-level meetings in two ways: naming specific students who exhibit behaviors across classrooms that may suggest social-emotional needs that interfere with their learning, and seeing students' responses to learning as a way to understand similar students. From her perspective, since the classroom and students are the most valuable resource for learning for all educators, knowing them through observation gives them the greatest voice and role in the classroom.

Her perspective brings a lot of credibility. She is well known for engaging students as learners and instilling in them a love for reading and writing. Further, she has high expectations for their learning and expects that every student in her classes of heterogeneous learners performs proficient on the state assessment. She has a record of ensuring that students live up to her expectations.

The visitors debrief in the principal's office after visiting the other 6th-grade teachers. Their discussion focuses on the predetermined question: How are teachers using standards-based grading and proficiency scales to communicate expectations with students? All teachers were using variations of "I can" statements, group work, and conferencing to have students share their progress in meeting the objectives. The principal leads the discussion to identify different approaches used by teachers to help students recognize and describe their learning. Following the principal's lead, visitors compare notes on the progress of students they have been watching over time and the nuances in the approaches among teachers and across content areas.

After a comprehensive discussion about the evidence gathered during the visit, the principal describes a few next steps and feedback she would share with teachers, plans to share effective practices, and her initial thoughts about conversations to help teachers recognize specific incremental steps that would help them. The principal then leads the give-and-take about the specific support that the district resource teachers would provide before deciding on the plan for support in the coming weeks.

On the drive back to the office, the principal's supervisor and I compare notes about the principal's actions during the visit. The supervisor selected the principal to lead the school because she was ready to advance the equity agenda. She has a strong instructional background, and, as a former instructional coach, she understands how to build trust through knowing her teachers well and can suggest the next step to move their practice. Nevertheless, his reflection on the visit quickly moves to his role in preparing the principal to execute her change strategy. He is considering the questions he would ask her in the "debrief of the debrief," which will be conducted one on one:

- Does she have the fiscal resources to release novice teachers to visit the English class to observe and reflect on the teacher's use of conferences and student notebooks as "real data" to know students as learners?

- How will she design her professional opportunities—monthly whole-school faculty meetings and instructional leadership team meetings—to identify and pilot the next steps of her change strategy?

- What is her plan for collecting feedback from families about the effectiveness of standards-based grading in communicating student progress?

He is also thinking about his work at the district level:

- What are the opportunities to engage teacher union leaders in creating flexibility in using meeting time for collaborative professional learning?

- What are the "politically appropriate" ways that he might improve coherence by engaging his colleagues in linking and communicating the district vision for advancing equity more closely with standards-based grading and proficiency scale implementation?

- He knows that the superintendent has helped board members understand that advancing equity is synonymous with strengthening the instructional core across the district for all students. They have responded by aligning policies, programs, and resources. How does he help the district leadership team communicate to the board the experiences and progress of schools on these two initiatives so that they remain committed to creating further coherence-making?

- How does he help his schools and the district tell their story and build public confidence in the district's efforts?

Teachers and classrooms like the ones described above provide all the evidence necessary to demonstrate that it is possible to advance equity by knowing and educating students so they have the tools that will enable them to think, learn, and act independently and to apply their skills to situations they face now and in the future. Equity warriors use politics, diplomacy, and, yes, warfare to advance equity so that each and every student in our charge achieves their individual potential. Equity warriors know it is in their power to do so. In the words of Ron Edmonds (1979):

> We can, whenever and wherever we choose, successfully teach all children whose schooling is of interest to us; we already know more than we need to do that; and whether or not we do it must finally depend on how we feel about the fact that we haven't so far. (p. 23)

Equity warriors, if you didn't before, you know now it is possible. Jesse and Juan are asking: What are you going to do?

References

INTRODUCTION

Biden, J. R. (2021, March 8). Executive order 14021: Guaranteeing an educational environment free from discrimination on the basis of sex, including sexual orientation or gender identity. https://www.govinfo.gov/content/pkg/DCPD-202100214/pdf/DCPD-202100214.pdf

Black, D. W. (2020). *Schoolhouse burning: Public education and the assault on American democracy*. Public Affairs.

Bostock v. Clayton County, Georgia, 590 U.S. 140 S. Ct. 1731 (2020).

Brown v. Board of Education of Topeka, 347 U.S. 483 (1954).

Butchart, R. E. (2020, September 16). Freedmen's education during reconstruction. *New Georgia Encyclopedia*. https://www.georgiaencyclopedia.org/articles/history-archaeology/freedmens-education-during-reconstruction

Carpenter, J. (2013). Thomas Jefferson and the ideology of democratic schooling. *Democracy and Education, 21*(2), article 5.

Collins, J. (2001). *Good to great: Why some companies make the leap and others don't*. HarperBusiness.

Cumming v. Richmond County Board of Education, 175 U.S. 528 (1899).

Deming, W. E. (n.d.). *Deming quotes*. The W. Edwards Deming Institute. https://deming.org/quotes/10141/

Dewey, J. (1902). *The school and society*. University of Chicago Press.

Gong Lum v. Rice, 275 U.S. 78 (1927). For more background, see also http://www.asianamericanlegal.com/historical-cases/gong-lum-v-rice/

Kaestle, C. F. (1983). *Pillars of the republic: Common schools and American society, 1780–1860*. Hill & Wang (a division of Farrar, Straus and Giroux).

Mendez v. Westminster School District of Orange County, 161 F2d 774 (1947). For more background, see also https://mendezetalvwestminster.com/case-history/

Orfield, G. (2001). *Schools more separate: Consequences of a decade of resegregation*. Harvard Civil Rights Project. https://eric.ed.gov/?id=ED459217

Reef, C. (2009). *American education and learning in America*. Facts on File.

Rothstein, R. (2017). *The color of law: A forgotten history of how our government segregated America*. Liveright Publishing.

Tape v. Hurley, 66 Cal 473 (1885). For more background, see also Asian American Legal Foundation. http://www.asianamericanlegal.com/historical-cases/tape-v-hurley/

PART I

INTRODUCTION

Cleary, T. (translator). (1988). *Sun Tzu: The art of war*. Shambhala Publications.

Kennedy, J. F. (1963, June 28). *Address before the Irish Parliament*. https://www.jfklibrary.org/learn/about-jfk/historic-speeches/address-before-the-irish-parliament

CHAPTER 1

Brown, B. (2018). *Dare to lead: Brave work, tough conversations, whole hearts*. Random House.

Campbell, D. T. (1976, December). *Assessing the impact of planned social change*. Occasional Paper No. 8. Dartmouth College. http://citeseerx.ist.psu.edu/viewdoc/download?doi=10.1.1.170.6988&rep=rep1&type=pdf

Charlotte-Mecklenburg Opportunity Task Force. (2018). *Leading on opportunity*. Author. https://www.fftc.org/sites/default/files/2018-05/LeadingOnOpportunity_Report.pdf

Childress, S. M., Doyle, D. P., & Thomas, D. A. (2009). *Leading for equity: The pursuit of excellence in Montgomery County Public Schools*. Harvard University Press.

City, E. A., Elmore, R. F., Fiarman, S. E., & Teitel, L. (2009). *Instructional rounds in education: A network approach to improving teaching and learning*. Harvard Education Press.

Harris, E. A., & Hu, W. (2018, June 5). Asian groups see bias in plan to diversify New York's elite schools. *New York Times*. https://www.nytimes.com/2018/06/05/nyregion/carranza-specialized-schools-admission-asians.html

Heifetz, R. A., & Linsky, M. (2002). *Leadership on the line: Staying alive through the dangers of leading*. Harvard Business School Press.

Kasperkevic, J. (2015, April 1). Georgia cheating scandal: 11 teachers found guilty of racketeering. *The Guardian*. https://www.theguardian.com/us-news/2015/apr/01/atlanta-teachers-found-guilty-cheating

Kotter, J. P. (1996). *Leading change*. Harvard Business School Press.

Lincoln, A. (1861, March). *Abraham Lincoln papers: Series 1. General correspondence. 1833–1916: Abraham Lincoln, March 1861 first inaugural address, final version*. Library of Congress. https://www.loc.gov/item/mal0773800/

Mizell, M. H. (2002). *Shooting for the sun: The message of middle school reform*. Edna McConnell Clark Foundation.

Roegman, R., Allen, D., Leverett, L., Thompson, S., & Hatch, T. (2019). *Equity visits: A new approach to supporting equity-focused school and district leadership*. Corwin.

CHAPTER 2

Mapp, K. L., & Kuttner, P. J. (2013). *Partners in education: A dual capacity-building framework for family-school partnership*. SEDL. http://www.sedl.org/pubs/framework/FE-Cap-Building.pdf

San Diego Unified School District. (2012, March). *A strategic process for creating quality schools in every neighborhood*. Author. https://issuu.com/sdusd/docs/sdusd-strategic-process

Soto, I. (2021). *Shadowing multilingual learners* (2nd ed.). Corwin.

PART II

INTRODUCTION

Brown, B. (2018). *Dare to lead: Brave work. Tough conversations. Whole hearts*. Random House.

Sergiovanni, T. J. (1992). *Moral leadership*. Jossey-Bass.

CHAPTER 3

Bennis, W., & Nanus, B. (1985). *Leaders: The strategies for taking charge*. Harper & Row.

Boston Public Schools. (2020). *Boston Public Schools FY21 Budget: Schools*. Author. https://www.bostonpublicschools.org/cms/lib/MA01906464/Centricity/Domain/184/FY21%20Budget%20Hearing%20School%20Budgets%20Presentation%202020-02-13.pdf (Slides 7–31)

Burns, J. M. (1978). *Leadership*. Harper & Row.

Collins, J. (2001). *Good to great: Why some companies make the leap . . . and others don't*. HarperBusiness.

Fullan, M. (2001). *Leading in a culture of change*. Jossey-Bass.

Koran, M. (2017, April 11). San Diego Unified's jaw-dropping grad rate is now official. Here's how it got here. *Voice of San Diego*. https://www.voiceofsandiego.org/topics/education/san-diego-unifieds-jaw-dropping-grad-rate-is-now-official-heres-how-it-got-here/

Levin, J., Manship, K., Hurlburt, S., Atchison, D., Yamaguchi, R., & Stullich, S. (2019). *Districts' use of weighted student funding systems to increase school autonomy and equity: Findings from a national study. Volume 1—Final report*. U.S. Department of Education, Office of Planning, Evaluation and Policy Development, Policy and Program Studies Service. https://www2.ed.gov/rschstat/eval/title-i/weighted-funding/report.pdf

Montgomery County Public Schools. (2018). *MCPS strategic plan, FY 2018–2021*. https://www.montgomeryschoolsmd.org/campaigns/Strategic-Planning-FY19-22/#boe-statement

National Research Council. (2002). *How people learn: Brain, mind, experience, and school* (6th ed.). National Academy of Sciences.

Perry, G. S., Jr. (2007, April). *Leadership development system for district, school, and teacher leaders in East Baton Rouge Parish Public Schools*. Stupski Foundation.

Quinn, T., with Keith, M. E. (2010). *Peak performing governance teams: Creating an effective board/superintendent partnership*. Quinn and Associates Ltd.

Roanoke School Board. (2019). *Strong students, strong schools, strong city*. Author. https://go.boarddocs.com/vsba/roacps/Board.nsf/vpublic?open# (search equity policy)

Roanoke School Board. (n.d.). *Equity scorecard, school year 2018–2019*. Author. https://go.boarddocs.com/vsba/roacps/Board.nsf/files/BJJGSB4509E0/$file/2018-19_equity%20scorecard.pdf

San Diego Unified School District. (2019). *Local control and accountability plan*. Author. https://sandiegounified.org/about/local_control_and_accountability_plan/what_is_the_lcap

San Diego Unified School District. (n.d.). *Vision 2020*. Author. https://sandiegounified.org/about/vision_2020_mission

Senge, P. M. (1994). *The fifth discipline: The art and practice of the learning organization*. Currency Doubleday.

Snowden, D. J., & Boone, M. E. (2007, November). A leader's framework for decision making. *Harvard Business Review*. https://hbr.org/2007/11/a-leaders-framework-for-decision-making

Tichy, N. M., & Cardwell, N. (2002). *The cycle of leadership: How great leaders teach their companies to win*. HarperCollins.

Virginia Department of Education. (n.d.). *Fall membership build-a-table*. Author. https://p1pe.doe.virginia.gov/apex/f?p=180:1:13801622393248

Vygotsky, L. (2002). *Thought and language*. MIT Press.

CHAPTER 4

Bryk, A. S., & Schneider, B. (2002). *Trust in schools: A core resource for improvement*. Russell Sage Foundation.

Casillas, C. (2018, September 4). Roosevelt staff professional development presentation.

Chenoweth, K. (2007). *"It's being done": Academic success in unexpected schools*. Harvard University Press.

Churchill, W. (1941, October 29). *Never give in, never, never, never, 1941*. Harrow School Speech. https://www.national-churchillmuseum.org/never-give-in-never-never-never.html

Haberman, M. (2010, October). The pedagogy of poverty versus good teaching. *Phi Delta Kappan, 92*(2), 81–87.

Marquet, L. D. (2012). *Turn the ship around! A true story of turning followers into leaders*. Penguin Random House.

Marshall, K. (2009). *Rethinking teacher supervision and evaluation: How to work smart, build collaboration, and close the achievement gap*. Jossey Bass.

Marzano, R. J., Waters, T., & McNulty, B. A. (2005). *School leadership that works: From research to results*. McREL.

Pfeffer, J. T., & Sutton, R. I. (2000). *The knowing-doing gap: How smart companies turn knowledge into action*. Harvard Business School Press.

Presentation to the San Diego High School Instructional Leadership Team, September 13, 2017.

Recommendations for the San Diego High School Campus, presented to the San Diego Board of Trustees, June 9, 2015.

Sergiovanni, T. J. (1992). *Moral leadership*. Jossey-Bass.

Tschannen-Moran, M. (2014). *Trust matters: Leadership for successful schools*. Jossey-Bass.

PART III

INTRODUCTION

City, E. A., Elmore, R. F., Fiarman, S. E., & Teitel, L. (2009). *Instructional rounds in education: A network approach to improving teaching and learning*. Harvard Education Press.

Fullan, M., & Quinn, J. (2016). *Coherence: The right drivers in action for schools, districts, and systems*. Corwin.

Mandela, N. (2003, July 16). *Address by Nelson Mandela at launch of Mindset Network,*

Johannesburg. http://www.mandela.gov
.za/mandela_speeches/2003/030716_
mindset.htm

CHAPTER 5

Arbinger Institute. (2010). *Leadership and self-deception: Getting out of the box.* Berrett-Koehler.

Boston City Charter. (2007, July). Boston City Charter, Section 73. https://www.cityofboston.gov/images_documents/2007%20the%20charter%20draft20%20%28final%20draft1%20with%20jumps%29_tcm3-16428.pdf

Boykin, A. W., & Noguera, P. (2001). *Creating the opportunity to learn: Moving from research to practice to close the achievement gap.* ASCD.

City, E. A., Elmore, R. F., Fiarman, S. E., & Teitel, L. (2009). *Instructional rounds in education: A network approach to improving teaching and learning.* Harvard Education Press.

Cleary, T. (translator). (1988). *The art of war by Sun Tzu.* Shambhala Publications.

Deming, W. E. (1994). *The new economics for industry, government, education* (2nd ed.). Massachusetts Institute of Technology, Center for Advanced Educational Services.

Dufour, R., & Marzano, R. J. (2011). *Leaders of learning: How district, school, and classroom leaders improve student achievement.* Solution Tree.

Fullan, M., & Quinn, J. (2016). *Coherence: The right drivers in action for schools, districts, and systems.* Corwin.

Harvard University Public Education Leadership Project. (n.d.). *Coherence framework.* Author. https://pelp.fas.harvard.edu/coherence-framework

Hattie, J. (2009). *Visible learning: A synthesis of over 800 meta-analyses relating to achievement.* Routledge.

Heath, C., & Heath, D. (2013). *Decisive: How to make better choices in life and work.* Crown Business.

Honig, M. I., Copland, M. A., Rainey, L., Lorton, J. A., & Newton, M. (2010, April). *Central office transformation for district-wide teaching and learning improvement.* University of Washington, Center for the Study of Teaching and Policy. https://www.wallacefoundation.org/knowledge-center/Documents/Central-Office-Transformation-District-Wide-Teaching-and-Learning.pdf

Honig, M. I., & Rainey, L. R. (2019). Supporting principal supervisors: What really matters? *Journal of Educational Administration, 57*(5), 445–462.

Johnson, S. M., Marietta, G., Higgins, M. C., Mapp, K. L., & Grossman, A. (2015). *Achieving coherence in district improvement: Managing the relationship between central office and schools.* Harvard Education Press.

Kardos, S. M., & Johnson, S. M. (2007). On their own and presumed expert: New teachers' experiences with their colleagues. *Teachers College Record, 109*(9), 2083–2106.

Marzano, R. J., & Waters, T. (2009). *District leadership that works: Striking the right balance.* Solution Tree Press.

McREL Intl. (2017). *Does your school have a guaranteed and viable curriculum? How would you know?* Author. https://www.mcrel.org/does-your-school-have-a-guaranteed-and-viable-curriculum/

National Center for Education Statistics. (2020, May). *The condition of education: Characteristics of public school teachers.* U.S. Department of Education, Institute of Education Sciences. https://nces.ed.gov/programs/coe/indicator_clr.asp

National Research Council. (2002). *How people learn: Brain, mind, experience, and school* (6th ed.). National Academy of Sciences.

National Study Group for the Affirmative Development of Academic Ability. (2004). *All students reaching the top: Strategies for closing academic achievement gaps.* Learning Point Associates. https://www.air.org/sites/default/files/downloads/report/All_Students_Reaching_the_Top_0.pdf

New York State Department of Education. (n.d.). *Culturally responsive-sustaining education framework.* Author. http://www.nysed.gov/common/nysed/files/programs/crs/culturally-responsive-sustaining-education-framework.pdf

Peters, T. J., & Waterman, R. H., Jr. (1982). *In search of excellence: Lessons from America's best-run companies.* Warner Books.

Portland Public Schools. (n.d.). PPS-HD: MTSS home-based distance learning resources. Author. https://www.pps.net/domain/5007

Russakoff, D. (2015). *The prize: Who's in charge of America's schools?* Houghton, Mifflin, Harcourt.

San Diego Unified School District. (2018). *Board governance policies.* https://sandiegounified.org/UserFiles/Servers/Server_27732394/File/About/Leadership/Board%20of%20Education/Overview/Board%20Governance%20Policies%20(12-11-18%20).pdf

Schein, E. H. (1992). *Organizational culture and leadership* (2nd ed.). Jossey-Bass.

Schein, E. H. (2013). *Humble inquiry: The gentle art of asking instead of telling.* Berrett-Koehler.

Simms, J. A. (2016). *The critical concepts (final version: English language arts, mathematics, and science).* Marzano Resources.

Teacher Union Reform Network. (n.d.). *TURN's Mission.* https://www.turnweb.org/about/

Texas Education Code. (various dates). https://codes.findlaw.com/tx/education-code/educ-sect-11-151.html

CHAPTER 6

American Institutes for Research. (2017). *Supporting English learners and students with disabilities: Strategies from turnaround schools in Massachusetts.* Author. https://www.air.org/sites/default/files/downloads/report/Supporting-English-Learners-and-Students-with-Disabilities-School-Turnaround-Sept-2017_0.pdf

American School Counselor Association. (n.d.). *National student to school counselor ratio, 1986–2018.* Author. https://www.schoolcounselor.org/getmedia/db3d19f8-0369-4a1b-b0f8-a21cdacebe75/Ratios-10-Year-Trend.pdf

City, E. A, Elmore, R. F., Fiarman, S. E., & Teitel, L. (2009). *Instructional rounds in education: A network approach to improving teaching and learning.* Harvard Education Press.

Cohen, D., & Ball, D. L. (1999, June). *Instruction capacity and improvement* (CPRE Research Report Series RR-43). University of Pennsylvania Graduate School of Education, Consortium for Policy Research in Education.

Goldring, R., Taie, S., & Riddles, M. (2014). *Teacher attrition and mobility: Results from the 2012–13 teacher follow-up survey* (NCES 2014–077). U.S. Department of Education, National Center for Education Statistics. http://nces.ed.gov/pubsearch

Hall, G. E., & Hord, S. M. (2001). *Implementing change: Patterns, principles, and potholes.* Allyn & Bacon.

Learning Policy Institute. (2017, February). *The role of principals in addressing teacher shortages.* http://learningpolicyinstitute.org/product/role-leadership-solving-teacher-shortages

Losen, D. J., & Whitaker, A. (2018). *11 million days lost: Race, discipline, and safety at U.S. public schools, part I.* American Civil Liberties Union. https://www.aclu.org/report/11-million-days-lost-race-discipline-and-safety-us-public-schools-part-1

McDonald, J. P., Moher, N., Dichter, A., & McDonald, E. C. (2007). *The power of protocols: An educator's guide to better practice* (2nd ed.). Teachers College Press.

Morris, E., & Perry, B. (2016). The punishment gap: School suspension and racial disparities in achievement. *Social Problems, 63,* 80–81. https://doi.org/10.1093/socpro/spv026

Moses, R. P., & Cobb, C. E., Jr. (2001). *Radical equations: Civil rights from Mississippi to the Algebra Project.* Beacon Press.

Moss, C. M., & Brookhart, S. M. (2012). *Learning targets: Helping students aim for understanding in today's lesson.* ASCD.

Muhammad, G. (2020). *Cultivating genius: An equity framework for culturally and historically responsive literacy.* Scholastic.

National Research Council. (2002). *How people learn: Brain, mind, experience, and school* (6th ed.). National Academy of Sciences.

Pearson, P. D., & Gallagher, G. (1983). The gradual release of responsibility model of instruction. *Contemporary Educational Psychology, 8,* 112–123.

Perry and Associates, Inc. (2014). *Bridging the gap between policy and practice: Best practice schools' experiences of New York City Department of Education special education reform.* New York City Department of Education. https://www.perryandas sociatesinc.com/NYC-SE_ReformBP_ Report_Final_4-23.pdf

Shafer, L. (2018, June 12). The experiences of teacher of color. *Usable Knowledge.* Harvard University Graduate School of Education. https://www .gse.harvard.edu/news/uk/18/06/ experiences-teachers-color

Simon, N. S., Johnson, S. M., & Reinhorn, S. K. (2015, July). *The challenge of recruiting and hiring teachers of color: Lessons from six high-performing, high-poverty, urban schools* (Working paper). Harvard University Graduate School of Education. https://robobees.seas.har vard.edu/files/gse-projectngt/files/the_ challenge_of_recruiting_and_hiring_ teachers_of_color_diversity_july_2015 .pdf

Sweeney, D. (2011). *Student-centered coaching: A guide for K–8 coaches and principals.* Corwin.

Sweeney, D. (2013). *Student-centered coaching at the secondary level.* Corwin.

U.S. Department of Education. (2014, March 21). *Civil rights data collection, data snapshot: School discipline.* Issue Brief No. 1. Author. https://www2.ed.gov/ about/offices/list/ocr/docs/crdc-disci pline-snapshot.pdf

Villani, S. (2002). *Mentoring programs for new teachers: Models of induction and support.* Corwin.

West, L., & Staub, F. C. (2003). *Content-focused coaching: Transforming mathematics lessons.* Heineman & University of Pittsburgh.

EPILOGUE

Edmonds, R. (1979, October). Effective schools for the urban poor. *Educational Leadership, 37*(1), 15–24.

Index

A SAGE Publishing Company

Helping educators make the greatest impact

CORWIN HAS ONE MISSION: to enhance education through intentional professional learning.

We build long-term relationships with our authors, educators, clients, and associations who partner with us to develop and continuously improve the best evidence-based practices that establish and support lifelong learning.

THE PROFESSIONAL LEARNING ASSOCIATION

Learning Forward is a nonprofit, international membership association of learning educators committed to one vision in K–12 education: Equity and excellence in teaching and learning. To realize that vision, Learning Forward pursues its mission to build the capacity of leaders to establish and sustain highly effective professional learning. Information about membership, services, and products is available from www.learningforward.org.

PERRY

Bridging knowledge and practice

Let's stay in touch!

We believe that all of us have much to offer and much to learn on the way to achieving equity for each and every one of our students. We want to learn from you about your journey to advance equity in your schools and districts.

Please reach out to share your stories and questions as we begin a dialogue with equity warriors across the country.

Join us at
www.equity-warriors.com